THE ANCIENT WORLDS OF ASIA

From Mesopotamia to the Yellow River

The
Ancient Worlds
of Asia

From Mesopotamia to the Yellow River

ERNST DIEZ

H8273

G. P. Putnam's Sons   *New York*

FIRST AMERICAN EDITION 1961

Translated by W. C. Darwell
from the French version by Louis Mézeray

Library of Congress Catalog
Card Number: 61-10333

ACKNOWLEDGEMENTS

The publishers would like to thank Messrs. Faber & Faber, Ltd., for permission to quote extracts from *The Development of Sumerian Art* by Sir Leonard Woolley; Penguin Books, Ltd., for permission to quote extracts from *What Happened in History* by V. Gordon Childe, *Ur of the Chaldees* by Sir Leonard Woolley, and *Prehistoric India* by Stuart Piggott; and Messrs. Routledge & Kegan Paul, Ltd., for permission to quote extracts from *Studies in Early Chinese Culture* by H. G. Creel.

TRANSLATOR'S NOTE

This translation of *Entschleiertes Asien* by Ernst Diez has been made principally from the French version published under the title of *Les Anciens Mondes de l'Asie*. Chapter XV was newly written and has been translated from the German by my colleague, Miss M. M. Middleton. The spelling of proper names has been standardised on the model of either the *Encyclopaedia Britannica* or the authorities named in the "Suggestions for further reading".

W.C.D.

CONTENTS

LIST OF ILLUSTRATIONS

The following illustrations are reproduced by permission
of the British Museum: 1, 2, 3, 4, 10, 11, 12, 13.

INTRODUCTION

This survey of Asian cultures ranges from the Euphrates to the Yellow River and covers a period of five thousand years from Noah to nineteenth-century Mandalay. It describes in accurate detail, both from contemporary sources and from the reports of the latest available archaeological expeditions, the artistic treasures of some of the greatest states, cities and temples the world has ever seen, and gives a compelling account of the daily lives, the hopes and the fears of many of our distant ancestors, for some of these people were the very founders of our Western civilisation.

There is a strange sense of unity in this survey, centred on the idea of the "god on a mountain" who may be represented in any one of the various types of tower from the Babylonian ziggurat to the Chinese pagoda. To assist our understanding of the art and architecture of the periods he describes, the author has included a brief account of certain aspects of the Islamic and Buddhist religions and the Chinese ancestor-cult.

I

THE GOLDEN AGE

Civilisation may be said to have begun when early man ceased his wanderings and took up a settled mode of life. This can only have been possible when he had found a dependable food-supply from tilling the soil and no longer had to hunt in nomadic tribes over wide tracts of land. Thus civilisation began with agriculture which assured man's settled existence.

Where was the first land cultivated? In the valleys of the great rivers—Nile, Tigris, Euphrates, Yang-tse? We now know that these were developed later than certain mountain table-lands in the Andes, East Africa and Iran. Here there was a natural growth of various grasses such as wild oats from which man was eventually to make bread. At first the grasses were harvested in their season, but later they were sown in the areas where man had settled and the cultivation of cereals began. With the spread of crops the settlements grew in importance and soon the tribes, at the mercy of drought in the mountains, moved down into the great valleys. Here they found an inexhaustible water-supply and they reaped a hundredfold.

These early civilisations go back to pre-history. Such is the strength of tradition, however, especially amongst the peasants, that many methods of land cultivation dating back five thousand years can still be seen today in the Balkans and certain areas of Central Asia.

One of the earliest regions to be cultivated was the Iranian plateau. In the palaeolithic period (the old stone age), when Europe lay deep under ice as far as the Alps, this region had a temperate climate. It was entirely surrounded by mountains and the hollow in its centre was an inland sea which eventually dried up to leave deserts of sand and salt. All that remains of this inland sea today is a series of oases, a day's journey apart, fed by mountain streams and rock springs and strung out along the southern slopes of the Elburz in Northern Iran as far as the Pamir. Ten thousand years ago these bare mountains were covered with forests and peopled with cave-dwellers who lived by hunting and fishing on the shores of the sea. From this sea a few islands emerged—the tops of what are now the mountain-ranges crossing the Kawir. The sea-shore, with its thick reeds, must have been very similar to the shores of the Hamoun today and to those of Lake Seistan with their tigers, leopards, wild asses, lions, gazelles and millions of water-fowl. In the thousands of years during which the climate here was as moist as it is now arid, man's settled existence was ensured by the natural fertility of the soil. As the centuries passed, however, the rain became scarcer, the mountain torrents dried up for months on end and the inland sea which had been fed by their waters gradually shrank. The vast marshes became grasslands and man came down to settle on the plain. Here he built reed huts and cultivated cereals. These prehistoric dwellings have been revealed by the grass mounds which cover them today. Here methodical excavations have yielded a wealth of information about the men who lived in them from three to six thousand years ago. Let us take a look at two or three of these excavated mounds or "tells" at Sialk near Kashan in Iran.

Kashan is situated on the eastern slope of the central Iranian mountains where they come down to the salt desert in the middle of the plateau. It is thus on what was formerly the western edge of the inland sea. The oldest strata of civilisation in Sialk date back to the fifth millennium B.C. Here a number of important discoveries were made. Clay spindles revealed the existence of a rudimentary textile industry. Small stone mortars and pestles in which colours were crushed showed that tattooing was practised. Both men and women were found to have worn necklaces and bracelets of small shells and stone beads. Amongst a number of carved bones, mostly the handles of knives, saws, sickles and various silex tools, there was an astonishing human figurine, one of the oldest so far found in Western Asia. This is now in the Louvre. It represents a man, perhaps a tribal chief or priest, standing, leaning slightly forwards, his arms crossed over his chest in hieratic style, dressed in a loin-cloth and wearing a cone-shaped cap. The man's clothing indicates that the climate of Kashan at this time was similar to that of Babylon and Egypt. It is now much hotter. The man's cap is similar to that worn by Iranian peasants today. Physically he differs from the Sumerians and the Egyptians in being thin, whereas they were mostly fat and their oldest statuettes appear to date from a somewhat later period than this one. This was evidently the end of the neolithic and the beginning of the copper age as several copper pins were found in the excavations. The dead were buried underneath their dwellings. In the tombs food and an axe were laid beside the bodies, showing that there was belief in the life after death.

The excavations at Sialk revealed eight successive and superimposed layers, the ruins of former villages. The three upper layers provided evidence of significant progress due to two major developments: the potter's oven and brick making. Previously the clay vessels, shaped by hand, had been laid out in the sun to dry, then stacked one on top of the other and covered with twigs to bake in the sun. The invention of the oven allowed the heat to be regulated and gave the clay an evenly red surface. The vessels, formerly very simply decorated with paint, could now be ornamented with representations of animals such as ibex, bears and water-fowl. Houses were made of brick which was then painted red.

In our machine-age, when so much is possible, it is hard to imagine what these discoveries meant to prehistoric man and what a long time was needed to perfect them. The brick, simple though it may appear to us, was the result of many experiments. In its rudimentary stage it was merely an irregular lump of hand-moulded clay. Its regular shape was achieved only after much trial and error.

The dead were found to be wearing exotic jewellery. Their shell necklaces and bracelets had come from the Persian Gulf and their turquoises from Eastern Iran. As early as the fourth millennium, therefore, the people of Sialk were trading. They were exporting their ceramics and perhaps also cereals and animals captured in hunting for other merchandise, notably such luxury goods as ornaments and jewellery. Bones found on this side indicate that horses, dogs and pigs were already domesticated. This very early domestication of the horse soon led to the breeding of the mule, a cross between a horse and a donkey and a far superior beast of burden. From the end of the fourth millennium this animal appears at Ur in scenes representing the Sumerian army, having been imported there from Iran.

The second tell at Sialk shows in its lower layers the progress of later civilisations. Here the houses were built of moulded brick and their inner walls were painted red and white. Elegantly shaped clay vessels were found painted with geometrical designs and figures of animals such as the ibex, wild sheep, leopard, dog and various birds as well as the Lord of Creation who is represented as a man leading an ox by a ring passed through the animal's nose. Copper vessels had almost completely replaced those of stone and the discoveries here included hammers, forged lumps of metal and hammered tools. Metal fusing was therefore known. A quantity of long copper pins with hemispherical heads, beads of turquoise, lapis-lazuli or jade, shell and rock-crystal pendants foreshadowed the rich jewellery later to be found in the tomb of the Sumerian queen Shub-ad at Ur. Further evidence that this civilisation had advanced to trading was found in the discovery of stone seals which were used to protect the merchandise. To Sialk came metals from the mountain valleys of Luristan, shells from the Persian Gulf, turquoises from Khorasan, lapis-lazuli from Afghanistan and jade from the fast-flowing rivers of Khotan on the other side of the Pamir.

The fourth millennium saw the beginnings of writing. This probably developed from trading. Signs representing the quantities and the value of goods such as barley, wheat, wine and butter, were scratched with a stylus on unbaked clay tablets. Some of these had holes bored in them so that they could be attached to the merchandise. Writing spread from Susa, probably over the plateau, when the kingdom of Elam extended its rule over the whole of Iran at the end of the fourth millennium. These lower layers of civilisation show us the end of the copper age at Sialk and the succeeding layers reveal periods which came some two thousand years later.

Mounds dating back to the neolithic period are found all over the Iranian plateau, but few excavations up to now have yielded such a store of information as we have been able to gather at Sialk. Near Persepolis, however, a neolithic village was discovered. This did not contain separate houses, like later villages, but consisted of an irregular cluster of courtyards and rooms. From this we may conclude that the inhabitants lived in clans, a form of community life inferior even to the polygamous family. These clans were most probably poly-androus, a form of society found in Elam during the following millennia and among a number of small Asiatic tribes. The possession of women in common between the members of one family or clan (hence among blood-relations only) implies that communal life is moving towards better organised social groups. Strabo (xvi, 783) gives the following account of a polyandrous community amongst the Arabs: "Brothers are considered more important than children. Leadership in the family and in high positions within the community is decided by primogeniture. All relatives hold possessions in common, but the eldest is the chief. They share one wife amongst them. The first to arrive enters and lives with her, leaving his staff in front of the door, for it is the custom to carry a staff. At night she stays with the eldest. Thus they are all brothers amongst themselves. They also cohabit with their mothers. Adultery is punished by death. The adulterer is the man from another family." The custom of planting a staff in the ground in front of the house where a man and woman lived together was very common in prehistoric times before the development of family life and occurs in all accounts of ancient marriage customs.

Let us, however, return to Sialk for a further glimpse of Iran's last prehistoric civilisation, the Indo-Iranian or Aryan, which within a matter of a few centuries was to enter the stage of history. Two thousand years have passed since the period described above. This could well have been called the Golden Age since here weapons were unknown and there was consequently no servitude, no despotism or caste and no warfare since there was no occasion for rivalry. But by the second half of the fourth millennium all this had changed. The Iranians settled in Sialk in the tenth century B.C. They either brought a much more highly developed civilisation or they developed very rapidly. They buried their dead, not under their houses, but in cemeteries outside their villages in graves marked with stone slabs. These were to yield much valuable information to archaeologists. Their men were buried with their weapons, which were of bronze. In these graves were also found bits, bridles and small round bells showing that these people were horsemen. They also forged weapons with a new metal, iron, at this time still rare and expensive, daggers and various iron objects being found together with weapons of bronze. A great number of earthenware vessels, probably full of food, were laid in the tomb. Some of them were of very fine quality, thin and elegantly shaped with a long spout. These were clearly ritual vessels for drink-offerings. The women wore rich jewels of iron, bronze and silver, lion-headed brooches and silver hairpins.[1]

The Iranian invasion brought the prehistoric period to an end. Where formerly there had been only villages on the plateau great cities now sprang up: Ecbatana, Persepolis, Pasargadae, Rhages (near Teheran) and Tus (near Meshed). Sumero-Babylonian cuneiform writing was adopted. Iran was entering the stage of history. With the founding of the Persian Empire by Cyrus it was soon to become of first importance in Western Asia and one of the great Empires of the Ancient World.

[1] R. Ghirshman: *Iran*, Pelican Books, 1954, pp. 73 ff.

2

THE DESCENDANTS OF NOAH

Can it be shown that the Flood had any basis in historical fact?
We can answer "yes" in so far as the occurrence of a natural
prehistoric event can be proved from archaeological excavations. Sir Leonard Woolley's work at Ur on the Lower
Euphrates has shown beyond doubt that a bed of clay eight
feet thick at a considerable depth below the surface and causing
a break between the levels of culture could only have resulted
from a flood of exceptional magnitude. It can scarcely be
doubted that this deluge and the Flood of the Bible were
identical. The origin of the Flood tradition is not biblical
but Sumerian and is recorded in the Babylonian epic of Gilgamesh where Ut-Napishti tells his great-grandson Gilgamesh,
in terms which coincide almost exactly with the later biblical
version, how he escaped from the great deluge. If we consider
where Ur lies in relation to the Persian Gulf today it seems
almost inconceivable that a great flood could have occurred
so far from the sea, but when we realise how this alluvial region
was continually spreading and that in about A.D. 400 the sea
still reached as far as Kurnah, where now the Tigris meets the
Euphrates, and that around 2000 B.C. the mouths of these
two rivers were still very far apart, we can see that Ur was in
fact near the coast and well within the range of catastrophic
flooding. At that time the Lower Euphrates valley was still
marshland out of which arose, like so many islands, areas of
alluvial land of great fertility which attracted like a magnet
those who tilled with the sweat of their brow the arid soil of
the neighbouring Arabian plateau or the middle Euphrates
valley. The annual floods which covered the whole of the area
with a uniform surface of water forced, as nowhere else, the

MESOPOTAMIA

inhabitants to live together in cities which, as in centuries passed, rose ever higher above the alluvial soil, for their mud-brick huts had a short life and had to be rebuilt with every generation. When these cities were first built, however, they were surrounded by a protective wall of unbaked brick ten to sixteen feet thick. This ensured their survival, and that of Ur among them, from the Great Flood.

These cities, the most ancient in Babylonia, had been founded by the Sumerians, a race whose ethnic origin has not yet been established, but who probably came from the eastern part of the plateau which extends from Mesopotamia to the valley of the Indus. Their tradition has it that when they reached the plain they already knew agriculture, the working of metals and writing. They were so far advanced in comparison with the original settlers that they at once reduced these to slavery.

The lists of the Sumerian dynasties reckon kings both before and after the Flood: "Then came the Flood and after the Flood kingship again descended from Heaven", say the clay tablet inscriptions. When Woolley's expedition of 1927-8 dug a trench alongside the hill of Ur they found first, to a depth of forty feet, household rubbish, ashes from hearth fires, decomposed bricks and masses of potsherds all in well-defined layers. This rubbish could only have come from the town above, flung out over its walls through the centuries, as happens in old walled towns today. Graves, including those of royalty, had been dug down into this rubbish-layer because more rubbish was found underneath them. The expedition then sank shafts below the level of the deepest graves; these yielded clay tablets inscribed with characters dating back to two or three hundred years before the graves were dug. On the other hand, the pottery and other objects found at this lowest level were identical with those found in the tombs, indicating that the material civilisation had not changed very much. The shafts were then driven deeper—this revealed a layer of perfectly clean clay, eight feet thick and bearing no trace of civilisation, which could only have been deposited by water. Below this were further layers of rubbish, potsherds, silex and stone implements similar to those found in the pre-Sumerian village of al 'Ubaid and therefore of greater antiquity. Thus a break in historical continuity had been revealed—above the clay the layers of pure Sumerian civilisation, below it the remains of a mixed culture, some Sumerian, others pre-Sumerian. But this town of Ur had a much higher civilisation than that of the surrounding villages whose inhabitants were still primitive: this was shown by a brick of burnt clay found at the lowest level and proving that the inhabitants of Ur were already living in solidly constructed permanent buildings and that Ur was a town, not a village of mud and reed huts like nearby al 'Ubaid. Thus Woolley's excavations, carried out with modern methods and an exacting technique, had achieved results of great importance. It was established that a bed of clay had in fact been deposited by the deluge, the Flood, and that the catastrophe had interrupted, but not destroyed, Sumerian civilisation, which was already advanced.

The royal tombs found on this site show the degree of civilisation attained. These were vaulted chambers made of stone or brick. In the tomb of a queen were found fluted gold vessels of exquisite shape and comparable with the finest of the Imperial Age. Their only decorative motif is a zig-zag line along the upper and lower edges. The tomb also contained two model boats, one of copper and the other of silver; the latter, very well preserved, is almost two feet long, with a raised stern and prow, five seats and, amidships, an arched support for the awning which was used to protect the passengers from the sun. The oars, which their leaf-shaped blades, were still in place. This type of boat is still in use today on the marshes of the Lower Euphrates. But the most surprising find was the queen's richly ornamented head-dress. Over a wig parted in the centre and thickly padded out at the sides were arranged three chains of lapis-lazuli and carnelian beads, the lowest hung with great gold ring pendants which came down over the forehead, the second wreathed with gold beech leaves and the third with willow leaves and gold flowers whose petals were of blue and white inlay. The queen also wore a golden "Spanish comb" with five points ending in gold flowers encrusted with lapis-lazuli. Spiral rings of gold wire were twisted into the side curls of the wig and heavy lunate ear-rings of gold hung down to the shoulders.

The whole court had been buried with the king and queen: palace guards, chamberlains and ladies-in-waiting. The latter also wore rich head-dresses; very little trace, however, remained of their clothing, but this must certainly have been of a fine brightly coloured material. Royal tombs also contained gold-encrusted mosaic harps. Transport equipment was found, too, notably a sledge chariot decorated with golden lions' heads and, lying beside the skeletons of the grooms and two asses, the tip of a remarkably interesting silver shaft fitted with a double ring through which the reins had passed; on the ring, and represented running round it, was the statuette of a most realistically modelled donkey. These Sumerian shaft-ends are the forerunners of countless others of the same type which were to be made in succeeding centuries and of which many examples, mainly from the Median and Achaemenian periods, have been found in the tombs of Luristan. The limitation of human sacrifice to the funeral rites of royalty may be explained by the deification of the sovereign who, according to belief, did not die but was merely transported into another world, so that the members of his court must have looked upon it as a privilege to be able to accompany him on the journey. The sacrifice of humans at the funerals of kings and princes was not only current practice with most primitive peoples, but persisted for centuries among peoples of a high standard of civilisation.

Among the most curious objects found in the tombs must be mentioned a pair of statuettes each representing a he-goat standing on its hind legs in front of a stylised tree with a cylindrical trunk and two symmetrical branches tipped with flowers. The animals' bodies are of wood, the more delicate parts of plaster coated with asphalt and covered with a layer of gold. The fleece is inserted white shell or lapis-lazuli. The most precious piece of chased gold uncovered in these tombs, however, was a helmet, fashioned to resemble a wig which fitted closely over the head, leaving only the eyes, nose, mouth and chin uncovered. The waves, curls and plaited band around the hair are of the most exquisite workmanship. The earpieces are perforated to allow the wearer to hear. These and other pieces, now in the Iraq museum in Baghdad, together with the gold vessels mentioned above, show that the goldsmith's art of almost five thousand years ago had already attained an unsurpassable mastery, whereas the art of representing the human figure is of interest only as an archaeological document. This is also the case of the mosaic "Standard" of Ur, which, together with all the other pieces mentioned, is illustrated in Woolley's publications on his excavations on this site. It consists of two rectangular panels twenty-two inches long by nine inches high and two triangular end-pieces. The standard was fixed to a pole and most likely carried in processions. It was found lying alongside the king's standard bearer and up against his shoulder. The mosaic is made of little mother-of-pearl figures on a lapis-lazuli background. The triangular sections represent mythological scenes and the main panels show, in rows one above the other, a royal banquet, beasts being led to slaughter, oxen, rams and fish, booty captured from the enemy, prisoners being brought before the king, a procession of warriors and war chariots in combat.

This standard shows us already objects which were later to be characteristic in Assyrian and Persian art. The warriors wear helmets similar to the one described above and cloaks held back on the shoulder by a clasp; they are armed with axes. The war chariots are drawn by mules and carry a driver and a soldier, the latter armed with javelins of which four are carried in reserve in a quiver mounted high up in the front. This standard gives us the earliest picture of the earliest army of the great Mesopotamian powers and is an historical document of the greatest value and importance. It shows us the army which carried the civilisation of Sumeria from the fringe of the Persian Gulf to the border of Mesopotamia and, much further still, to the shores of the Mediterranean Sea. The weapons found in the tombs, particular the daggers, bear witness to a hitherto unsuspected perfection of craftsmanship. The standard tells us finally that the Sumerians introduced the chariot into the history of warfare at the end of the fourth millennium, the chariot with which the Babylonians and Assyrians were later to found their empires and which was still to win battles for Alexander the Great.

On the mound of al 'Ubaid there came to light one day a foundation stone on which was inscribed the name of the second king of Ur. This established the historical accuracy of the lists of the Sumerian kings, lists which had been previously known but of which the first dynasties were not recognised as historic. The third dynasty after the Flood is called the First Dynasty of Ur; its founder was Mes-anni-pad-da, whose son A-anni-pad-da is mentioned on the foundation stone of the building of al 'Ubaid which it was thus possible to date around 3100 B.C., together with the objects found in it. So, thanks to the discovery of this foundation stone, the First Dynasty of Ur entered the domain of history and a whole epoch was brought to light.

Woolley then attempted a reconstruction in model form, from the foundation walls still standing and fragments of metal overlay found on the site, of the dwelling of Mes-anni-pad-da, the oldest building known so far in Mesopotamia. Four copper statues of bulls standing upright had been found, as well as friezes representing reclining cattle, cows moving, pigeons, a farm with a reed cattle-shed in the middle and on each side men milking cows, straining and beating milk. These were not herdsmen, however, but priests or servants of the temple. Everything indicates that this building was one of those temples to which were attached sacred farms on which priests prepared, according to the rites, the milk of the mother-goddess Nin-Kharsag which was the nourishment reserved for priests and kings. The façade of the temple consisted of a wall ribbed with vertical grooves, a common feature in Mesopotamia, and a staircase leading to the raised doorway in front of which was a porch with a penthouse roof whose supporting columns were of wood overlaid with copper. Columns of mosaic held up the lintel over which there was a copper bas-relief seven feet nine inches long and three feet six inches high representing an eagle grasping a stag in each of its claws. At the edge of the platform, on each side, stood copper bulls in an imitation meadow represented by coloured terra cotta flowers. Above ran the copper frieze of reclining cattle, higher up the mosaic frieze with the farm, and higher still the pigeon frieze. This was quite an idyllic façade with its pastoral calm, a rare thing amongst all the scenes of military campaigns, battles and offerings of tribute which were later to occur again and again on the façades of Mesopotamian monuments.

The particular feature of this art, the oldest found in the "Land between the two rivers", is the technique of overlaying. In this alluvial land of Lower Mesopotamia, where there was no stone, the natural building material was sun-baked brick with wooden pillars used as supports. For ordinary living-huts these two materials were used in the raw state. Taking the normal present-day dwellings as an example, the palm-tree trunks used in their construction were not even squared off. On the other hand, the columns used in temples and palaces were overlaid with sheets of copper and geometrically designed mosaics of shells, lapis-lazuli and slate, and the rough-cast whitened walls appear to have been topped with friezes of metal. The glazed brick which was later to be used in mural decoration in Western Asia is not found here yet.

For thousands of years the site at Ur was conspicuous by a great knoll, the ruins of the "Ziggurat", the terraced temple dating from the Third Dynasty of 2300 to 2180 B.C. Seven centuries have passed since the first period of Ur's prosperity—an enormous gap in the history of a city, but the Western world has known similar periods of decline, as in the case of Rome's thousand years between the end of the Empire and the beginning of the Renaissance. The land of Sumer, which had become a great empire by the year 2900 B.C., had had to yield its sway over Mesopotamia to the Semite kings of Akkad who styled themselves "Kings of Sumer and Akkad" and whose capital was on the Euphrates some fifty miles north of Babylon. Sumerian preponderance returns, however, in the rule of city-states, firstly Lagash which lasted for a century, then Ur which under the Third Dynasty, about 2100 B.C., became the chief city of Sumer and Akkad.

The Ziggurat at Ur, at its time of building the largest in Sumer and still the best preserved in Mesopotamia, was built by the first two kings of the Third Dynasty Ur-Nammu and

Dungi. A century ago the British Consul at Basra, Mr. J. E. Taylor, excavated the top of the knoll and found clay cylinders bearing inscriptions showing that they had been placed there by the last king of Babylon Nabonidus in about 550 B.C. to record his completion of the tower founded by Ur-Nammu and his son Dungi, but left unfinished. These established not only the age of the Ziggurat itself but the identity of the site with the biblical Ur of the Chaldees, the home of Abraham. Only interested, like other archaeologists of his time, in digging out museum pieces such as were being unearthed in plenty from the hills of Assyria, Taylor did not pursue his investigations and unfortunately left the upper part of the Ziggurat exposed to the weather and the ravages of Arab builders in search of cheap material. In 1922 a joint expedition of the British Museum and the Museum of the University of Pennsylvania under the direction of Woolley began an excavation of the tower. The work of clearing the ground was costly and unrewarding, bringing very little to the museums beyond an occasional rare piece, but archaeologically it proved of great interest. It was only after two winters had passed and tons of rubbish had been removed that the nucleus of the tower came to light.

Ziggurat means "Hill of Heaven" or "Mountain of God" and each Mesopotamian city contained one or more of these staged temples. Staged towers and stepped pyramids are found amongst ancient civilisations all over the world, in Ancient Egypt, all over Indo-China, in the Indian Archipelago, in Chinese Turkestan, China (pagodas), Oceania, Peru and Mexico. They cannot be said to have been purely local in origin: it has been assumed, for example, that, as the Sumerians came from a mountainous country, they were accustomed to worshipping their gods in high places. We shall see later that these temples had a cosmic significance, their stages corresponding to different mythocosmic spheres, to degrees of ascent towards the divinity, such as Dante shows in his "Mountain of Purification" which was based on Eastern models. They symbolise the Mountain of the Universe; in India they represent Meru, the Mountain of the Gods, and in Mesopotamia something certainly very similar.

The Ancient Worlds of Asia

The Ziggurat of Ur, built within the temple of the Moon God Nannar, is about two hundred feet long and one hundred and fifty feet wide and was originally about seventy feet high. It is solid, the centre being of unbaked brick about eight feet thick. The first terrace is about fifty feet high and strengthened by flat buttresses. The second and third terraces were appreciably smaller; on top of the third stage stood a shrine. On the north-west face of the building, opposite the temple of Nannar, three flights of stairs each of a hundred steps led upwards to the next storey, one projecting at right angles, the other two running parallel with the wall. The processions climbed together in three different directions, slowly and solemnly, with the god-king, the priests and ministers at the head, on the central stairway, the procession of boys and girls singing hymns and the notables of the city and the nation on the two lateral stairways. From an inscription found here we can imagine these terraces laid out with earth and trees to form hanging gardens and picture to ourselves what the Ziggurat, the "Mountain of God", must have looked like. At the foot of the Ziggurat, opposite the central stairway, rose the great temple of Nannar, the principal divinity of Ur, whose shrine on the topmost platform of the tower was, however, only a part of the panoply devoted to his cult. Attached to the temple was a college of priests engaged in every kind of economic activity.

Like our medieval monasteries, each temple owned vast lands whose revenues were paid to the god, making necessary a whole system of granaries, cattle-sheds and shops as well as an administration to run it. As the king was the visible representative of the god on earth, the members of the court and the personnel of the state, the Secretaries for Finance, War, Agriculture and Transport, the tax-collectors and the whole body of the civil service all lived within the precincts of the temple. The peasants paid in the tenth part of their cattle, sheep, goats and donkeys, barley and cheese, jars of butter and olive oil, dates, rushes, wine and bales of wool, all weighed and recorded on the clay tablets which in their thousands bear accurate witness to this intense commercial activity. The scribe took a blank clay tablet, inscribed on it with a stylus in cuneiform script a list of the goods delivered and handed over a receipt. The tablets were rapidly baked in the oven and have thus survived the passage of time better than any documents of paper.

Four other temples from different periods, two shrines, one to Nannar and the other containing the Moon God's ship, and finally Ur-Nammu's palace formed a Royal and Sacred Area which was later rebuilt by Nebuchadnezzar II (604–561) the son of Nabopolassar the founder of the last Babylonian dynasty. The whole area was surrounded by a vast wall of unbaked brick.

One of the oldest parts of the city of Ur lay close against this Sacred Area. From about 2000 B.C. the houses in this district were built on terraces formed by the rubbish left behind from centuries of previous building. By the time of Abraham the houses in Ur were standing on many different levels and when the city was destroyed in 1885 B.C. those on the lower level were buried under the rubble of those higher up, which preserved them so well that "they appeared to have been abandoned on the previous day rather than thirty-eight centuries ago." These houses were built of baked brick, roughcast and whitewashed, on foundations of unbaked brick; they were of two storeys and contained thirteen or fourteen rooms grouped round a central courtyard. From the street the main door opened into a hall which usually had a small pool for the washing of feet. This led into the brick-paved courtyard, in the middle of which was sunk a pipe to drain away rain water. The rooms had no windows, sufficient light entering through the doorways. A staircase led to the upper floor where the rooms were approached from a wooden gallery which overhung the courtyard all the way round. The flat roof was made of rammed clay laid over mats and supported by beams. The houses of Ur and other cities of Lower Mesopotamia were thus very similar to those found today in many Eastern countries and even in southern Europe where Moorish houses, in Spain in particular, are built on this plan.

Ur was only one city among the city-states of the Chaldees. According to their own traditions the Sumerians had come from over the sea. The affinities between the Sumerian civilisation and the pre-Aryan culture of the Indus, which flourished at the same time, lend support to the thesis that these two peoples had a common origin. The Sumerians, who came perhaps from the mountainous region where the Indus rises, may have come by sea to the shores of the Persian Gulf. This would seem to correspond with the cult of the Sea God Enki (Ea in Semitic) at Eridu, a town south of Ur and formerly on the shores of the Gulf. It is probable that each clan founded its own town and took up its own form of worship: the towns of Isin and Larsa worshipped the Sun God Babbar (Shamash in Akkadian), Uruk was the centre of the cult of Anu, the God of Heaven "looked upon as the supreme God from the remotest historical times"[1] who was later supplanted by his daughter Ishtar, the planet Venus and Goddess of Sensual Delight. Uruk will later be the home of Gilgamesh. Nippur worshipped Enlil, the God of the Air and the Surface of the Earth, also called "the Lord of the vast earth", who proceeded to divide up the kingdoms; Kish worshipped the God of War, Zbaba, as well as Ishtar; Babylon, whose name means the "Gate of God", worshipped Marduk, and Sippar was another centre of the Sun God cult. Lagash (Tello), a little further west, on a canal linking the two rivers, worshipped Ningirsu, the God of War.

Until the First Dynasty of Babylon (2057–1758) united the lands of Sumer and Akkad, that is for more than two thousand years, the city states passed through a troubled period of continual struggle for a supremacy which passed successively to the great Sumerian cities of Kish, Ur, Uruk, Lagash, Isin and Larsa, thence to Sargon, the king of Akkad, and his successors, and thence to the Guti, a mountain people from the Zagros valleys who invaded Mesopotamia. In addition to these foreign conquests there were continual incursions by the Bedouins, but, as in China, all the barbarian conquerors were eventually to yield to Chinese civilisation, so in Mesopotamia Sumerian culture survived all invasions, influenced them and shared with them the benefits of a well-ordered life. First among these benefits was that of the law.

Everyone has heard of the famous Code of Hammurabi, the seventh and greatest king of Babylon who reigned about

[1] L. Delaporte: *La Mésopotamie* (L' Evolution de l'Humanité—Albin Michel).

1800 B.C. over the whole of Mesopotamia. Its text is known from the great stela found in 1902 at Susa, whence it had been taken by the Elamites in the twelfth century during one of their invasions. It is nothing less than a compilation of ancient Sumerian laws and customs which, with certain modifications, were at this time in the process of being accepted over the whole state of Babylon. It was not, moreover, the first code of laws—one had already been drawn up by the second king of the Third Dynasty of Ur and yet an earlier one by Uru-kagina, a "patesi" (provincial governor) of Lagash about 2630. There were also collected laws of local application in different cities. The modifications made by the Semitic jurists of Babylon were mainly in the direction of heavier punishment for certain offences, particularly offences against the sacredness of the family tie, and crimes committed by slaves. Adultery, for example, is punished by death for both guilty parties whereas under Sumerian law it did not even necessarily mean divorce. It is evident from the inscriptions deciphered on numerous Sumerian tablets that every act of civil life was subject to the law: buying and selling, inheritance, contracts and loans, marriage, divorce and adoption. There were two courts—civil and religious; in the former the judges were nominated by the king, in the latter they were priests. High officials such as provincial governors also had certain juridical powers. The principal difference between this legal system and ours is that, in common with all ancient civilisations, it recognised distinctions of class: all were not equal before the law. Society was divided into three classes: patricians, free men and slaves. A crime against a patrician was punished much more severely than the same crime against a member of the second class, but the patrician himself received a heavier punishment for the dishonouring of his own class. Marriages were arranged by the parents of the betrothed, and engagements sanctioned by a gift of silver from the fiancé to his future father-in-law which would be surrendered if he broke off the engagement but returned to him in double if the girl broke it off. A man who seduced a girl was obliged to ask her of her parents in marriage. The marriage formalities were simply the drawing up of an act establishing reciprocal rights and duties. When the ceremony was over the bride entered into possession of the engagement gifts and herself contributed a dowry and a trousseau to the new home. These are a few of the more important elements of what was a very complete legislation concerning marriage.

Like our monasteries in the Middle Ages the temples of Sumer were centres of learning. The schools attached to them trained both boys and girls to be scribes, which was not easy in view of the nature of cuneiform writing. It was not merely a matter of learning several hundreds of signs: it was also necessary to know their various meanings, as is still the case today in Chinese. The discovery of a number of clay tablets has given us a very accurate picture of the teaching methods employed. The scholar was required first of all to memorise a long list of simple signs with their phonetic values, then grouped lists of signs in alphabetical order and ideograms expressing certain words or concrete ideas or defining a quality or a class. Thus the sign for "wood" would come to be written in front of the signs for "seat" or "tree". Then the pupils learnt short phrases, common commercial formulae, current expressions and titles of honour. Lastly came grammar, which can today be reconstructed from tablets of conjugations and declensions. The master would write the text on one side of a blank tablet, the pupil read it and then tried to reproduce it from memory on the other side.

Mathematics were taught also, as is shown by clay tablets bearing multiplication and division sums, square and cubic roots. Lists of weights and measures were found as well as lists of Sumerian and Semitic synonyms arranged in parallel columns. Boy and girl students were often employed as scribes in the temples themselves, where they copied ancient texts, transcribed hymns and litanies as well as dealing with important business and administrative correspondence. In addition there were the learned scribes, true scholars to whom modern oriental studies are indebted for important documents relating to even older periods. There were also schools for doctors and architects. The statue of Gudea seated (he was a "patesi" of Lagash about 2100 B.C.) with a tablet showing the plan of a temple on his knees, as well as many tablets inscribed with plans of properties, houses, towns and canals, show that the taste for architecture was widespread among both sovereigns and people. The practice of medicine and surgery seems to have been of doubtful advantage to both parties: whereas current medical practice and the exorcising of demons seem to have been reasonably safe, this was not the case with surgery, where any failure could be severely punished. "If a doctor operate on a man's eye with a copper lancet and the man loseth his eye thereby, the doctor shall also have his own eye removed with the same lancet." This "eye for an eye and tooth for a tooth" kind of justice can hardly have encouraged the practice of surgery.

The natural resources of the population lay in agriculture and cattle-raising. Where irrigation was sufficient, the soil was extremely fertile. These Eastern lands, where the peasant toils all day in field and garden to make the soil productive, must be seen if we are to realise the hard work and the amount of irrigation required to achieve fertility. The distribution of this precious water is exactly calculated and strictly allotted. The soil was worked by the plough, of very ancient invention although the first time it is represented in Sumeria, where it is pictured being drawn by a pair of oxen, dates only from the fourteenth century B.C. After harvesting the cereals were spread out over a circular threshing-floor, where the grain was trodden out by oxen pulling a kind of sledge, a process still seen today in Greece and Eastern countries as far as China. The grain was ground between stones or roasted and crushed to make a kind of porridge; it was also used to brew beer. Wine was made from dates as well as from grapes. There was plenty of fish in the streams and canals. The Sumerians were thus self-sufficient as far as food was concerned. They were also able to provide themselves with the raw materials for clothing, as they had sufficient wool, cotton and flax. The town of Mosul was later to give its name to "muslin", known the world over.

On the other hand, there was a notable lack of certain important raw materials such as wood and metals, which were brought by water from mountainous countries: cedars from the Lebanon and walnut and iron from the mountains of Armenia. The towns on the coast of the Persian Gulf became ports of transit for overseas trade from Egypt and India. The goods were transported on the Euphrates as far as Carchemish, a Hittite town north-east of Aleppo, whence they were dispatched by caravans towards Syria. The trading houses of the Sumerian cities had their agents in distant places with whom they maintained correspondence and regulated their business by letters of credit. As there was still no coinage, trade was done by barter. For local dealing values were calculated in measures of barley. For external trade the standards were ingots of gold or silver, the shekel of silver being the unit. Every trading transaction had to be made in writing in the presence of witnesses; failure to conduct business in this way was a punishable offence.

The Sumerians were polytheistic and had very many gods. There were patron gods of cities, to whom the great temples were consecrated: they were the lords of the land, the other gods being merely guests within the sacred enclaves who were worshipped with more modest rites. The patron god set high on the top of the Ziggurat was too aloof from his people who worshipped in their homes tutelary gods whom they would also ask to intercede on their behalf with the supreme deity. In spite of his unapproachable supremacy, the patron god in his sanctuary—the temple—partook of the life of his subjects, eating their food, marrying human women and having children by them, interesting himself as a landlord in the crops, seeing to it that these were abundant, provided that the proper rituals were carried out. City gods took part in wars and victory was not complete until the statue of the enemy's deity was captured and brought back in triumph. Thus Marduk, the god of the city and supreme god of the empire, was captured at the seizure and destruction of Babylon by Tukulti-Nimurta, the king of Assyria, and taken to Assur, where he was installed in a new temple. The power and prestige of the Assyrian capital were thereby increased. The gods thus shared the joys and griefs of their peoples.

But the supreme power of the gods was limited to this world, as the world beyond was not for man. The Sumerians did in fact believe in the survival of the spirit or the soul, but in dark and desolate Hells which had something in common with the Hades of the Greeks. The dead are therefore given a decent burial with offerings of food and drink, but this is merely to prevent an unsatisfied ghost from haunting the living. What counts is life on earth. "To Nannar his King, Ur-Nammu consecrates this in the interest of his own life" runs the usual form of dedication, or "May Nannar my King rejoice in my work; may he reward me with a decree of life, a prosperous reign and a secure throne; may I be Nannar's beloved shepherd, may he grant me long life."

Originally all the gods had their own functions, and it is only later that these were duplicated or confused. Enki of Eridu was Lord of the Ocean and the God of Wisdom who had invented crafts and writing, Enlil was Lord of the Rain and Wind, Nabu Lord of Vegetation, Nergal Lord of the Plague, Shamash the Sun God was Lord of Justice, Isthar the Goddess of Love and Fecundity, and Nin-khursag watched over childbirth. These were their original functions, which later came to be a projection of the earthly success of the king who represented the god. The god shares with the priests and servants of the temple the daily sacrifices of food and drink. The god is offered meat, bread, dates, milk, wine and beer. If the god is required to exercise his power for particular favours, special magical and symbolic rites are performed, such as the pouring of pure water into a vessel, then over ears of barley and branches of date palm to ask for the necessary water for the crops. An illustration of this was found at Dura on the Euphrates, showing the priests making a similar offering on behalf of a family which was present at the ceremony. In this respect also Sumerian traditions were to outlive by thousands of years the original civilisation which created them. Only the coming of Christianity put an end to these traditions and even then some of them survived. When in certain countries on Easter Saturday the village priest visits the principal farms in the parish to bless the fruits of the earth which are offered to him in baskets, this ritual act is within the tradition of the Sumerian sacrifices. The "Lamb of God" of the Christian New Testament was already the symbol of human sacrifice in Sumerian times. When a lamb is sacrificed to a god it is proclaimed that "the lamb is the representative of man, man hath sacrificed a lamb for his own life, he hath sacrificed the head of the lamb for his own head". This idea was, however, magical, and had none of the profound religious significance conferred upon it by Christianity. In the same way soothsaying and astrology had a natural place in this kind of religion and had great influence on the lives of men.

The Sumerian state was theocratic, like the Chinese under its oldest dynasty. The god was the true sovereign of the city and the governor or king only his visible representative, his vicar. Consequently the governor or king was also the god's priest and this is often mentioned on the tablets. Kings governed in the name of the god and the deification of royalty was the natural conclusion. Church and State were so closely allied that the State is to be regarded as a theocracy and the Church as a political institution.

Berossus, a priest and historian of the Hellenic period following the conquest of Babylonia by Alexander, describes a race of beings, half men and half fish, which, led by a certain Oannes, came out of the Persian Gulf and founded the coastal towns of Sumer where they introduced agriculture, writing and metalwork. "In a word," he says, "everything which makes for a better life was given to man by Oannes, since when there have been no further inventions." This Oannes turns up again as a god on the façades of Assyrian temples. Thus Berossus considered that in his time there was nothing of importance which had not been known to, or invented or practised by the Sumerians. Sumerian civilisation was assimilated and spread by the Babylonian and Assyrian Empires; its cuneiform writing was used by the Akkadian Semites, the Assyrians, the Hittites, the Persians and even the Greek successors of Alexander; the Sumero-Babylonian diplomatic language was introduced into the courts of Syria and Egypt. The cylindrical seals of Syria and Cappadocia were Mesopotamian, that is Sumerian, in origin, and Sumerian influence is to be found in the sculpture of the Assyrians, the Hittites and the Phoenicians. The arch, and the cradle vault, were already being used in the oldest royal tombs in Sumer in the fourth millennium, and their history can be followed in Mesopotamian architecture for thousands of years to come.

In addition to its material civilisation, the spiritual heritage of the Sumerians, through its influence on Hebrew literature, is still a source of strength today, greater even than the heritage of Rome. Horace and Ovid are read only by the cultured few, whereas the Bible is known to all. The story of the creation from the Fall to the Flood, the best known story on earth, came into Hebrew literature from the Sumerians and during the captivity of Babylon the Jews came to know of Babylonian spiritual culture, examples of which abound in the Old Testament. The Laws of Moses, which were to become one of the cornerstones of Western civilisation, were laid down on the principles of Sumerian justice.

We will ask Sir Leonard Woolley, to whom the world owes much of the resurrection of the civilisation of Sumer and from whose works we have largely borrowed, to conclude this chapter. His account of the Sumerians ends thus: "Their civilisation, lighting up a world still plunged in primitive barbarism, was in the nature of a first cause. We have outgrown the phase when all the arts were traced to Greece and Greece was thought to have sprung, like Pallas, full-grown from the brain of Olympian Zeus; we have learnt how that flower of genius drew its sap from Lydians and Hittites, from Phoenicia and Crete, from Babylon and Egypt. But the roots go farther back: behind all these lies Sumer. The military conquests of the Sumerians, the arts and crafts which they raised to so high a level, their social organisation and their conceptions of morality, even of religion, are not an isolated phenomenon, an archaeological curiosity; it is as part of our own substance that they claim our study, and in so far as they win our admiration we praise our spiritual forebears." [1]

[1] C. Leonard Woolley: *The Sumerians*, Oxford, 1928.

3

ASSYRIAN TEMPLES AND PALACES

Six hundred years before Christ, Nineveh was destroyed and with it the great Assyrian Empire came to an end. At the head of a powerful army of Medes, Persians and Babylonians, Cyaxares, king of the Medes, captured the city after a brief siege, laid low its walls, destroyed its palaces and reduced it to ruins. Assyria was incorporated into the Kingdom of the Medes and was never to play any further part in history as an independent state. The saying of the prophet was fulfilled.

Assyrian power had lasted 1500 years and had twice built up a great empire which dominated Western Asia. Tukulti-Enurta seized Babylon in the mid-thirteenth century B.C. and took its god Marduk into captivity. Assurnasirpal II (885–860) extended the frontiers of his empire and Salmanasar III (860–825) conquered the hereditary enemy Israel and forced her to pay tribute. Tiglath-Pileser III (745–727) regained the provinces lost by his predecessors and brought the Jews into captivity. Salmanasar V (727–722) besieged Samaria, the capital of the Kingdom of Israel, and his successor Sargon II (722–705) captured it, dismembered the state and deported its inhabitants. Sargon conquered the Egyptians, re-established Assyrian power in Babylon and waged war in Elam. Sennacherib (705–681) once more subjugated a rebellious Babylonia, waged war in Palestine, conquered Hezekiah, King of Judah, and finally destroyed Babylon in 689 B.C. Esarhaddon invaded and occupied lower Egypt (671), and his son Assurbanipal (668–626) set off to conquer the land of the Nile, pillaged Thebes its capital in

666 B.C. and completely overran Elam. This was the height of Assyrian power; from then onwards it never ceased to decline. Egypt and Lydia threw off the yoke and in the East the Empire was threatened by the Medes. Shortly after the death of Assurbanipal, Cyaxares conquered the Assyrians and for the first time laid siege to Nineveh. Held back by an invasion from Scythia, he joined forces with Babylon and finally destroyed Nineveh. Although Assyria then lay in the power of the Medes, an Assyrian general, Nabopolassar, captured Babylon and founded a new dynasty.

The destruction of Nineveh was certainly not as complete as Lucian would have us believe when he makes Mercury say to Charon: "My good pilot, Nineveh is so badly destroyed that it is impossible to say where it stood; no trace of it remains." Excavations have abundantly shown that the contrary was true. The city, moreover, had not been founded in a day by an Assyrian despot wishing to immortalise his victorious name by the creation of a new capital. In the third millennium the Akkadian city on the site had been built on five layers of civilisation. King Hammurabi in about 1750 B.C. mentions the famous temple of Ishtar, built on a hill in the centre of the city, in honour of the great goddess who was worshipped throughout Mesopotamia. She was also called Nin and gave her name to the city. In the period of Amarna, in the middle of the fifteenth century, Nineveh was part of the kingdom of the Mitanni, a people of Indo-European origin, and was only incorporated into the Assyrian kingdom, then fully expanding, by the kings of Assur, the older capital. It was, however, to remain a city of little importance for several centuries more, and it is only under King Sennacherib, in the early years of the seventh century, that its period of brilliance begins. Sennacherib had destroyed Babylon and wished to make Nineveh the greatest city of the East, which it became under his successors.

For a hundred years Nineveh, the loveliest and perhaps the largest city in Asia Minor, filled the world with astonishment and fear. It was from here that the dreaded armies and emissaries of the Assyrians set out to conquer and demand tribute. It was the centre of trade: "The merchants of Nineveh are more numerous than the stars of the firmament." It also became a great school of Chaldaean science. In his palace Sargon amassed a library whose treasures still bring us knowledge of the Assyrian-Babylonian civilisation. Even today, every child who reads the Bible knows the name of Nineveh, whilst Assur and Calah, the previous capitals, have remained mere names. Even the men who dug up the Assyrian cities about A.D. 1850, Botta, Place and Layard, hardly knew what to call them, knowing them more by the names given by the natives to the tells, or artificial hillocks, on which they had stood—Kelle Shergat and Nimrud. The first tell, under which lay buried the oldest Assyrian capital, is fourteen hours' journey by road southwards from Nineveh on the right bank of the Tigris, whilst Calah, under the hillock of Nimrud, is only three hours' ride to the south of Mosul on the left bank of the river near its junction with the upper Zab. Calah had replaced Assur as a royal residence by about 1300 and became the capital again later under Assurbanipal II and his successors. Sargon himself lived there also after building in Nineveh his palace which he inaugurated in 706, the year before his assassination.

The resurrection of the buried civilisations of Mesopotamia began a little more than a century ago, stimulated by stories from the Bible and the Romantics' love of the exotic and the Orient in particular. The veil of this historical night began to lift over the vast steppes and deserts of Mesopotamia until gradually the two or three thousand tells which rise above the buried cities began to be uncovered and to yield up their mysteries.

The Western world knew of Nineveh and Babylon only through the Bible. The first scientific information of any value about these two cities was the work of C. J. Rich. Rich began the study of Oriental languages at the age of nine and at fourteen was learning Chinese. He served for several years in India and at the age of twenty-four was appointed Resident of the East India Company in Baghdad. In two remarkable books he has left us an account of his journeys through ancient

Babylonia and Assyria and of his researches on the sites of ruined cities. He died in 1820 of cholera at the early age of thirty-three. It was a Frenchman, Botta, who acknowledged Rich as the true pioneer of Mesopotamian excavations. Botta, then French consul at Mosul, started digging on the knoll of Kuyunjik, the site of Nineveh, but soon abandoned this for Khorsabad, a few miles North of Mosul. Here he had the great joy of unearthing a palace of Sargon (722–705). His work at Khorsabad was continued from 1851 to 1855 by a French expedition led by Victor Place. The ancient city was called Dur-Sharrukin, after its founder Sargon. Its outer walls were oriented with their four corners at the cardinal points. Built into the walls were eight monumental gates, each one bearing the name of an Assyrian divinity.

The greatest triumphs in this heroic age of excavation, however, were achieved by Austen Henry Layard in 1845, two years after Botta's first expedition. Layard dug on the knoll of Nimrud, the site of the ancient city of Calah, and uncovered the palace of Assurnasirpal, the most important of seven royal palaces. A second expedition under Layard discovered Sennacherib's palace at Kuyunjik. Layard was not only an exceptionally gifted archaeologist and excavator, but also a clever diplomat and a remarkable writer. His enthusiasm for nature and art, which he expressed with a great nobility of style, makes the reading of his books a great pleasure even today. The account of these expeditions is best recorded in his own words:

"During the autumn of 1839 and winter of 1840 I had been wandering through Asia Minor and Syria, scarcely leaving untrod one spot hallowed by tradition, or unvisited one ruin consecrated by history. I was accompanied by one no less curious and enthusiastic than myself. We were both equally careless of comfort and unmindful of danger. We rode alone; our arms were our only protection; a valise behind our saddles was our wardrobe, and we tended our own horses, except when relieved from the duty by the hospitable inhabitants of a Turcoman village or an Arab

43

tent. Thus unembarrassed by needless luxuries, and un-
influenced by the opinions and prejudices of others, we
mixed amongst the people, acquired without effort their
manners, and enjoyed without alloy those emotions which
scenes so novel, and spots so rich in varied association,
cannot fail to produce.

"I look back with feelings of grateful delight to those
happy days when, free and unheeded, we left at dawn the
humble cottage or cheerful tent, and lingering as we listed,
unconscious of distance and of the hour, found ourselves,
as the sun went down, under some hoary ruin tenanted by
the wandering Arab, or in some crumbling village still
bearing a well-known name. . . .

"I had traversed Asia Minor and Syria, visiting the ancient
seats of civilisation, and the spots which religion has made
holy. I now felt an irresistible desire to penetrate to the
regions beyond the Euphrates, to which history and tradition
point as the birthplace of the wisdom of the West. Most
travellers, after a journey through the usually frequented
parts of the East, have the same longing to cross the great
river, and to explore those lands which are separated on the
map from the confines of Syria by a vast blank stretching
from Aleppo to the banks of the Tigris. A deep mystery
hangs over Assyria, Babylonia, and Chaldaea. With these
names are linked great nations and great cities dimly
shadowed forth in history; mighty ruins, in the midst of
deserts, defying, by their very desolation and lack of definite
form, the description of the traveller; the remnants of mighty
races still roving over the land; the fulfilling and fulfilment
of prophecies; the plains to which the Jew and the Gentile
alike look as the cradle of their race. After a journey in
Syria the thoughts naturally turn eastward; and without
treading on the remains of Nineveh and Babylon our pilgrimage is incomplete.

"I left Aleppo, with my companion, on the 18th of March.
We still travelled as we had been accustomed—without
guide or servants. The road across the desert is at all times
impracticable, except to a numerous and well-armed

caravan, and offers no object of interest. We preferred that through Bir and Orfa. From the latter city we traversed the low country at the foot of the Kurdish hills, a country little known, and abounding in curious remains. . . . We entered Mosul on the 10th of April.

"During a short stay in this town we visited the great ruins on the east bank of the river, which have been generally believed to be the remains of Nineveh. We rode also into the desert, and explored the mound of Kalah Shergat, a vast ruin on the Tigris, about fifty miles below its junction with the Zab. As we journeyed thither we rested for the night at the small Arab village of Hammum Ali, around which are still the vestiges of an ancient city. From the summit of an artificial eminence we looked down upon a broad plain, separated from us by the river. A line of lofty mounds bounded it to the east, and one of a pyramidical form rose high above the rest. Beyond it could be faintly traced the waters of the Zab. Its position rendered its identification easy. This was the pyramid which Xenophon had described, and near which the ten thousand had encamped; the ruins around it were those which the Greek general saw twenty-two centuries before, and which were even then the remains of an *ancient* city. Although Xenophon had confounded a name, spoken by a strange race, with one familiar to a Greek ear, and had called the place Larissa, tradition still points to the origin of the city, and, by attributing its foundation to Nimrud, whose name the ruins now bear, connects it with one of the first settlements of the human race.

"Kalah Shergat, like Nimrud, was an Assyrian ruin: a vast shapeless mass, now covered with grass, and showing scarcely any traces of the work of man except where the winter rains had formed ravines down its almost perpendicular sides, and had thus laid open its contents. A few fragments of pottery and inscribed bricks, discovered after a careful search amongst the rubbish which had accumulated around the base of the great mound, served to prove that it owed its construction to the people who had founded the

45

city of which Nimrud is the remains. There was a tradition current amongst the Arabs, that strange figures carved in black stone still existed amongst the ruins; but we searched for them in vain, during the greater part of a day in which we were engaged in exploring the heaps of earth and bricks, covering a considerable extent of country on the right bank of the Tigris. . . .

"Were the traveller to cross the Euphrates to seek for such ruins in Mesopotamia and Chaldaea as he had left behind him in Asia Minor or Syria, his search would be vain. The graceful column rising above the thick foliage of the myrtle, ilex, and oleander; the gradines of the amphitheatre covering a gentle slope, and overlooking the dark blue waters of a lake-like bay; the richly carved cornice or capital half hidden by the luxuriant herbage; are replaced by the stern shapeless mound rising like a hill from the scorched plain, the fragments of pottery, and the stupendous mass of brickwork occasionally laid bare by the winter rains. He has left the land where nature is still lovely, where, in his mind's eye, he can rebuild the temple or the theatre. . . . He is now at a loss to give any form to the rude heaps upon which he is gazing. Those of whose works they are the remains, unlike the Roman and the Greek, have left no visible traces of their civilisation, or of their arts; their influence has long since passed away. . . . The scene around is worthy of the ruin he is contemplating; desolation meets desolation: a feeling of awe succeeds to wonder. . . . These huge mounds of Assyria made a deeper impression upon me, gave rise to more serious thoughts and more earnest reflection, than the temples of Balbec and the theatres of Ionia." [1]

Layard returned to Mosul in 1842. He was then employed in the Diplomatic Service in Constantinople. He tried persistently to obtain the means and permits he needed for further excavations but had very little success. His determination was strengthened by events at Khorsabad. Here Botta, on the

[1] Austen Henry Layard: *Nineveh and its Remains* (London, 1849), vol. i, pp. 1–7.

advice of a local peasant, had sunk a shaft in a mound and had discovered, not far below the surface, a wall dressed with stone slabs carved in relief. This turned out to be the first Assyrian monument to be uncovered since that empire fell. Finally in 1845 Sir Stratford Canning, British Ambassador to the Sublime Porte, put at Layard's disposal the necessary means for a first campaign. On the 8th of November of that year Layard left Mosul and went down the Tigris to try his luck on the hill of Nimrud.

A trench cut out of the side of the hill soon led him to a wall covered with inscriptions and fragments of reliefs. He was now certain that monuments lay buried underneath the mound. The next day he cleared a chamber with walls dressed at the base with a ten-foot-high frieze of vertical slabs of stone. It soon turned out that this was the usual method of dressing Assyrian walls. The bottom third of the wall was covered with stone slabs and the remainder was rough-cast and decorated with paintings. At the end of November the first slabs of two friezes were uncovered. These were separated by a band of inscriptions and contained bas-reliefs of human figures. They depict military campaigns, sieges, building and hunting in the time of the Assyrian kings. Every museum of importance today possesses some of these bas-reliefs. Visitors pass them by with a glance, scarcely realising that they are the story in pictures of a bygone civilisation. For Layard and his companions the discovery of this art of bas-relief was a revelation. The wonder of it all still echoes in his words:

"On each slab were two bas-reliefs, separated from one another by a band of inscriptions. The subject on the upper part of No. 1 was a battle scene. Two chariots, drawn by horses richly caparisoned, were each occupied by a group of three warriors; the principal person in both groups was beardless, and evidently a eunuch. He was clothed in a complete suit of mail, and wore a pointed helmet on his head, from the sides of which fell lappets covering the ears, the lower part of the face, and the neck. The left hand, the arm being extended, grasped a bow at full stretch;

whilst the right, drawing the string to the ear, held an arrow ready to be discharged. A second warrior urged, with reins and whip, to the utmost of their speed three horses, which were galloping over the plain. A third, without helmet, and with flowing hair and beard, held a shield for the defence of the principal figure. . . . I observed with surprise the elegance and richness of the ornaments, the faithful and delicate delineation of the limbs and muscles, both in the men and horses, and the knowledge of art displayed in the grouping of the figures and the general composition." [1]

This partial description of a single war-chariot gives an idea of the wealth of material provided by these Assyrian bas-reliefs. If all the bas-reliefs taken from the dozen or so temples and palaces at Nimrud and Kuyunjik had been put end to end they would have measured several miles in length. The first plaques found by Layard had been considerably damaged by fire. He therefore attacked the north-west corner of the mound where various objects and the remains of walls had previously been found. This gave him reason to believe that another palace lay buried underneath. His efforts were immediately rewarded. One morning he was hastily summoned to a part of the site where it was thought that Nimrod himself had been discovered. This turned out to be a colossal alabaster head of a winged lion: the body was found later. Layard says:

"I saw at once that the head must belong to a winged lion or bull, similar to those of Khorsabad and Persepolis. It was in admirable preservation. The expression was calm, yet majestic, and the outline of the features showed a freedom and knowledge of art, scarcely to be looked for in the works of so remote a period." [2]

The news quickly spread amongst the Bedouin encamped around. They sprang to horse and arrived at the gallop. At the sight of the head they all cried with one voice, "God

[1] Op. cit. vol. i, pp. 40–41.   [2] Op. cit., vol. i, p. 65.

1. Assyrian sculpture. The last great Assyrian ruler, Assurbanipal (668–626 B.C.), hunting lions. Shortly after the death of Assurbanipal the Assyrian Empire came to an end at the hands of Cyaxares, King of the Medes, who captured Nineveh, the Assyrian capital, and laid it in ruins.

2. Assurbanipal and his queen feasting in their garden in great state. The Assyrian Empire reached the height of its power under Assurbanipal and collapsed quickly after his death.

3. Assyrian sculpture. Hunting wild asses and slaying lions.

alone is great, and Mohammed is his Prophet!" Great persuasion was required to make the Sheik go down into the trench to convince himself that this was really only a stone image and not a miraculous apparition. Layard records:

> "'This is not the work of men's hands,' exclaimed he, 'but of those infidel giants of whom the Prophet—peace be with him!—has said that they were higher than the tallest date-tree; this is one of the idols which Noah—peace be with him!—cursed before the Flood.' In this opinion, the result of a careful examination, all the bystanders concurred." [1]

One of the workmen, however, had dropped his basket of earth at the sight of this fantastic head and galloped off to Mosul. Here he spread panic throughout the bazaar with the news that the great Nimrod had appeared in the neighbourhood. This rumour at once reached the ears of the Caliph who summoned the Mufti and the Ulema to take counsel on the matter. Accompanied by an excited crowd they went to the Governor's residence to protest against this open violation of the laws of the Koran. No one knew, however, whether Nimrod had been an orthodox prophet or an unbeliever. The Pasha, to be on the safe side, ordered Layard to respect the "remains" and put a stop to the excavations for the time being. This was not the first time that Layard had been held up by fanaticism and superstition as well as by the officials at Mosul. He went to see the Pasha and the matter was soon settled. A *firman* by the Sultan finally enabled him to proceed.

Several more examples of these mythical winged animals, half man half beast, soon came to light. They flanked all fronts of buildings and the doors of all the great halls. We now know that they represented the astral gods of the four corners of the earth: Marduk, the winged bull, Nebo the man, Nergal the winged lion and Ninib the eagle. All these statues still bore traces of polychromatic painting. Layard was greatly impressed by these magnificent examples of Assyrian art:

[1] Op. cit., vol. i, pp. 66–67.

"I used to contemplate for hours these mysterious emblems, and muse over their intent and history. What more noble forms could have ushered the people into the temple of their gods? What more sublime images could have been borrowed from nature by men who sought, unaided by the light of revealed religion, to embody their conception of the wisdom, power and ubiquity of a Supreme Being? They could find no better type of intellect and knowledge than the head of the man; of strength, than the body of the lion; of ubiquity, than the wings of the bird. These winged human-headed lions were not idle creations, the offspring of mere fancy; their meaning was written upon them. They had awed and instructed races which flourished 3000 years ago. Through the portals which they guarded, kings, priests and warriors had borne sacrifices to their altars, long before the wisdom of the East had penetrated to Greece, and had furnished its mythology with symbols long recognised by the Assyrian votaries. . . . For twenty-five centuries they had been hidden from the eye of man, and they now stood forth once more in their ancient majesty. But how changed was the scene around them. The luxury and civilisation of a mighty nation had given place to the wretchedness and ignorance of a few half-barbarous tribes. The wealth of temples, and the riches of great cities, had been succeeded by ruins and shapeless heaps of earth. Above the spacious hall in which they stood, the plough had passed and the corn now waved. Egypt has monuments no less ancient and no less wonderful; but they have stood forth for ages to testify her early power and renown, whilst those before me had but now appeared to bear witness, in the word of the prophet, that once 'the Assyrian was a cedar in Lebanon with fair branches and with a shadowing shroud of an high stature; and his top was among the thick boughs . . . his height was exalted above all the trees of the field, and his boughs were multiplied, and his branches became long, because of the multitude of waters when he shot forth. All the fowls of heaven made their nests in his boughs, and under his branches did all the beasts of the field bring forth

their young, and under his shadow dwelt all great nations'
for now is 'Nineveh a desolation and dry like a wilderness,
and flocks lie down in the midst of her: all the beasts of the
nations, both the cormorant and the bittern, lodge in the
upper lintels of it; their voice sings in the windows; and
desolation is in the thresholds.' (Ezekiel, xxxi, 3, etc.;
Zephaniah, ii, 13 and 14.)"[1]

This north-western palace at Nimrud, from whose ruins
Layard exhumed these majestic representations of astral
divinities, and whose halls were later to yield him the finest
bas-reliefs, was subsequently identified as the palace of Assurnasirpal II (885–860), the king who had transferred his residence
from Assur to Calah. It was the oldest and the finest palace
in the city and its discovery made the name of Henry Layard
famous. As well as many scenes of military campaigns, battles,
sieges and building works, the royal residence contained those
famous hunting scenes showing wild animals in flight, wounded,
or being put to death. The dramatic naturalism of these
scenes was to make Assyrian art famous throughout the world.
The Assyrian kings were the first of a line of hunting monarchs
which continued over thousands of years; the last examples
were to be found in the early years of our own twentieth century. Hunting afforded them the opportunity of exercising,
in times of peace, their courage, skill and strength. Nimrud,
the mythical founder of the kingdom of Assyria, was "a great
hunter before the Lord". Ninus, the legendary builder of
Nineveh, was as famous for his combats with lions and leopards
as for his triumphs over warring peoples. The Babylonians,
Assyrians and Persians, the Byzantine Emperors and the
ancient Caliphs decorated their palaces and their hunting
lodges with scenes from the chase. The same kind of decoration
also recurred in clothing and carpets. Then, as now, all kinds
of wild animals from wild asses and gazelles to lions and tigers,
were kept in a "paradise" (park) at the disposal of the king
whenever he wished to hunt. Assyrian bas-reliefs show us the
king standing in his chariot, drawing his bow on the wild

[1] Op. cit., vol. i, pp. 69–71.

animals which often attacked his horses, whilst warriors on foot run up ready to assist in case of danger. This art was only in its early stages in the period of Assurnasirpal. It reaches perfection in the palace of Assurbanipal (668–626) at Kuyunjik which yielded the striking pictures of the "lion pierced by an arrow" and the "lioness fatally wounded" now to be admired in the British Museum.

After discovering the winged bulls and the human-headed lions one of Layard's first problems was to get two of these colossal statues to London. The danger of incursions by tribes of thieving Bedouins, made desperate by recent bad harvests, only served to hasten the project. The two least enormous and best preserved pieces, a bull and a lion, were chosen and mounted on a massive waggon specially made for them at Mosul. Greatly intrigued by the operation, the whole population turned out to watch the waggon, drawn by a pair of buffaloes and a whole army of Arabs and Chaldaeans, as it left the town and crossed the river on the worm-eaten boat-bridge. To get the bull out of the ruins a trench had to be dug twenty-three feet deep, ninety-eight feet long and over sixteen feet wide. The huge load was then hauled along on rollers, with enormous difficulty, by hordes of Arabs who shrieked wildly as they pulled on the ropes. Nothing can better describe the natives' feelings than the words of Sheik Abd-ur-rahman whom his friend Layard reports as saying:

"Wonderful! Wonderful! There is surely no God but God, and Mohammed is his Prophet. In the name of the Most High, tell me, O Bey, what you are going to do with those stones. So many thousands of purses spent upon such things! Can it be, as you say, that your people learn wisdom from them; or is it, as his reverence the Cadi declares, that they are to go to the palace of your Queen, who, with the rest of the unbelievers, worships these idols? As for wisdom, these figures will not teach you to make any better knives, or scissors, or chintzes; and it is in the making of those things that the English show their wisdom. But God is great! God is great! Here are stones which have been

buried ever since the time of the holy Noah—peace be with
him! Perhaps they were under ground before the deluge.
I have lived on these lands for years. My father, and the
father of my father, pitched their tents here before me;
but they never heard of these figures. For twelve hundred
years have the true believers (and, praise be to God! all
true wisdom is with them alone) been settled in this country,
and none of them ever heard of a palace under ground.
Neither did they who went before them. But lo! here comes
a Frank from many days' journey off, and he walks up to the
very place, and he takes a stick, and makes a line here, and
makes a line there. Here, says he, is the palace; there,
says he, is the gate; and he shows us what has been all our
lives beneath our feet, without our having known anything
about it. Wonderful! Wonderful! Is it by books, is it by
magic, is it by your prophets, that you have learnt these
things? Speak, O Bey; tell me the secret of wisdom." [1]

Festivities, music and dancing to celebrate the success of
this first day went on all night long. The second act began on
the following day: the transporting of the winged bull as far
as the river. The buffaloes harnessed to the waggon proved
incapable of moving it and it had to be drawn by men. Layard
rode at the head with the Sheik, to show the way, and was
followed by musicians playing with all their might on drums
and fifes:

"The cart followed, dragged by about three hundred
men, all screeching at the top of their voices, and urged on
by the Cawasses and superintendents. The procession was
closed by the women, who kept up the enthusiasm of the
Arabs by their shrill cries. Abd-ur-rahman's horsemen
performed divers feats round the group, dashing backwards
and forwards, and charging with their spears." [2]

The waggon got stuck twice before it reached the river bank.
The human-headed winged lion followed by the same route.

[1] Op. cit., vol. ii, pp. 84–85.   [2] Op. cit., vol. ii, p. 88.

Finally the two colossi were laid on the river bank ready to be loaded on to a raft and floated downstream to Basra. Then the third act began. Layard's previous shipments had been plaques. These had presented no problems as they were comparatively light. They had been shipped down to Baghdad by Mosul boatmen, thence to Basra by boatmen from Baghdad and finally transferred to ocean-going vessels. As the transshipment of these colossi at Baghdad would have caused great difficulties, Layard insisted on their being ferried down direct to Basra. The Mosul boatmen, however, who had never gone farther than Baghdad, would have none of this. The problem was eventually solved by finding a Baghdad boatman, under the threat of prison for debt, who was willing to take charge of the whole operation.

The first expedition was now almost over, and Layard prepared to leave Nimrud. Before doing so, however, he was anxious to rebury the walls covered with plaques and the doors guarded by the winged colossi to protect them from the depredations of the "true believers" who had been known to tear out the eyes from the statues of human beings to prevent them from exercising any magical power. Before again sealing up these exhumed treasures, Layard took the readers of his *Nineveh and its Remains* once more through the ruins of the great palace:

"On approaching the mound, not a trace of building can be perceived, except a small mud hut covered with reeds, erected for the accommodation of my Chaldaean workmen. We ascend this artificial hill, but still see no ruins, not a stone protruding from the soil. There is only a broad level platform before us, perhaps covered with a luxuriant crop of barley, or may be yellow and parched, without a blade of vegetation, except here and there a scanty tuft of camelthorn. Low black heaps, surrounded by brushwood and dried grass, a thin column of smoke issuing from the midst of them, are scattered here and there. These are the tents of the Arabs; and a few miserable old women are groping about them, picking up camel's-dung or dry twigs. One or two girls, with firm step and erect carriage, are just reaching the top of the mound, with the water-jar on their shoulders, or a bundle of brushwood on their heads. On all sides of us, apparently issuing from under ground, are long lines of wild-looking beings, with dishevelled hair, their limbs only half concealed by a short loose shirt, some jumping and capering, and all hurrying to and fro shouting like madmen. Each one carries a basket, and as he reaches the edge of the mound, or some convenient spot near, empties its contents, raising at the same time a cloud of dust. He then returns at the top of his speed, dancing and yelling as before, and flourishing his basket over his head; again he suddenly disappears in the bowels of the earth, from whence he emerged. These are the workmen employed in removing the rubbish from the ruins.

"We will descend into the principal trench, by a flight of steps rudely cut into the earth, near the western face of the mound. . . . We descend about twenty feet, and suddenly find ourselves between a pair of colossal lions, winged and human-headed, forming a portal. . . . In the subterraneous labyrinth which we have reached, all is bustle and confusion. Arabs are running about in different directions; some bearing baskets filled with earth, others carrying the water-jars to their companions. The Chaldaeans . . . in their striped dresses and curious conical caps, are digging with picks into the tenacious earth, raising a dense cloud of fine dust at every stroke. The wild strains of Kurdish music may be heard occasionally issuing from some distant part of the ruins, and if they are caught by the parties at work, the Arabs join their voices in chorus, raise the war-cry, and labour with renewed energy. . . . We issue from between the winged lions, and enter the remains of the principal hall. On both sides of us are sculptured gigantic winged figures; some with the heads of eagles, others entirely human, and carrying mysterious symbols in their hands. . . . One of them has, however, fallen across the entrance, and there is just room to creep beneath it. Beyond this portal is a winged figure, and two slabs with bas-reliefs; but they have

55

been so much injured that we can scarcely trace the subject upon them. Further on there are no traces of wall, although a deep trench has been opened. The opposite side of the hall has also disappeared, and we only see a high wall of earth. On examining it attentively, we can detect the marks of masonry; and we soon find that it is a solid structure built of bricks of unbaked clay, now of the same colour as the surrounding soil, and scarcely to be distinguished from it.

"The slabs of alabaster, fallen from their original position, have, however, been raised; and we tread in the midst of a maze of small bas-reliefs, representing chariots, horsemen, battles and sieges. Perhaps the workmen are about to raise a slab for the first time; and we watch, with eager curiosity, what new event of Assyrian history, or what unknown custom or religious ceremony, may be illustrated by the sculpture beneath.

"Having walked about one hundred feet amongst these scattered monuments of ancient history and art, we reach another doorway, formed by gigantic winged bulls in yellow limestone. One is still entire; but its companion has fallen, and is broken into several pieces—the great human head is at our feet.

"We pass on without turning into the part of the building to which this portal leads. Beyond it we see another winged figure, holding a graceful flower in its hand, and apparently presenting it as an offering to the winged bull. Adjoining this sculpture we find eight fine bas-reliefs. There is the king, hunting, and triumphing over, the lion and wild bull; and the siege of the castle, with the battering-ram. We have now reached the end of the hall, and find before us an elaborate and beautiful sculpture, representing two kings, standing beneath the emblem of the supreme deity, and attended by winged figures. Between them is the sacred tree. In front of this bas-relief is the great stone platform, upon which, in days of old, may have been placed the throne of the Assyrian monarch, when he received his captive enemies, or his courtiers.

"To the left of us is a fourth outlet from the hall, formed by another pair of lions. We issue from between them, and find ourselves on the edge of a deep ravine, to the north of which rises, high above us, the lofty pyramid. Figures of captives bearing objects of tribute—ear-rings, bracelets, and monkeys—may be seen on walls near this ravine; and two enormous bulls, and two winged figures above fourteen feet high, are lying on its very edge.

"As the ravine bounds the ruins on this side, we must return to the yellow bulls. Passing through the entrance formed by them, we enter a large chamber surrounded by eagle-headed figures; at one end of it is a doorway guarded by two priests or divinities, and in the centre another portal with winged bulls. Whichever way we turn, we find ourselves in the midst of a nest of rooms; and without an acquaintance with the intricacies of the place, we should soon lose ourselves in this labyrinth. The accumulated rubbish being generally left in the centre of the chambers, the whole excavation consists of a number of narrow passages, panelled on one side with slabs of alabaster; and shut in on the other by a high wall of earth, half buried in which may here and there be seen a broken vase, or a brick painted with brilliant colours. We may wander through these galleries for an hour or two, examining the marvellous sculptures, or the numerous inscriptions that surround us. Here we meet long rows of kings, attended by their eunuchs and priests—there lines of winged figures, carrying fir-cones and religious emblems, and seemingly in adoration before the mystic tree. Other entrances, formed by winged lions and bulls, lead us into new chambers. In every one of them are fresh objects of curiosity and surprise. At length, wearied, we issue from the buried edifice by a trench on the opposite side to that by which we entered, and find ourselves again upon the naked platform. We look around in vain for any traces of the wonderful remains we have just seen, and are half inclined to believe that we have dreamed a dream, or have been listening to some tale of Eastern romance. Some, who may hereafter tread on the spot when the grass again grows over the ruins of the Assyrian palaces, may indeed suspect that I have been relating a vision."[1]

Layard returned to Mosul in the autumn of the following year, 1849, to undertake his second campaign. This time he dug on the two mounds of Kuyunjik and Nimrud. At Kuyunjik he found, amongst other objects, bas-reliefs representing the transporting of the winged colossi and of enormous blocks of stone. These have appeared many times in illustrations. A complete building was cleared and identified as the palace of Sennacherib (705–681). The south-east front of the palace was decorated with figures of humans and winged bulls in high relief. From Nimrud Layard shipped a further pair of human-headed lions via Basra to London. Leaving a reliable overseer at the Kuyunjik site, he set off to visit other ruined cities in Mesopotamia and Kurdistan, then sailed down the Tigris in a kellek, followed by a great raft loaded with the treasures he had found in Nineveh. His goal was now the ruins of Babylon on the Euphrates, near the town of Hillah. This may be reached from Baghdad south-west across the marshy plain, crossed by canals, which lies between the Tigris and the Euphrates.

The true discovery of the civilisation of Assyria, for the Western world at least, took place, not on the banks of the Tigris, but in London in the Crystal Palace. This had housed the Great Exhibition of 1851 in Hyde Park and was transferred in 1854 to Sydenham for use as a museum. In addition to its Egyptian, Greek and Roman "courts" it included a "Nineveh court". A façade and two halls of a palace gave the visitor the most accurate impression possible of the architecture and decoration of Nineveh. This was, of course, intended for the general public and not for archaeologists. The winged colossi and bas-reliefs were moulded in plaster and shown in their many bright colours. The large hall was a reconstruction of a ceremonial hall and the smaller one that of a royal apartment.

Fifty years after Layard and the French archaeologists who followed him had uncovered Assyrian temples and palaces, the

[1] Op. cit., vol. ii, pp. 109–114.

German Oriental Society decided to excavate the ruins of Assur. This was the oldest capital of Assyria and was buried under the mound of Kelle Shergat. The campaign was begun in 1903 by Robert Koldewey, well known for his excavations at Babylon, and continued until 1914 by Walter Andrae and his collaborators. In the fifty years that had passed, the technique of excavation, improvised and amateurish at first, had improved and developed into a truly scientific method. Today the work is directed by a staff of experienced specialists: engineers, architects, epigraphists, numismatists, ceramists, chemists, illustrators and photographers. The site is dug out in successive layers and examined with the greatest care to establish the dates of the successive periods of history of these ancient cities. The merest fragment of pottery is kept for examination by the competent specialist. Each new layer of civilisation is photographed and described in the greatest detail as it comes to light. The soil is sieved and the remains are assembled and classified before the earth is cleared ready for the excavation of the next layer. Compared with modern excavators Layard and his contemporaries might almost be said to have been pillagers like our ancestors who rushed to exploit the richest seams in the gold mines and abandoned whole shafts and galleries which today still yield considerable treasure to those who are patient enough to sieve and wash the earth.

It often happened in Layard's time that the excavators did not know when or under which king these palaces and temples had been built. The prize exhibits were torn down from the walls and the rest was left exposed to the elements until, as Layard has said, "the grass has grown once more over the ruins of the Assyrian palaces". Ruins such as Nineveh, Calah, and Khorsabad, which yielded such magnificent remains at so little cost, were exceptions. Excavators usually had to be content with much less and to proceed "ex ungue leonem". Assur yielded far less to the archaeologists than Layard found in the other royal palaces, yet we know more about it today. Andrae, in fact, like Koldewey on Babylon, has written a book on *The Rediscovery of Assur*. Let us now pay a brief visit to the city with Andrae as our guide.

The city which bears the name of Ashur, the god and ruler of the land of Assyria, lies on a rocky promontory falling sheer on to the plain and former bed of the Tigris. The eastern edge of this promontory rises steeply above the present west bank of the river. To the south and west it falls gently down to the plains. This was the natural way of approach to the city, and it is here that the monumental gates are to be found. The city was thus naturally defended on two sides of its triangular platform—a classical example of the siting of a prehistoric town. There were three entrances: the south gate, the west gate and the Gurgurri gate. The latter led to the north side of the town. Here, along the edge of the plateau, the façades of palaces and temples rose proudly in line: the temple of Ashur, the tower of Ashur-Enlil, the Old Palace, the temple of Anu-Adad and the New Palace. Behind them stood the temples of Ishtar and Sin-Shamash. Outside the town, in the plain below and beside the former river bed, a third of a mile from the Gurgurri gate, stood Ashur's festival temple. These buildings all date from different periods and were several times restored, firstly in the third millennium in the time of the Akkadian priest-kings and the national state which lasted until 2000, then in the time of Hammurabi when Assur took over from Babylon, then in the fifteenth and the thirteenth to the ninth centuries and finally in the eighth and seventh centuries under the last Assyrian kings. Under the latter Assur enjoyed its last splendour before its decline in about 600. Later, however, in the Babylonian, Persian, Seleucid, Parthian and Sassanian periods, Assur was again inhabited and again enriched with new buildings.

The gods of Assur lived on the northern fringe of the city, high in the heavens in their temple towers, or in the dark sanctuaries of the lower courts. They dominated the city and the surrounding plain. There was Ashur, the king of the gods and the Assyrian national deity, Anu and Adad, the gods of the heavens and the fertilising rains, Enlil, the lord of the lands, Sin and Shamash, the moon and sun gods and Ishtar the queen of the gods, the mother-goddess. Their temples had tall façades with crenellated tops. Higher still, above the flat temple roofs, rose the terraces of the ziggurats. The external walls were lined with vertical grooves like organ-pipes and dressed with brightly coloured glazed bricks. The city was protected by a crenellated wall. This was double on the south and west sides where it was exposed. This was a very old system of defence which can still be seen in Constantinople. There were also double gates on these sides. The houses were of unbaked brick and had flat roofs. The rich family's house had an inner and an outer courtyard which were separated by the men's quarters. The walls were painted red with a black and white painted frieze. There were altars in recesses for worship in the home. The inner courtyard and the rooms leading off it were for the use of the mistress of the house, the children and the servants. In size and arrangement the men's living-room was similar, but the women's had an adjoining bedroom, bathroom and other rooms. The ordinary family's house was small with an inner courtyard only and a main living-room. There were high wooden chairs with backs, stools and benches to sit on, and, for sleeping, couches with rounded ends. The floor was covered with carpets or matting. At night-time it was customary to stroll on the terraces to enjoy the cool air and to try to read the stars from which it seemed that the gods were looking down.

The fronts of the temples were resplendent with many-coloured glazed brick. The plinths and the walls were ornate with lions, sphinxes and representations of battle-scenes. These decorations dated principally from the time of Sennacherib. The alabaster plaques found in the northern capital cities give place here to glazed brick mosaics of Babylonian origin. This was a new technique and showed up the battle-scenes, sieges and processions of tribute-bearers in the brightest of colours. As on the walls of the Persian mosques two thousand years later, the inscriptions were in white on a turquoise-blue background. As later in Persia also, the favourite colours used were black, yellow and blue. The interior of the temples consisted of a number of courts lined with halls. The god's sanctuary, like the private suites of rooms in our large houses of a few generations ago, was in the part of the temple facing the longest side of the courtyard. In some cases it was pre-ceded by an antechamber. The statue of the god was not at the end of the central axis, but in a recess in the shorter side. This arrangement was peculiar to Assyria.

As throughout Asia Minor, the New Year Festival com-memorated annually the god's death and resurrection. The solemn procession left the temple of Ashur to the singing of plaintive hymns. The statue of the god was brought down, veiled, from the temple to the river-bank and thence carried into the festival temple. It was followed by the images of the other gods which were accompanied by the colleges of priests. The arms of the Tigris symbolised the river of Hell. All the sacred emblems, headed by those of Ashur, under canopies glittering with gold, were brought down and put on to boats. Accompanied by priests and priestesses they glided silently down the peaceful waters of the river. On reaching the *akitu* the procession slowly entered the tree-lined court and the priests arranged the statues of the gods in the sanctuaries prepared for them. This temple differed from other Assyrian temples in that all its rooms were arranged along the main axes. Sennacherib had conquered and destroyed Babylon in 689 and had transferred to Assur the cult of Marduk, the principal Babylonian god. He offered this conquest as a hom-age to the Assyrian national god whose prestige was thereby considerably enhanced. The god Ashur-Marduk was then entitled to a Sacred Way such as Marduk had had in Babylon and he was given a festival temple.

4

THE TOWER OF BABEL

Originally Babylon was merely a trading-place for Eridu and Ur, the two great Sumerian centres of commerce at the mouth of the Euphrates, but she surpassed them both, and all the other cities of Mesopotamia, making her name famous for all time. The choice of her name already foretold her future: Bab-Ili, "Gate of God". By her civilisation she overcame her enemies and conquerors, Assyrians, Kassites, Hurrians and Hittites, and forced them to contribute to her glory. She was forever in rebellion, forever impatient to throw off the barbarian yoke; she paid for her temerity often and cruelly with her blood and her ruins. The Assyrian kings punished her: Tekulti-Enurta, Sargon, Sennacherib, Assurbanipal and Xerxes the Persian. Each one destroyed also the sacred tower of her great patron god Marduk, who shared her defeats as well as her victories, who grew with her and with her knew captivity under the Assyrians. Just as earthly kings assume the title and powers of the rulers they conquer, so do the victorious gods appropriate the spheres of influence of the divinities they subject; thus did Marduk assume the power of Anu, the king of the gods, of Enlil the "Lord of the Lands" and of Bel the "Ruler of the Kingdom of the Air".

> "Thy name everywhere in the mouths of men bringeth
> happiness.
> Marduk, great king, may I by thy holy will
> Enjoy health and adore thy holiness,
> May my prayer be answered.
> Put truth into my mouth
> And good thoughts into my heart. . . .

Marduk, great king, give life unto me!
My soul is thine to command!"[1]

Marduk's blue and gold sanctuary could be seen from afar over the plain of the Euphrates, shining out from the top of the staged tower. It was indeed a proud edifice, well worthy to be his dwelling, that the Assyrian kings Asshardon, Assurbanipal and Nabopolassar had built for him. The base of the tower was nearly a hundred yards square and the tower itself was of the same height; the first stage was one hundred and eighteen feet high, the second fifty-nine feet, the third, fourth, fifth and sixth each nineteen feet. The sanctuary rose nearly fifty feet above the top stage, shining with its splendour of blue bricks under a gold roof. Here it was that the god, reclining on a gold couch, consumed the sacrificial offerings. Such was Etemenanki, the upper temple, the "House of the Foundation of Heaven and Earth", towering above Esagil, the lower temple. In the sanctuaries arranged around the inner courtyard dwelt the other gods, Marduk's guests: Nabu, Tashmetum, Ea, Nusku, Anu and Sin. "I have employed many peoples . . . from many lands out of all the nations to build Etemenanki" wrote Nebuchadnezzar on the clay tablets which record the annals of his reign. It is not surprising, therefore, that Alexander, the conqueror of the world, could not clear away from the enormous ziggurat the rubble under which it had lain buried since its last destruction by Xerxes, even though he set to the task ten thousand men who worked for two months, and finally his whole army. His intended reconstruction of the temple was prevented by his death, and what his successors rebuilt was but a shadow of its former greatness. . . .

Ceremonies were held throughout the year in the different temples. The influence which these may have had on Chris-

[1] The old poems and epics of Mesopotamia go back in many cases to an unknown date in the third millennium B.C. What we know of them has been pieced together from clay tablets preserved in Old Babylonian sites (second millennium B.C.), and in greater numbers from the remains of Assyrian and Neo-Babylonian libraries (*circa* 900–500 B.C.). The use of the very durable clay tablet has saved a treasure of early literature and governmental and financial accounts for the modern world.

4. Stele from Babylon engraved with a
charter. About 1140 B.C.

5.&6. The ruins of Persepolis.

tian festivals will be clear from a description of the festival
of the New Year, the most important in Babylon. This was
called the Akitu and was held at the Spring equinox in the
first days of the month of Nisan. Before dawn the high priest
of the temple of the Esagil went alone into Marduk's sanctuary,
drew back the curtain which hid the statue of the god, and
addressed to him a secret prayer known as the "Mystery of
the Esagil":

"Lord who in thy fury knowest no equal,
Lord, king of goodness, master of the lands,
Thou who hast made the happiness of the powerful gods,
Lord whose glance layeth low the mighty;
Ruler of kings, light of men who shareth out our fortunes,
Oh Lord, Babel is thy throne and Bosippa thy crown,
The wide heavens are thy whole belly.
Oh Lord, with thine eyes thou gazest upon the universe ...
With thine arms thou seizest the mighty . . .
With thy glance thou grantest them mercy.
Make them to see thy light so that they may proclaim thy
    power,
Lord of the lands, light of the Igigi [1] whose word is
    benediction,
Who would not proclaim the acts of thy power,
Speak of thy greatness or celebrate thy almighty rule?
Lord of the lands who dwellest in E-ud-ul,
Whose hand raiseth the fallen,
Ever look with pity on thy city of Babel,
Towards Esagil, thy temple, turn thy face,
Secure the freedom of thy children of Babel!"

Each morning the high priest addressed another prayer to
Marduk and on the third day he also prayed to Marduk's
wife, Zarpanit, the merciful "Madonna":

[1] The Igigi are the circumpolar stars, thought to be celestial spirits, which never
go below the horizon. E-ud-ul, "House of the far-off days" means the temple
of the Esagil. The German translations of the hymns are from Heinrich
Zimmern's *Das Babylonische Neujahrfest*, Der alte Orient, vol. 25.

"She is powerful, divine, the highest of goddesses,

Zarpanit, the brightest of the stars, who dwelleth in the E-ud-ul.

The most radiant among the goddesses, whose raiment is light. . . .

Zarpanit, whose throne is most high in the heavens!

My mistress is radiant, sublime, most high,

Among the goddesses she hath no equal!

She who accuseth and defendeth,

Who maketh the rich to be poor and the poor to be rich,

Who layeth low the enemy and feareth not his divinity,

Who saveth the prisoner and raiseth the fallen with her hand!

Bless the slave who blesseth thy name.

Make sure the fate of the king who feareth thee.

Give life to thy children of Babel;

Intercede for them with Marduk the king of the gods,

So that they may proclaim thy glory, raise high thy rule,

Proclaim thy acts and celebrate thy name!

(To me) to the servant who blesseth thee, grant thy grace,

In danger and in need, take him by the hand,

In sickness and in suffering give him life!

So that he may forever walk in joy and happiness,

So that he may in all places proclaim thy acts to man!"

The high priest then went into the main courtyard of the temple, open to the stars, and turning towards the constellation of the Ram he said three times: "Ram, image of Heaven and Earth!" This constellation, which had not been visible for a long time, was in fact reappearing over Babylon at this time of the year, each day a little earlier, and was therefore worshipped as the symbol of the Feast of the New Year and the Spring. In the evening of the same day the high priest recited in front of the statue of Marduk the "Poem of Creation" which begins thus:

"When on high the Heavens had no name,
Nor the earth below,
When Apsu, the First of gods, their Creator,
And Tiamat, the mother of them all,
Caused the waters to run together. . . ."

The epic describes the origin of the world of the gods and the deadly struggle between the first and the second generations, which was similar to the struggle between the Greek gods and the Titans. Apsu and Tiamat produce generations of gods. The conflict arises between the parents and the new gods, Ea and his wife Damkina, who gives birth to a prodigious child destined to overthrow the forces of darkness and to create the present world. Tiamat, in her revenge, gives birth to eleven fearful monsters, some of which seem to have passed into the signs of the zodiac: scorpion-men, fish-men, snakes, dragons and salamanders. Marduk, the child of Ea and Damkina, has in the meantime grown up, and is begged by the gods, now helpless, to wage battle against the first generation and its monsters. Marduk agrees on condition that after his victory he will be recognised as king of the gods. They give their consent at a banquet the description of which foreshadows the festivals of Homer's Olympus:

"All the great gods, all those who rule the world
Went in before Anshar, filling the hall,
Embraced each other, stood together,
Conversed and took their places for the feast.
They broke bread, drank the wine,
The sweet drink bewitched their senses. . . .
Intoxicated now, their feelings were inflamed,
To Marduk, their saviour, they gave the command of the
    world."

Is there anywhere a more exquisite testimony to man's unchanging behaviour through time and race? The gods, befuddled and carefree, rashly hand over to Marduk nothing less than supreme power:

"Be therefore the most venerated among the great gods,
May thy destiny surpass all others, thy will be all-powerful!
From this hour may thy command be irrevocable,
Thy hand hath the power to raise up or bring down!
Oh Marduk, since thou wilt be our avenger,
We commit to thy hands the command of the Universe!"

Whereupon Marduk, well armed and equipped, goes off to attack Tiamat, kills her and, dividing her body in two, creates the sky and the earth with the sun, the moon and the stars, the plants, the animals and man. The "Poem of the Creation" ends with a majestic hymn to the glory of Marduk.

There then followed the great purification of the temple and the preparations for the procession. Before the god was brought out, the king handed over the insignia of his office to Marduk; these insignia were then handed back to the king by the high priest after the king had recited a humble confession, by which he made penance for all his people and received the god's pardon. On the sixth day of Nisan, the god Nabu from the sister-town of Borsippa was brought in. Nabu, originally "Guardian of the World" and "Lord of the World", had had to cede these titles to Marduk and, as the inventor of writing, was worshipped as the "Scribe of the Fates". He was also the God of Trade, the Babylonian Hermes. His statue was then placed in a chapel of the Esagil and the emblems of numerous other gods from Kish, Uruk, Nippur, Sippar and other cities were placed in the temple.

During the New Year Festivals there was also performed the sacred drama, or "mystery". In this, Bel-Marduk, the sick and humiliated god, descended into Hell to rise up again into the light, a suffering, a passion, which he had to endure, like Tamuz-Ishtar and all the other gods whose lot it is to die as the dark days of winter begin and to rise again with the coming of spring. This sacred play was also an ancient Sumerian tradition which had come down into the cult of Marduk; this light myth appears to have been foreign to the lands of the Euphrates and was brought there by the Sumerians from their northern mountain country. Like the Christian Saviour,

Bel-Marduk suffered his Passion, was tortured, put to death and rose again, the god of light who triumphed over the powers of darkness. . . .

One of the most important New Year ceremonies was the "Decreeing of Destiny". This took place on the eighth and the eleventh days of Nisan in the "Chapel of Destiny". There Marduk, king of the gods, of heaven and earth, stayed to receive homage from the other gods and decreed the fates for the coming year. These decrees were inscribed on tablets by Nabu, the "Scribe of the Universe".

Then began the famous New Year procession: the gods, leaving the Chapel of Destiny, passed in procession through the gate of Ishtar and along the sacred way to the river, where they embarked for the House of Prayer outside the city. The German Oriental Society has completely excavated this sacred way and its massive Gate of Ishtar, a building in two parts which crosses the double outer wall and is decorated with brightly coloured glazed brick reliefs of lions, bulls and dragons. Whilst the procession halted on the river bank to transfer the statues from waggon to boat, hymns were sung to the various gods, such as this one to Marduk, in which we may notice some slight irony:

"Oh Lord, why dost thou not sojourn in Babel?
Is not thy throne in the Esagil?
Art thou no longer Lord of Babel?
Art thou no longer so called by Zarpanit?"

Perhaps at this moment also was sung this lovely hymn to Ishtar:

"Oh thou sublime Ishtar, armed for the fray,
Mistress adorned in splendour and clothed in anger!
Gentle-sounding flute, heifer which butts the corners of
    the earth with its horns,
Burning brand which wages war, which threatens heaven
    and earth,
Mighty Ishtar who hast created man,

69

Who walkest in front of the cattle, who lovest the shepherd,
Shepherdess of all lands, of the whole universe!
Keeper of the flocks, we kneel before thee, we search for
   thee,
Thou healest the ill-treated and the downcast and givest
   him back his right. . . ."

The gods' statues remained for three days in the temple of
the New Year feast outside the city, during which time hymns
were sung and sacrifices made to them. On the eleventh day
of Nisan the procession returned to the Esagil and after a
further congregation of the gods in the Chapel of Destiny the
New Year feast came to an end.

In the old quarter of the city the palaces of the former kings
were strung out along the eastern bank of the Euphrates and
the vast temple of the Esagil rose up, topped by the Etemenanki. There was not sufficient room here for the new palace
which Nebuchadnezzar planned to build. On a basalt tablet
found amongst the ruins and relating to the building works at
Babylon and Borsippa, the monarch declares that, as he is
unwilling to interfere with the sacred dwellings of the god
Marduk or the processional way or the Arahtu canal which
runs east alongside the temples and the palaces, he has chosen
to build his new palace outside the city gates. He did in fact
build at the northern exit of the city on the east bank of the
river and his palace had mighty foundations and magnificent
terraced gardens. These came to be known as "the hanging
gardens of Semiramis". The palace, as the king himself
proudly proclaimed, was "made to be admired by all men for
its magnificence, to be respected for its richness and grandeur,
and is truly majestic in its splendour". It rose above the outer
wall of the town like a citadel. The view from its terraces,
above the sea of roofs of the city, embraced the palm groves
and orchards of the oases, irrigated by the canals, and, still
further beyond, the staged tower of Borsippa. Immediately in
front of the palace, on the south side, lay the inner wall of the
city, behind the mighty walls of the former royal palace.
Further on, rising from its gardens, the crenellated Esagil

was topped by the high tower of the Etemenanki. All these buildings were reflected in the waters of the Euphrates over which glided sailing vessels without number. Downstream could be seen the great Euphrates bridge, built by the king. This connected the eastern part of the city, containing the temples and palaces, with the western districts on the other bank. How easily we can understand the pride in the builder-king's words: "Is not this the great Babel which in my almighty power I have raised up as my royal throne in honour of my majesty?" The king's pride was justified: this new Babel, which had risen like the phoenix from the ruins left by the Assyrians, although begun by his father Nabopolassar, was largely his own creation. Marduk rewarded him with a long reign of more than two score years. Twenty years later Cyrus, king of the Persians, captured the city without a struggle. He commanded that there should be no pillaging or destruction, and the proud city made such an impression on him that he preferred it to Susa as a winter residence. In his summer residence at Pasagardae on the Iranian plateau, he had a tomb built in the form of a miniature ziggurat: his last resting place was raised on a six-stage building in the middle of a park—a small Etemenanki.

Babylonia knew two great periods of splendour: the first under Hammurabi (1792–1750 B.C.) and the second under Nebuchadnezzar (604–562) who aimed at a revival of the age of Hammurabi whose history he knew well. An interval of over a millennium separates these two periods, an interval which saw the Hittite and Kassite invasions and the supremacy of the Assyrians, and is almost as long as the time between the ages of Augustus and Charles V. So solid was the organisation of the two empires of Rome and Babylon that they outlived centuries of foreign domination and revived in the splendour of a brilliant renaissance. The two capitals of ancient Asia and ancient Europe have several common features. They did not invent anything new: their strength lay in their powers of assimilation and organisation. They assimilated the ancient civilisations of the Iranians and Sumerians, the Carthaginians and the Greeks and from them produced new civilisations which have ruled the world. The Babylonians, for example, adopted the cuneiform writing of the Sumerians to transcribe their own language which became one of the main languages of the world. Tablets found at Tell el Amarna in Egypt show that the whole of the Near East was using Sumero-Babylonian writing towards the middle of the second millennium B.C., and that the Babylonian language, in a garbled form like levantine French or pidgin English, was the lingua franca of the Oriental peoples. The Babylonians adopted the ancient juridical principles of the Sumerians to make up the Code of Hammurabi, whose two hundred and eighty paragraphs, inscribed on a diorite stela, make it a forerunner of the Codes of Justinian and Napoleon.

The influence which Babylonia has exerted over all other civilisations, the revelation of which, some fifty years ago, led to the theory of "pan-Babylonianism", is unique in the history of the human race. How can this influence be explained? Firstly by the intensive trading activities between the various tribes and peoples from the very earliest times, then by the similarity in the structure of men's minds and in their reactions and attitudes to cosmic processes and natural events. It was thus possible for a civilisation, after striving for a thousand years for a coherent system in the relations between man and nature, to impose its pattern on neighbouring peoples.

Primitive man was particularly impressed by the night sky with its multitude of stars. The explanation of phenomena which filled him with fear and astonishment naturally led to a particular conception of the world, to a cosmography. The cosmography elaborated by the Babylonians was so clear and logical that no other nation at the time failed to come under its influence. We know as little about the origins of Babylonian astronomy as we do about when its inventors, the Sumerians, settled in the Euphrates valley, or where they came from. They enter history in about 3500 B.C., but by then they had a basic religious system. They were the first we know of to worship the stars; their gods were the constellations and they worshipped the sun and the moon. This led to the belief in a solid and comforting bond of union between the destiny of the god and that of man. We on earth must behave as the gods behave in heaven; we are the microcosm of this macrocosm in the skies. This voluntary submission to the will of the gods reassured man, giving him a feeling of being protected, and calmed his anxieties about the world and life. When this conception broadened out into a religion it became widely accepted, triumphing over the totemic system of the Egyptians and in time occurring in India, China and Central America.

Astronomy was thus at once the fundamental and the highest science of the Sumerians and the Babylonians, and astrology was its practical application. If it was required to know the will of the gods, the stars must be studied accurately and continually. In ancient civilisations there was no ethical relationship between man and god and the moral notion of sin was unknown. The only thing which mattered was to follow the "etiquette" indicated and ordained by the stars, taught by astrology and comparable to court ceremonial. This "etiquette" was the origin of court procedure in Babylon, whose kings were held to be the sons and representatives of the gods. Life on earth was organised to be the counterpart of the life beyond and had to follow fixed laws prescribed by the priests, the interpreters of the divine will. Man's prosperity depended on his observance of the pre-established rules of universal order as revealed in the movement of the stars. The highest representatives of heaven, through which the divine will became manifest, were the planets Mercury, Venus, Mars, Jupiter, Saturn, the Moon and the Sun. Like the Earth, heaven had three dominions: air, earth and water (ocean) which were shown in descending order from north to south, corresponding to the geographic structure of Babylonia which was limited in the north by mountains and in the south by the sea. The region between the air and the water, in the heavens, was the "celestial dike" which corresponded to the Earth. Just as in the fluvial plain of Babylon the dikes were used as a means of communication, so, in the heavens, the planets moved along the "celestial dike" of the zodiac.

If the heavens were a projection of the earth, then the various countries of the earth must correspond to celestial regions.

Only those satisfying this condition were considered as "countries", that is each complete in itself under the sovereignty of a king, just as a heavenly region was under the sovereignty of a god whom the king represented on earth, the king being of divine origin and ruling "by the grace of god". This link between god and king has survived in modern times in several Asiatic Empires, notably in Burma, Siam, and Japan whenever these countries have been independent or have retained their monarchy.

The Babylonian heaven, therefore, was conceived in the image of the earth, both in the main and in greater detail. It had a Tigris and a Euphrates and it contained all the great cities of Babylon. Each of these was the seat of one of the gods who reigned in the celestial Babylon, Sippar, Eridu and Nippur, just as their representatives reigned over their earthly counterparts.[1]

The three dominions of heaven were embodied in Anu, the northern sky (Uranus) with the polar star as its centre; Enlil-Bel, Lord of the Earth, therefore of the zodiac and "Lord of the Lands" (Kronos); and Ea, god of the ocean depths (Poseidon). But the universe was governed, not so much by this first generation of gods as by a second: Sin, the Moon God, Shamash, the Sun God and Ishtar, the planet Venus. When Bel's supremacy was threatened by hostile forces he turned to these three to govern the "celestial dike" and thus they ruled over the earth also, as the earth was the counterpart of the "dike", and the worship of this triad became everywhere paramount. In Babylon, however, Shamash was replaced by Marduk. The emblems of the three gods were the discs of the moon, the sun and Venus. To these were added four others corresponding to the four quarters of the sun: Marduk (Jupiter), god of the spring until the summer solstice, Ninib (Mars), god of the autumn from the summer solstice, Babu (Mercury), the autumn sun until the winter solstice and Nergal (Saturn), the winter sun. This gave the number seven for the seven days of the week which in some countries still bear the names of the planets.

[1] Cf. Hugo Winkler: *Die Weltanschauung des Alten Orients.*

The Tower of Babel

This is only one of the ancient numerical systems which cannot be fully discussed here but which have all come down to us. Numbering by fives gave the five colours of the planets—blue, black, yellow, white and red—used to paint the stages of the towers. The addition of two, gold and silver, the colours of the sun and moon, gave seven, which was the number of the stages. The number five also rules minerals and metals and many other objects of daily life. Another number system of the Babylonians, of Sumerian origin and still in use today, is the division into 60 (hours and minutes) and the 360 degrees of the circle.

Perhaps the most decisive influence which Babylon has had on the Western world is that of quite a different kind: superstition, which has affected like a curse the lives of millions of people. In the form of astrology it was more or less harmless, but as magic and witchcraft it has done untold harm. From the Old Testament Book of Daniel we have learnt of the arts of the many astrologers, magi and Chaldeans in the time of Nebuchadnezzar, but it is only after the decline of Babylon that the false science of Babylonian astrology and soothsaying began to poison the Mediterranean world. For centuries it deceived Rome and today it is still in evidence in the ridiculous horoscopes of the popular press. The origin of these beliefs, fraught with such grave consequences, lay in the powerlessness of Babylonian medicine to deal with the sickness and plagues which attacked man so often and so suddenly. As both cause and remedy were unknown, these evils were attributed to evil spirits and devils which tortured and killed men either directly or through the intermediary of dreaded female persons. A text running through eight tablets and entitled "Torture by fire" describes most exactly how this evil originated in Babylonia. "By magical formula, by her look, by her saliva, the witch is able suddenly to bring all manner of evil on the body, the house and the property of man. She wanders through the streets, enters houses, deprives a man of his procreative powers, prevents a woman from conceiving, hinders the married couple in their conjugal duties, inflicts sickness on a man, drives the good god from his body and puts a demon in his

75

place. An image of the man, be it made of earth, wax or any other material, is all the witch requires to do him harm or destroy him: she may lay the image beside a body in a coffin, in a doorway or on a bridge where it is trampled under foot. . . . There is only one way of exorcising the witch's evil power: by fire. As the Babylonian rarely managed to catch her in the act he usually fell back on burning her in effigy. Most Babylonian exorcisms end with a prayer to the god of fire to whom the witch is consigned after a duly conducted trial."[1]   Whereas in Babylonia the burning in effigy was usually considered sufficient, in Europe this superstition led to the dreadful burning at the stake. The second paragraph of the Code of Hammurabi gives the penalty of death and the sequestration of all property for the crime of unjustly accusing a person of witchcraft, yet in the Western world thousands of innocent people died at the stake.

The clay tablets of the ruins of Babylon have revealed to us kings' proclamations, priests' hymns, trade contracts and judicial acts. They have also given us a glimpse of the thoughts and feelings of the average man of Babylonia: "I am a man of low degree, destiny overwhelmed my father and the mother who bore me has departed for the land of no return." "I am bowed under the curse which has afflicted me; I, a man of little substance, am scorned by the rich and the powerful. The strong man is wise and full of circumspection; if thy belly rumbles it is because of thy injustice towards thy god! The heart of god is as far away as the centre of the heavens. . . . Take heed, friend; hear my counsel! The word of the man of substance who has yet learned to kill is still held in respect, but the weak man who has not sinned is humiliated. The wastrel who has committed a crime can easily find witnesses in his favour but the just man who seeks God's counsel is persecuted; the pockets of the man whose name is thief are filled with *pasallu* and the powerful rob the purses of those who can scarce buy enough to eat." "Wherever thou lookest, thou seest nought but stupid men. The mind of the rich man is accounted good and he is made powerful. Who has ever troubled the rich and

[1] F. Delitzsch: *Mehr Licht.*

powerful man? He who bears the face of a god has a god to protect him; the man who is afflicted, even if he fears the goddess, is defeated by death." These are the words of the ordinary man of Babylon, of the Babylon of the common people with their complaints, their confessions, their wisdom the truth of which is almost frightening, coming down to us through five thousand years, which seem to have passed like a day without bringing any essential alleviation of man's unhappiness. Of all great Babylon's heritage, that is the most touchingly human.

5

"KING DARAYAVAUSH PROCLAIMS . . ."

From Assyrian inscriptions we know that certain Aryan tribes came into Iran through the Caucasus passes and the valley of Lake Urmia in the middle of the ninth century B.C. Other tribes of Aryans from the steppes to the east of the Caspian Sea had also penetrated to the Iranian plateau through the northern mountains. Two of these tribes became peoples with a strong political organisation and were to play a decisive part in the history of this part of Asia. They were the Medes, who occupied what is now an area bounded roughly by the north-western Iranian towns of Tehran, Hamadan, Kashan and Kasvin, and the Persians, who settled farther south in the valleys of the Zagros mountains as far as what is now the province of Fars. With the help of the Scythians, who had also crossed the Caucasus mountains, and the Babylonians, the Medes conquered the Assyrians in 612 B.C., destroyed their capital Nineveh and put an end forever to their supremacy. The Median conqueror was Cyaxares, but his son Astyages who succeeded him fell a prey to the soft luxuries he inherited from the Assyrians in his residence in the capital Ecbatana (near the modern Hamadan) and lost his throne to Cyrus, king of the city of Anshan. Cyrus had succeeded to the throne of Anshan and other cities in 559; in 550 he conquered the Medes and afterwards Lydia, whose king was Croesus, occupying its capital Sardis in 546, and then he took Babylon in 539. Thus in the space of a mere twenty years he had won control of the whole of Asia Minor. There still remained Egypt, however, but his projected invasion of this country was cut short by his death in 530 as he was fighting off an invasion of Eastern Iran by tribes of Aryans. With the help of his own people, the Persians, whom he made into a "people of lords" he had founded an empire. He exempted the Persians from taxes, requiring them only to follow him into war, and rewarded them by grants of land in the countries they conquered. With its satrapies (provinces ruled by a governor, or "satrap") royal Persia was a kind of federal state with a central administration which reached out over the whole empire, and a court of supreme justice with seven Persian judges who bore the title of "benefactors of the King".

Egypt was conquered by Cyrus's son Cambyses, who ruled from 529 to 522. He died on the way home, however, and the task of bringing back the army fell to the twenty-year-old Darius, who came from a different branch of Cyrus's Achaemenian family. Persia was in the throes of a general revolt led by Gaumata, a false Magian, who was passing himself off as Bardiya, the brother of Cambyses (whom Cambyses had in fact had secretly assassinated) and laying claim to the throne. With the help of the leaders of faithful tribes Darius defeated Gaumata, but owing to the jealousy aroused by the gifts and honours he had showered on his favourites, he had to contend with a further general revolt which broke out soon after his succession in 522 and spread immediately over the whole country from Babylonia to Bactria. The latter, like other lands beyond the Euphrates, had remained faithful to him. Order was not restored until 518, when Darius was at last able to devote himself to the organisation of his vast empire.

The empire was divided into twenty satrapies, whose governors, or "satraps", were chosen from the noblest Persian families. The position of these provincial governors was as exalted as it was responsible. They were, amongst other things, the tax collectors. The administrative centre was the capital, Susa, the nerve-centre of the network of great roads which criss-crossed the vast territory. Existing roads, such as the old Assyrian military and trade route from Assur and Nineveh over the Zagros mountains and the Iranian plateau to Ecbatana, were remade and connected with newly-made roads such as the "royal way" from Ephesus on the Aegean

Sea through Ionia and Lydia to Susa. This was four hundred and fifty *parasanges* (1666 miles) long and had one hundred and eleven staging places. The journey from Ephesus to Susa via Sardis took ninety-three days. The speed of the couriers who transmitted their orders or messages on horseback was said to equal that of the flight of a crane. Official messages, bearing the royal seal, were carried with all speed, but all private communications were subject to censorship. Not until the Mongol empire of Genghis Khan will the postal services be as swift and as sure.

Not content with Susa, his permanent capital on the plain, the king had another residence built on the plateau which became known to the Greeks as Persepolis, "the city of the Persians". Everything made of wood or brick was destroyed when Darius's palaces were burnt by order of Alexander in 330 B.C. All that remained of Persepolis was the stone framework of the buildings and the many columns which make it even today the loveliest and proudest ruined city on earth. It was at Persepolis that, during the Nauruz, or New Year feast, the Achaemenian kings received the tribute of the satrapies. This solemn procession is shown in relief on the walls of the huge terrace on which Darius's palace is built. In the building of Persepolis Darius employed architects from Egypt and other advanced civilisations whose influence is shown amongst features of Assyro-Babylonian, Ionian and Median architecture. This collaboration gave rise to an eclectic imperial architecture, with elements from all the Western satrapies. Taken as a whole, however, it has an undeniable unity and an unequalled grandeur and ostentation. The Assyrians and Babylonians built their temples and palaces on terraces, but that was no longer necessary here, on the rocky soil of the plateau. The two types of palace, housing either the residence or the throne, had a portico with a colonnade, flanked by two massive corner towers, and, behind, a hall with columns, surrounded, in the case of the residential palace, by rooms and adjoining quarters. This type of building, as well as the capitals and columns, is Chaldaean and Median in origin and goes back to the type of old peasant houses in the mountainous country which the Medes had occupied. The stone door and window frames and the palm-leaf fluting were of Egyptian origin. The winged sphinx and the winged human-headed bull on the monumental doorway of Xerxes were Babylonian and Assyrian, as were also the plaques in relief which covered the walls of the outer stairways. These borrowed features did not, however, spoil the beauty of the whole and no king has ever been able to create an entirely new style of architecture owing nothing to the past. We should rather wonder that Darius, in a reign of thirty-six years (522–486), was able to create a style representative of the Persian monarchy and still worthy of our admiration. Darius and his successors also built at Susa, the former capital of the kingdom of Elam on the banks of the Kerkha at the foot of the western edge of the Iranian plateau. Here, on the plain, the predominant material is brick and, as in Babylonia, the symbolical figures and marching bowmen are in glazed brick.

The tombs of the Achaemenian kings which were dug out of rock were also inspired by older Chaldaean and Median types. They were sculptured high above ground-level in the face of the rock and externally were made to resemble a hall with four columns and a door—formerly closed with a stone slab—which led into the burial chamber where the coffin was laid in a deep hole in the rock. Above the entrance façade was sculptured the dais bearing the royal throne: a platform on four legs carried symbolically by two ranks of men representing the different peoples of the Empire. The King of Kings is shown standing on a three-step platform, his left hand supporting a bow, his right hand raised in a gesture of veneration towards the emblem of Ahuramazda, the winged solar disc bearing the figure of the god, a variant of the very ancient solar symbol of the Sumerians. Opposite the king stands the fire altar from which a flame rises. High on the right the crescent disc of the moon shows that the fire-worship was to take place at night. On the two side walls of the stone recess on either side of the platform carrying the throne, the priests and noblemen stand in three superimposed ranks watching the sacred ceremony. Between the columns of the façade an inscription has been cut into the rock-face. At Naqsh-i-Rustam, on the edge of the plain on which Persepolis is built, are the four rock tombs of the Achaemenian kings— Darius I, Xerxes, Artaxerxes and Darius II. In front of them there still stands today a rectangular tower with a flat roof and blind windows. This was the fire altar where the royal standards were kept and where the sacred flame flickered in the half-light.

With the creation of a new imperial organisation there came a new and dazzling court ceremonial inspired by the Assyrians. The king's suite consisted of several thousand Persian noblemen, and membership of the court was looked upon as the highest honour and the sign of the king's private favour. Access to the sovereign was, however, reserved for the select few. Anyone daring to come before the king without permission could be put to death; only the heads of the Persian tribes were exempt from this ruling but even for them such a procedure would have been very risky. Fifteen thousand persons (the number is probably exaggerated) had the honour of daily eating with the king—at a distance, of course, and according to strict etiquette. This entailed a daily expenditure of four hundred silver talents.

Iran owes to the government of Darius its excellent agriculture and gardens. These, in this land of poor rainfall, depended on artificial water-supplies and irrigation canals, often several miles long and mainly underground. Irrigation cost the state a lot of money. The king toured the satrapies in person to find out for himself the progress being made and to reward governors who showed themselves able and willing to improve the lot of the people. Thus, in a decree to the satrap of Magnesia in Asia Minor, he shows his satisfaction at the introduction of plants from Babylon. Darius's greatest merit lay in his constant anxiety to educate the Persian people. The cuneiform alphabet had already been adapted from Babylonian syllabic writing during the time of Cyrus. It became widespread in the reign of Darius, largely owing to the great number of inscriptions. Like those at Behistun, these are documents of the greatest importance and constitute the very beginnings of

Persian literature. The sons of Persians were introduced to the arts of war and riding, to love of truth and to ancient songs. The physical and mental training of the youth of Persia as practised in the court of Susa was admired by Plato and other Greek writers, and it was on the model of Susa that the satraps organised educational establishments in their provincial capitals. The supreme court of justice, created by Cyrus, was continued and several recorded anecdotes speak of the impartiality of the judges. Persian law brought great improvement to society by suppressing private revenge. Neither in public nor private matters was anyone permitted to take the law unto himself: this is the basis of every society which is based on law. On the other hand it would be preferable to pass over the question of penal law which was, as it has always been all over Asia, harsh and cruel.

Darayavaush—the Persian name of the Great King—has recorded the events of his reign for us on inscriptions. These, in the case of the two rock-faces at Bagistan and at Naqsh-i-Rustam, are virtually his autobiography. At Bagistan (the modern Behistun) a mountain with two peaks rises on rock cliffs in the district of Bagistana which has been sacred from time immemorial. This "land of heaven" which in the preceding millennia had been consecrated to the gods of Babylon, stands beside the former trade-route from Hamadan in Babylonia via Kermanshah. Along this route, once a military road, stand several monuments dating back to ancient kings and carved out of the local rock. Darius chose a vertical rock-face, some distance away from the route and about one hundred and sixty feet above ground level as a precaution against the hand of sacrilege, to record and commemorate his victories in figures and inscriptions. These figures are not in high relief, but carved in the round, framed in stone and set against the rock-face. The great king, as on his tomb described above, is leaning on his bow with his right hand raised to the emblem of Ahuramazda, but here his left foot rests on the body of the defeated Gaumata. Behind him stand two Persians, one with bow and quiver and the other holding a two-handed lance. In front of him, their names carved on the stone, stand the nine "kings of untruth," the rebels conquered by the king, bound to each other by a rope round their necks and with their hands tied behind their backs. Plaques on each side and underneath have an inscription in three languages, old Persian, Elamite and Babylonian, cut into the rock in cuneiform characters. It begins thus:

> "King Darayavaush proclaims:
> The mighty King,
> King of Kings,
> King of Persia,
> King of the lands,
> Descended from Arsames
> The Achaemenian."

There follow the king's genealogy, a list of his territories and the principles of his government, the history of the Persian kingdom from the death of Cambyses to the campaign against the Scythians, a large proportion of which is taken up by the account of the crushing of Gaumata, the impostor who tried to pass himself off as Cambyses' brother, and the defeat of the nine rebel "kings of untruth". The text stresses the veracity of the facts it reports, puts the reader on his guard against untruth and proclaims the axioms of good government:

> "King Darayavaush proclaims:
> King, thou who shalt reign
> In the days to come,
> Keep and protect thyself
> From insolent imposture.
>
> King Darayavaush proclaims:
> Oramazda and all the other gods of the universe
> Have come to my aid
> Only because I was not the servant of evil,
> Not a servant of imposture,
> Because I have committed no act of violence,
> Neither I nor any of my race.

I have chosen the way which was as straight as a javelin,
I have chosen the right way.
To no knight, to no man-servant
Have I ever done violence.
The vassal who built my house
Have I raised up as the support of my house,
But the vassal who brought down my house,
Him I have punished severely according to right and the
    law.

King Darayavaush proclaims:
Thou who shalt read this inscription
In the days that are to come
Shalt see that I have caused it to be engraved in the rock
Together with these figures of men.
Efface it not nor destroy it!
See that thou keepest it whole
So long as thy seed shall live!"[1]

As far as their form is concerned, these royal annals go back
to the inscriptions of the Assyrian kings. The text was taken
from annals drawn up on tablets and constantly kept up to
date, then it was engraved in the diplomatic language in use
at the time. The historiographers eulogised their royal master
more extravantly for posterity than doubtless he would have
done himself, but the remarkable thing about these inscriptions
is the way in which the whole Persian Empire is assimilated
into the royal household, whose servant it was held to be.
This is why only events affecting the royal household are
recorded and why we constantly come across the concepts of
"imposture", "untruth" ("droga" in old Persian), and "kings
of untruth". "Imposture" is the chaos, disorder and reign
of violence which the king found on his accession to the throne,
the disorder provoked by the conspiracy of the false Bardiya
and fed by the intrigues of the nobility.

The Great King states on several occasions that his rule
comes from the god Ahuramazda (Oramazda):

[1] From F.-W. Koenig: *Relief und Inschrift des Königs Dareios I am Felsen von Bagistan.*

"King Darayavaush proclaims:
Oramazda hath entrusted to me the lordship of these
  lands.
Oramazda hath lent me his aid,
That I might win this lordship and hold it.
It is the will of Oramazda
That I keep the lordship of these lands."

This affirmation of the divine right to rule is not a convention as it became with later monarchs, but was based on the words of the prophet whose doctrine the Great King had made safe by killing Gaumata, his hereditary enemy. In one of the *gathas* or hymns collected in the Avesta, Zoroaster calls on the future legitimate king to put the Magian to death:

"The deceivers shall themselves be deceived, they shall be abandoned and shall cry aloud: with the faithful satraps he shall bring death and slaughter and shall defeat them and bring peace to the people whose generations shall rest contented: he shall bring them torment and the bond of death and shall soon be the Great King. The impostors are vowed to decay, they who scheme to bring down the just and darken the light of heaven. Where is the prince of light who shall take from them life and liberty? For, Mazda, thine is the Kingdom through which thou givest a better fate to the weak who live under thy law."

In defeating the Magian and professing the doctrine of Zoroaster, Darius had brought about the *frasam*, the illumination, and thus the mission of Zoroaster was accomplished. This is why he proclaims in an inscription at Susa: "This have I done by the will of Ahuramazda so that I might bring about the illumination over all the earth.

In investing Darius with sovereign dignity, Ahuramazda brought to men the peace of the Achaemenian Empire which lasted more than two hundred years. The pride of the inscriptions of the King of Kings was justified: he was the Saoshyant, the Soter, the liberator of Iran.[1]

---

[1] *Archaeologische Mitteilungen an Iran*, Band. III.

6

THE COURT OF THE SASSANIANS

"Firstly my well-being. Nothing giveth man so lawful a cause of grief as the want of a leader whose absence maketh him to believe that his comfort shall cease, that disorders shall break out and that all manner of evils shall fall upon the just, one after the other, in their persons, their vassals, their fortunes and all that hath value to them. In short, we find no fear or lack which sticketh harder at a man than that he should be without a good king."[1]

These are the words of the young king Chosroes I (A.D. 531–579) to one of his governors shortly after his accession to the throne. He was certainly referring to his late father, King Kavad (A.D. 488–531), who, by his tolerance of the Mazdakite movements, had brought the Empire to the verge of ruin. The Mazdakite sect demanded equal distribution of all possessions, including women, the suppression of the privileges of the nobility and the prohibition of the killing of any living being. Not until shortly before his death did the king change his attitude towards this sect; by then their revolution had led to excesses and the king had them massacred. It took some time, however, to make good the harm done by the movement. Possessions which had been expropriated were returned to their former owners and wives to their lawful husbands. Women who had been unmarried before they were carried off were made to marry their captors if the latter were of sufficiently high rank; if not the women had to break off the union with compensation of a double dowry. The State looked after the families of grandees and nobles which had

---

[1] A. Christensen: *L'Iran sous les Sassanides*, Copenhagen, 1936.

lost a father or a husband. The daughters were married off according to their station and with a dowry from public funds; the sons were brought up to enter State service. Chosroes thus created a new nobility absolutely devoted to his service.

Landowners also received State assistance for the reconstruction of damaged property and the repair of canals and were given cattle to restock depleted herds. Ruined villages were rebuilt, bridges repaired and new fortifications erected. The fiscal system was reformed: taxes were fixed according to the area of land under cultivation and the number of fruit trees. This system lasted so well that it was later adopted by the Caliphs. A personal tax, to be paid quarterly, was imposed on all men from twenty to fifty years of age, except the nobility and the grandees of the Empire, soldiers, priests and court officials and secretaries. These reforms considerably increased the State income and filled the public coffers against times of war for which Chosroes always strove to be prepared. The army was also reformed. Previously the lower nobility, the core of the army, had been obliged to serve both without pay and at its own expense. Chosroes had the army lists reviewed and allotted arms, a horse and pay to those soldiers without means of their own. A cavalry soldier's complete equipment consisted of armour for his horse, and for himself a coat of mail, a breast-plate, leggings and thigh-pieces, a sword, lance and round buckler, a number of weapons hung on a belt, an axe, a quiver, two bows, thirty arrows and two spare bowstrings carried at the back of the helmet. The main weapons were the lance and the bow which the Iranian Aryans had wielded with great skill from time immemorial. The elite of the mounted troops were the knights, comparable to those of the Middle Ages. They were all noblemen and from them the king recruited his bodyguard.

Chosroes appointed four *spahbads* to command his armies. These were both military commanders and governors of the four great provinces of the Empire: in the east Khorasan, Seistan and Kerman; in the south Persis and Susiana; in the west an area corresponding to the present Iraq as far as the frontiers of the Byzantine Empire; in the north Great Media and Azerbaijan.

It was not long before Chosroes had the opportunity of making war. Once begun, it occupied him for more than half his reign of nearly fifty years. His chief enemies were the Byzantines with whom he made a lasting peace, but only after many campaigns, in 562. He had to defend his empire in the east against the Ephthalites, or white Huns, and later against the ancestral enemies of Iran, the Turkish tribes of Turanians, hordes of wild nomads who for centuries had been swarming into the empire from Transoxania.

There is a well-known fable about Chosroes I Anorchivan ("of the immortal soul") which was later often to be retold by Islam poets. According to this the king, out hunting, got separated from his suite in the ardour of the chase and found himself alone with his vizier. As they were riding over a plain they came across a village in ruins and abandoned except for two owls which were perched on a crumbling wall and screeching. The king, afraid and superstitious in this lonely place, asked his vizier what secrets the two birds might be discussing. "Sire," replied the cunning vizier, "I crave your pardon before telling you what those birds are saying. One bird, about to give his daughter in marriage to the other, is demanding a suitable dowry. 'Give her this ruined village,' he says, 'and others as well.' 'With pleasure,' replies the other bird, 'if our mighty sovereign continues his present activities and abandons his people to hunger and misery, it isn't a mere two or three ruined houses I shall be giving you, but a hundred thousand.'"

Chosroe's justice became proverbial and the subject of many legends. It is said that once, on his return to Ctesiphon, he was receiving the envoys of different monarchs who had sent him gifts and messages. One of these envoys, sent by the Emperor Justinian of Byzantium, visited the royal palace and wondered at its splendour. He was struck, however, by what he considered a fault in the design of the square in front and asked the reason for it. He was told: "An old woman's house stood there and as the king could not persuade her to sell it and did not wish to force her to do so, he had to suffer this irregularity in the plan of the palace." "In truth," replied the Greek, "this irregularity is more beautiful than any symmetry."

Another anecdote tells of the chain of cattle-bells which the king had caused to be fixed to a wall of the palace so that any of his subjects who felt that he had suffered an injustice might ring it and bring his complaint to the attention of the king in person. The bells hung untouched for seven years until one day they began to ring furiously. It was a donkey rubbing its back against the chain. Chosroes sent for the animal's owner and requested him to take better care of his charge.

These more or less amusing examples of the justice of the Sassanian king do not, however, excuse the typical Oriental cruelty meted out to the guilty, and even to the innocent, who when put to death were impaled.

The capital of the Sassanian Empire and the residence of most of the kings of the dynasty, was Ctesiphon, twenty miles south of Baghdad on the Tigris. Defended by a semi-circle of walls and ditches, the capital contained seven different towns and for this reason was called "El Madain" ("the towns"). In the east was the district of Aspanbar, still visible today in the majestic ruins of the palace of Taq-i-Kesra. This contained the royal park and gardens. A corner of a wall, still standing, may possibly have been part of the enclosure of the king's great deer park. This district has been thought by some to have been the site of New Antioch, or Veh-Antiokh-Khosru. This was also called Rumaghan, or the town of the Greeks, and was built near Ctesiphon by Chosroes to house the former inhabitants of Antioch in Syria which he had captured. From towns in Syria and from Rhodes he brought to El Madain marble slabs and columns and the necessary materials for the making of stone and glass mosaics so that the houses in the new town could be decorated in the Syrian manner. By the time of the Arab historian Masudi in the tenth century, however, New Antioch was in ruins. Legend has it that the new town was rebuilt on the plan of the old so exactly that every inhabitant was at once able to recognise his own house. Chosroes also built hot baths and a hippodrome, two indispensable features of Roman and Greek life. The citizens were granted special privileges such as the free exercise of Christianity. They were ruled directly by the king and their town enjoyed the rights of asylum. There is today a colonial town of this kind, Julfa, opposite Isfahan. This was founded in A.D. 1604 by Shah Abbas for the former inhabitants of the Armenian town of Julfa on the Araxes in Azerbaijan. It still retains its original character.

On the western bank of the Tigris stood Seleucia, the oldest of these cities. It was founded about 300 B.C., as its name indicates, by Seleucus Nicator, Alexander the Great's general and the first Seleucid king. The Roman emperors Trajan and Verus destroyed it in the second century A.D. and the first Sassanian king Ardashir (224–241) rebuilt it as Veh-Ardashir (New Ardashir). It was a spacious city with neatly paved streets. There were private enclosures near the houses, as the wealthier inhabitants owned herds of cattle. These grazed during the day in a valley near Mahoza, the adjoining town. There was a large bazaar and, in the streets, strolling merchants hawked goods of every description. The wine-trade, as everywhere in the East, was carried on by the Jews. A flourishing commerce brought prosperity to the town. Gold chains and bracelets were sometimes so little esteemed that they were given to the poor as alms instead of money. If the inhabitants were not noted for their culture, they were famous as eaters and drinkers. "The women eat, but do not work", it was said. Seleucia was also the Christian centre of the Sassanian Empire and the residence of the *catholicos*. Here stood the Cathedral, the "great church of Seleucia", as well as other churches and convents. The inclusion of two other small townships within its borders gave the seven districts which made up Great Ctesiphon, called El Madain by the Arabs.

It is not difficult to picture this vast capital on the banks of the Tigris. Most of the houses were hidden in luxuriant green gardens. The tall, imposing "White Palace" could be seen from far away, and part of one of its wings, the famous Taq-i-Kesra, is still standing today. This was the ancient throne-room, ninety-five feet high, eighty-two feet long and one hundred and forty-one feet wide. It was covered with an elliptical vault and flanked on each side by five perpendicular vaulted chambers. Its façade was a long five-stage wall. The right wing of this wall crumbled in 1888 but the left wing is still standing. This was, however, only half of the palace. There was another matching symmetrical building. Both buildings had two wings and the whole formed the framework of an enormous court with ornamental flower-beds divided into four by two intersecting canals. In the centre of the courtyard was a fish-pond. So that he might enjoy the brilliant colours of his flower-beds in winter-time as well, the king had them copied into a vast carpet some thirty-five yards square. This carpet, called "Chosroes's Springtime", was laid in the throne-room in the winter for use by the king and his court at festivals. It was the largest carpet ever made and was woven in threads of silk, gold and silver and set with precious stones. The design represented a pleasure-garden with streams, paths, trees and flowers. The yellowish soil was made of gold with the banks of the streams in a darker colour; the water was represented by threads of silver and the pebbles at the bottom and the fish were woven in their natural colours. The gravel of the paths was worked in small stones the size of pearls; the stalks of the plants and the branches were in silver and gold, all the leaves were made of silk and the fruits were many-coloured precious stones. This eighth wonder of the world had a modest posterity which continued down to the "garden-carpets" of the eighteenth century. According to Arab and Persian historians of the time, the walls of the throne-room, of which the bare bricks are still standing, were once covered with mosaics. These portrayed, amongst other things, a scene from the siege of Antioch and the fighting round the town. Here Chosroes, in a green tunic on a red-roan horse, is reviewing his troops. The lower part of the walls was hung with carpets and the back of the room, containing the throne, was divided off by a huge brocade curtain.

On the days when the king gave audience the room was filled with visitors and guests. The king's suite took their places according to the three classes into which they were divided: firstly the king's sons and the knights stood ten cubits away from the curtain; secondly, twice this distance away, stood the "intimates" of the sovereign—those who shared his table and the learned men who recited to him; thirdly, and further away still, stood the jesters, artists, singers and the like. Behind this third rank stood visitors who did not belong to the court. There were minstrels who, at the king's request, would sing to musical accompaniment. The hierarchy was maintained even at this level, and a singer could only be accompanied by a musician of his own rank.

When the grandees were assembled in their dazzling armour and wearing cone-shaped caps, with the ranks of the other two classes and the musicians and guests behind them, the curtain would rise to the sound of horns and cymbals and reveal the magnificent spectacle of the sovereign on his throne. According to contemporary historians this was an awe-inspiring sight. Chosroes's successor, Hormizd IV, was described in his kingly apparel by Theophylact. The king's golden tiara set with rubies, emeralds and pearls was dazzling in its brilliance. His breeches and tunic were embroidered with gold. His two hands rested on his sword which was held between his legs. Wide ribbons of gold stiffened with wire jutted out from his shoulders like flames; these symbolised the royal *hvarnah*, or fire of victory. The dais behind the throne was also of brilliant gold. The room was in shadow, as the light came in only through relatively small openings in the ceiling. The spectacle of the enthroned king so impressed the onlookers that they involuntarily fell to their knees. Visitors who had audience were led before the king by a high court dignitary. The visitor advanced holding a handkerchief to his mouth. This handkerchief, called a *padham*, was carried in the sleeve and was used to prevent the desecration of holy objects (the sacred flame for example) by human breath. The holy object in this case was the air breathed by His Majesty. On reaching the king the visitor remained prostrate until told to rise. He then bowed, with his arms raised or crossed over his breast. When invited to speak he had to preface his words with conventional wishes such as

"May your divinity be immortal!" or "May Ahuramazda grant your desires!" Only then could he address his request to the monarch.

The palace had hundreds of rooms. It was the central seat of government of the empire with its *divans*, or ministries, where bureaucracy was as rife as it is today. The number, names and organisation of these ministries are unknown, but we have the various seals of the Privy Council, the Ministries of Justice and Finance and the Ministry responsible for nominations to offices and titles. We can assume that there were also *divans* for military affairs, the Mint, the Post, the Crown Lands and others.

The king's suite consisted of a number of dignitaries: the Grand Steward, the Grand Master of Ceremonies and the Keeper of the Curtain, the stewards of the palace, the wine-stewards, the cup-bearers and the chefs, the chamberlains, the Grand Falconer, and the Master of the Horse. The bodyguard, under the Captain of the sentries, protected and accompanied the king. The bodyguard commander was one of the most influential court officials and one of those closest to the king. When the king mounted horse, the bodyguard stood in two ranks wearing breast-plate, helmet, sword and buckler and carrying a lance. As the king passed by, each officer of the guard raised his buckler so that it touched the edge of the royal saddle and then bowed his head until his forehead touched the buckler.

There was, however, another important body of men at the Sassanian court. These were the astrologers and soothsayers. When a prince was born all the astrologers of the court had to devise a horoscope. Before any important step was taken the astrologers and soothsayers were always consulted. The former exorcised demons according to a very complicated ritual. Chosroes II called together his three hundred and sixty soothsayers, astrologers and magicians to find the most propitious date for the building of a causeway across the Tigris. The project failed, however, and a great many of them paid for it with their lives. There was also a body of doctors attached to the court, and a body of poets. A quotation at the end of this chapter gives a typical example of their style. The harem, of course, was in the charge of the eunuchs.

When the king was away the conduct of the courtiers remaining behind was closely watched by special officials. The same etiquette had to be observed as when the monarch was in residence. Those who observed it were said to be "single-faced" whilst the remainder, the "two-faced", were open to the dangerous accusation of hypocrisy. The king's person was protected by the minutest precautions against threats of assassination. No one knew where he was going to sleep. Four beds were prepared every night in different rooms and it sometimes happened that he did not use one of them but went to sleep in an empty room, resting his head on his arm instead of a pillow.

No one, not even his own son, could enter the king's private chamber without permission. There is a tale which tells how one day Yazdgard I, a Sassanian king of the early fifth century, found his son Vahram, then thirteen years old, in a forbidden part of the palace. He asked him if the door-keeper had seen him come in. "Yes," replied the boy. "Then go and give him thirteen strokes with the rod," said the king, "dismiss him and appoint Azadhmard in his place as keeper of the curtain." Vahram obeyed. Some time later the boy again tried to get into the forbidden room but the door-keeper stopped him and, tapping him on the chest with his fist, said: "If I catch you here again, I'll give you sixty strokes, thirty for the injustice you did to the previous door-keeper and thirty more for making me risk the same punishment." This reached the ears of the king and Azadhmard the door-keeper was sent for and rewarded with a cloak of honour and various gifts.

It was both tradition and good policy for the king to show a certain liberality towards his subjects. Generosity enhanced his prestige and ensured the entire devotion of his immediate entourage. It is said that the moment one of his subjects received approval for an action or a proposal by the king's uttering the word "zih" he was given one thousand drachmae which the treasurer was required to hand over at once. Court officials bringing good news to the king were often rewarded by being allowed to fill their mouths with gold, rubies or pearls. . . . Officers of the court were paid by the king according to their style of living. If they had estates of their own the revenues from these was taken into account, but regardless of this they received from six thousand to twelve thousand drachmae a month for expenses.

When one of the king's ministers or high dignitaries was honoured with a personal visit from the sovereign, he dated all his future letters from this event. For a certain period he was exempted from property tax and his horses and other equipage were marked with a special sign. A high police official came to his house every morning with three hundred horsemen and a hundred foot soldiers, and this detachment was stationed in front of his house until sunset. Whenever he went out he was preceded by the foot-soldiers and followed by the cavalry. The king was given presents by his host and, on leaving, was preceded by a swift horseman carrying a precious harness and a gilded saddle: this was the equipment which his host had put at his disposal during his stay. The honour of a personal visit from the sovereign brought lasting privileges to the host. No member of his family could be imprisoned for a felony and none of his servants could be condemned to death without his master's consent. The gifts he brought to the king at the New Year Festival (held at the Spring Solstice) and the Feast of Mithra were presented before all others. He had precedence in audiences and took his place on the right of the king even when accompanying him on horseback.

The king received gifts at these two annual festivals from the grandees of the empire and from his wealthier subjects. Each gave what he himself prized most: amber, musk, valuable clothing or other costly goods. Warriors gave horses or weapons, the rich gold or silver, the governors part of the excess revenue of their provinces. Poets recited verses composed for the occasion, orators pronounced speeches and those who shared the king's table brought a symbolic gift of first fruits. If one of the king's wives gave him a beautiful richly adorned slave girl this wife had a claim to be preferred above all the other wives in the harem. The king was obliged to give similar presents in return. At the Spring Festival he usually distributed his winter clothing amongst the court dignitaries; at the Feast of Mithra he gave his summer clothing.

The custom amongst Eastern monarchs of rewarding their subjects or honouring other sovereigns with ceremonial robes is a very ancient one. It was practised by the Caliphs of Islam, the court of Byzantium and in China. The Armenian general Manuel received from Shapur II a ceremonial robe, an ermine cloak, a pair of gold buckles for his helmet, a diadem, a clasp similar to those worn by the king, a purple tent bearing the emblem of an eagle, sky-blue carpets for the entrance to the tent, and gold vases for his table. A diadem woven with threads of gold and set with pearls conferred the greatest distinction and was ranked next to royal dignity. When a person had rendered to his sovereign or to the state a service deserving to be recorded for posterity, his name was mentioned in the inscriptions carved on the royal monuments.

Another mark of distinction, already used by the Achaemenians, was the granting of titles of honour. Herodotus reports that the Achaemenian kings bestowed upon those who had particularly distinguished themselves in their service the title of "Benefactor". Under the Sassanian monarchs this practice was greatly extended. Generals received the title of *Harzahmard* ("Thousand men," that is, strong as a thousand men). The titles were usually associated with the name of the king, as in Tahm-Yazdgard, Tahm-Kusro, where *tahm* meant "brave". This custom was followed by the sovereigns of Islam whose servants are often known to us only by their titles and not by their names.

In war-time, when conditions were difficult, the great royal banquets were cancelled and the king received at his table only the three highest dignitaries of the state. The meal, on these occasions, consisted simply of bread, salt, vinegar and vegetables with an omelette as the main dish. If the war ended in victory the great feasts began again and the occasion was celebrated by a speech from the vizier. The high dignitaries took their places with the king on the dais, the other guests sitting at a lower level. Prayers were said before the eating began. It was forbidden to speak during the meal, orders being given by signs. When the meal was over jesters and minstrels were brought in.

The royal princes were brought up at court with the sons of knights under the "knights' tutor". First of all they learnt reading, writing and arithmetic, riding and hunting, polo and chess. Particular care was given to weapon-training, especially the handling of the bow and the lance. Education finished at the age of fifteen. At this age the boy was required to know the religious dogma of the *Avesta* and to have a clear idea of a man's rights and duties. At the age of twenty he was examined by the scholars and the high priests. The daughters of good families also received a thorough intellectual training, as is shown in the following anecdote. A lawyer on his way to court was once approached by a group of five women one of whom asked him certain points of detail concerning bail. He was unable to answer her last question, whereupon one of the women retorted: "Don't rack your brains any longer. Just admit you don't know. We'll get the answer from the Lord High Justice's Commentaries."

All these institutions and practices mostly concerned the court and the nobility only. Chosroes's reforms had affected the lives of the ordinary people very little. They continued to live, as in the past, in wretched poverty and insecurity. The following passage of rhetoric is an eloquent protest by Burzoe, an eminent doctor of the time. It shows how the conscience of an enlightened scholar was affected by the condition of the poor:

"Our times, having become old and decayed, have the appearance of purity but are in fact very troubled. For if god has granted our king happiness and success, if our king is at the same time prudent, very powerful, magnanimous, searching in examination, just, human, liberal, a lover of truth, grateful, concerned with rights and duties, unwearying, persevering, intelligent, ready to help, endowed with a tranquil mind, reasonable, thoughtful, gentle, sympathetic, clement, well-acquainted with men and things, a friend of science and the scholar, of goodness and the good, but harsh with the oppressor, fearless and not easily led, knowing how to procure an abundance of what his subjects need and to keep from them that which they do not—in spite of all this we see that our age is everywhere falling into decadence. It seems, indeed, as if truth has fallen from the hand of man, that that of which we are in great need is no longer with us, that what is with us is harmful, that what is good fades away, that what is bad grows apace, that error advances laughing whilst the good conscience draws back weeping . . . that governments are with us only to follow their pleasure and to violate the laws, that the oppressed resigns himself to humiliation and that the oppressor puffs himself up with pride, that greed everywhere opens her mouth and swallows everything both near and far, that frugality exists no more, that the wicked are raised to heaven and the good cast down, that the noble in heart are fallen from the greatest height to the lowest depths, whilst the most contemptible have honour and might, that power has passed from the capable to the incapable. It is as if the world, drunk with joy, were saying 'I have shut away that which is good and brought out that which is bad.' "[1]

[1] A. Christensen: *L'Iran sous les Sassanides*, Copenhagen, 1936.

7

THE CITY OF PEACE

There are few towns in Asia as disappointing as Baghdad to the visitor who hopes still to discover some reminder of the exotic romanticism of the Arabian Nights. Damascus still has its great Friday Mosque from the time of the Omayyads, Jerusalem its famous Dome of the Rock built by the Omayyad Calif Abd el Malik, Ctesiphon its grandiose ruin, the Arch of Chosroes. Baghdad, on the other hand, has simply nothing left to offer the visitor who cares at all for archaeology. Not only was this great city destroyed several times, but its ruins were pulled down and the bricks used for new buildings.

When the founder of the Abbasid dynasty Abu Jafar Abdallah el Mansur ("The Victor by the help of God") was looking for a suitable site for his new capital he chose a little village, Baghdad ("a Gift from God") on the west bank of the Tigris at its junction with the Diyala. The site had every advantage for trade, communications and water-supplies (the waters of the Diyala flowed down in abundance from the Zagros mountains) and was in no way inferior to that of Babylon, a day's journey south-west on the Euphrates, or Ctesiphon, a similar distance south on the Tigris. These two ancient cities, whose power and prestige Baghdad was to inherit, supplied the Caliph with building material and work was begun with a great army of forced labour. The canals in the area were improved, developed and covered over, aqueducts and fortifications were built with great zeal, and the city was planned so as to absorb near-by small settlements. The most important of these was Karkh, which stretched from the centre or "Round City" to the Isa canal whose long arc linked the Tigris with the

Euphrates. The only construction work undertaken by Mansur on the eastern bank of the Tigris, where modern Baghdad now stands, was the establishment of a military encampment for his son Mahdi. He gave lands surrounding the city as fiefs to his relatives, followers and officers. He called his new city Dar-es-Salaam ("Dwelling of Peace") or Medinat-es-Salaam ("City of Peace") and his huge citadel, the Round City, was called Medinat-es-Mansur.

Mansur's Round City, surrounded by three ramparts and a moat, was about a mile and a half in diameter. In the centre stood the Caliph's palace, next to the Friday Mosque. Surrounding these, and arranged symmetrically like the decorative motifs of a carpet, stood twenty administrative buildings divided equally into four sectors. The circular ramparts had four gates. These were arranged in accordance with the natural features of the site and not, as was more usual, at the cardinal points. The axes between them connected the middle of the sides of the inscribed rectangle. Here were the gates of Khorasan (NE), Basra (SE), Kufa (SW) and Syria (NW). The two roads connecting them diametrically across the city were the shortest cuts between the outlying districts but the Round City was closed to all ordinary traffic.

The outline of the Round City was marked out on the ground in the oriental fashion of laying down cotton sacks impregnated with naphtha. These were set alight and the area which the fire had cleared marked the foundations of the surrounding walls. There were three of these, the centre one being the biggest. The inner ring between the inner and centre walls was nearly three hundred feet across and was built up with houses. The outer ring between the centre and outer walls was left empty. The centre wall was nearly a hundred feet high and a hundred and fifteen feet wide at its base; it tapered gradually to the top and was crenellated and turreted. The inner and outer walls were smaller and had rounded crenellations. The four gateways in the outer wall were very similar to those still seen in certain Asian towns today. The moat was crossed by a vaulted passage-way built into the wall. Two lateral walls then led through the outer ring to the central enclosure, whose monumental gateways were domed and had an upper storey containing a *madshlis*, a large room giving a view over the whole city. Vaulted ramps led to the flat-topped ramparts and Caliph Mansur liked to ride on horseback from the Khorasan gate to the *madshlis* to look out eastwards towards the region bordering on the Iranian plateau where the Abbasid dynasty originated. According to one story, when the Caliph was standing here one day an arrow fell at his feet bearing a message warning him that his life was in danger. The domes of the gateways stood on columns of teak and were green outside and gilded inside. No one except the Caliph was allowed to go into the inner town on horseback; horses had to be left outside the gates. Only certain members of the royal household were permitted to be carried in as far as the palace in litters.

Mansur's great palace at the centre of the Round City was called the "Golden Gate" or the "Palace with the Green Dome", as the centre of it was topped by a large green ceramic dome. On top of this, some one hundred and thirty feet above the ground and visible from a great distance, stood the statue of a man on horseback. On the ground floor under the dome was the audience chamber, some thirty-three feet long and the same width and height. Above this was another room of the same size of which the dome formed the roof. The audience-chamber was reached by an *iwan*, or cradle-vaulted room open at the front. Around this central part of the building, which was intended for receptions, were arranged the courtyards lined with private dwellings. The palace was badly damaged in A.D. 841, scarcely eighty years after it was built, at the siege of Baghdad during the war between Caliph Amin and his brother Harun al-Rashid. The proud green dome was still standing in A.D. 941, however, when it was destroyed by lightning.

Mansur soon found his residence inside the Round City too small for him, and in 775 he moved to the Kasr-el-Khuld, the "Castle of Eternity", which he had built outside the walls beyond the Khorasan Gate on the banks of the Tigris. The new palace took its name from the gardens which seemed to rival those of Paradise, or "Khuld" in the Koran. The building was completely destroyed in the thirteenth century and all we know of it is that it was a wonderful sight with its galleries, domes and high walls. Mansur was only to enjoy it for a short time, for he died in the same year on his way back from a pilgrimage to Mecca.

Mansur was only the second representative of the Abbasid dynasty. This had been founded by his brother Abdul Abbas, called "Saffah" ("the bloodthirsty"). The dynasty brought glory to Baghdad for five centuries. Mansur, however, was already showing some of the dangerous family traits with his thirst for pleasures, his morbid irritability and his unlimited cruelty. He lived in perpetual fear of treachery and surrounded his residence with an extraordinary system of defences. He only felt safe amongst his faithful and when surrounded by his troops. The common people were all made to live outside his fortified walls. More than once he had his victims buried alive and cut off the hands and feet of political suspects. His son and successor Mahdi was no better. He was a drunkard and formed such an attachment to his own daughter that he would never be separated from her, making her go everywhere with him, even on horseback when he disguised her as a man. Like his father, however, he had bouts of goodness and generosity when he distributed lavish gifts. These traits showed themselves particularly in his two sons Hadi and Harun al-Rashid. Hadi tried to poison his mother and issued death sentences without flinching. A courtier relates:

"I was in Hadi's close confidence, yet I was always on my guard because of his well-known tendency to put people to death. Once he sent for me at midday, in spite of the terrible heat and without my having had lunch. I hastened to him and was led from one room to another until I found myself near the women's apartments. There I found him. He immediately dismissed everyone else and ordered me to close the door. He then confided to me that he was displeased with Yahya Ibn Khalid who was stirring up the people against him in favour of his brother Harun al-Rashid.

Finally he commanded me to bring him forthwith the head of his brother Harun. When I objected he threatened to have me put to death. After assassinating Harun I was to go to the state prison and kill all the Alides[1] and their followers, then hasten to Kufa with all available troops and massacre all the Abbasids and their followers, sack the town and everything in it."

Chance decreed that Hartama, the courtier in question, should hear shortly afterwards from the Caliph's mother that the Caliph was dead.[2] Hadi's brother Harun is the only Abbasid whose name is widely known today. This is due to his frequent mention in the Tales from the Arabian Nights. There is no doubt that under his reign the kingdom achieved a period of splendour. This was due not so much to the Caliph, however, as to excellent viziers and other capable men to whom the Caliph entrusted the reins of government. He cared less about governing than the stories, which arose from a certain popularity he had with his subjects, might lead us to believe.

To know what the Caliph was really like, we go to Ibrahim, a court minstrel, who says:

"I was at home one evening when a court eunuch brought me an order to present myself forthwith to Harun. I hastily mounted my ass, but when we arrived at the palace the eunuch turned away from the entrance-gate and led me by a secret way to a newly-built summer-house. There we entered one of those large inner courtyards which Rashid likes so well. He was sitting in the middle of it with a page at his side who now and then replenished his goblet. He was wearing his summer clothing, that is a light tunic held in place by a brocade shawl embroidered with large and brightly coloured designs and so fastened around his waist as to fall over and reach down to his knees. When he saw me he smiled and bade me keep him company. He then

[1] The members of the family of Ali, the husband of Fatima and son-in-law and cousin of the Prophet.

[2] A. von Kremer: *Kulturgeschichte des Orients unter den Chalifen.*

summoned his servants and immediately a hundred slaves appeared from behind the arches of the courtyard where they had been standing in readiness for their master's command. He ordered a cushion to be brought for me and had it placed on the ground in front of him. Then he commanded a harp and bade me sing. I was just about to pluck the strings when Masrur, the chief of police, appeared and stood some distance away as was his custom when he had some secret to communicate to the prince. The latter motioned him to approach and Masrur whispered some words in his ear. The prince then burst forth in anger, his eyes became bloodshot, the veins of his neck swelled out and he shouted: 'How much longer will the Alides try my patience? But, by Allah, I shall kill them all and all their followers.'"

The minstrel, fearing that the Caliph might first of all vent his rage on him, plucked his strings and began to sing:

"I prize most highly as a cure for all anger and grief
Three full bubbling goblets and three more
And four more still, making ten,
Quickly filled and as quickly emptied,
Held out to me by the beautiful hands
Of perfumed girls with dazzling charms.
Those are all the joys, for, in truth
Without lovely women life has no value."

The Caliph immediately ordered three goblets of wine, then three more, and, finally, after hearing the song again, four more to make up the ten. When he began to feel the effect of the wine he rose to retire and at the same time ordered the minstrel to be given a hundred thousand *dirhems*. When the minstrel returned home he found that the money had already been sent.

The Caliph also liked to visit his minstrel in his own house in the evening. He used to go there on an ass, accompanied by the chief of police and surrounded by a troop of white Caucasian slaves and palace servants who ran along at his side. These excursions naturally increased his popularity and gave rise to a number of anecdotes which have been preserved in popular tradition.

Harun's highly-strung nature revealed itself in other ways than in violent attacks of fury. He was very easily moved to tears. One evening, as he was walking along the banks of the Tigris, he burst into tears on hearing the plaintive song of the boatmen and it was a long time before he recovered. Immoderate both in hatred and in friendship, he was equally immoderate in his prodigality. One day, a story goes, he had received a gift of a beautiful slave-girl. In her honour the Caliph ordered a feast at which all the women singers in the palace took part. Together with the slaves they numbered two thousand. When his wife Zobayda heard of this she was angry and complained to Olayya the Caliph's half-sister. Olayya quickly made up a song, rehearsed it with Zobayda's slaves and at one o'clock in the afternoon Olayya and Zobayda, followed by their thousand slaves and dressed in their richest attire, came out into the garden and sang their song to the Caliph. The prince was so moved that he distributed amongst those present all the silver in his treasury. This was said to amount to six million *dirhems*. These fits of prodigality were not by any means rare.

The whitewashing of Harun by historians of the time, who praised him and ignored as far as possible his excesses, was due principally to his frequent pilgrimages to Mecca. These blinded his pious subjects to his faults. Each pilgrimage kept him away from Baghdad for several months. The conduct of the State was then left in the capable hands of his vizier Yashya the Barkemid who, with his sons Fadl and Djafar, governed from Harun's accession in 786 until 803. Djafar was for a long time a favourite of the Caliph and shared some of his popularity. He fell into disgrace, however, and was put to death in 803 when the Caliph returned from a journey to Mecca. His head was exposed on the central bridge in Baghdad and the two halves of his severed body on the other two bridges. His father and brother were both imprisoned and their possessions seized. The Barkemids were descended from high priests of the Buddhist monastery of Naubehar in Balkh. This was the end of their rule, which had brought such benefits to the country. After this outburst of violence Harun transferred his residence to the quiet provincial town of Rakka on the Euphrates. The story of the exchange of ambassadors and gifts between Harun al-Rashid and Charlemagne would appear to be legendary, as no Arab sources mention it. It is probable that Arab merchants appeared one day at Charlemagne's court and claimed to be the envoys of the Caliph merely to gain access to the Emperor and improve their prospects of trading.

Musical entertainment was very popular at Harun's court. So also was horse-racing. This took place on a race-course near the palaces. One race is described in a contemporary poem:

"On the morning of the appointed day we were there amidst the crowd which had gathered for the festival. We led our horses there. We led them just as everyone else did, but we knew better how to train them. We took horses as slender as arrows whose running is governed by favourable stars. They were ridden by black jockeys, small in stature whose race goes back to Ham, the ancestor of the black-skinned people. On their swift horses they look almost like black starlings skimming the roof-tops. The horses were lined up in front of a taut rope, in charge of a faithful believer, a most trustworthy man. He is willingly chosen as judge and he decides between them according to what is right. See! The horses rush forward at our signal like a streaming rainstorm. They follow each other in pairs or singly, as pearls scatter from a broken necklace or like a flight of *kata*[1] frightened by the threatening shadow of the vulture high in the clouds. And now we rejoice in the victory which brings us fame, honour and profit, for the steeds are laden with precious objects and we share the booty: dazzling cloaks of gilded brocade, cloths of Indian satin and velvet spread out over the horses' backs so that they seem to be covered with blood. They also carry a little sack of silver

[1] Desert birds common in Mesopotamia and Syria.

which the winning owner can scarcely lift. Quickly the seal is broken and we seize its contents, we who never seal our sacks of silver, and we distribute it amongst the grooms. They are better skilled than we in rubbing down our horses and even in times of famine they need never suffer hunger. The horses stand there, around the tent, hobbled or leaping freely and their neighing rings out through the air." [1]

The noble sport was enjoyed in the most varied ways: hunting, fishing and bird-catching. Harun was particularly fond of dog and cock fights. These were later to become a favourite form of sport. Tradition has it that he himself introduced the Persian game of horse-croquet, the forerunner of modern polo, archery and a game resembling cricket. Cross-bow shooting, for which lead shot was used, appeared a little later. Chess, already played at the court of the Omayyads, was very popular in Baghdad. Rashid paid the chess-players he kept at his court, and an Arab historian describes a scene where the Caliph played chess on a pleasure-boat during an excursion on the Tigris. The game was always highly appreciated at the court and much later one of the Caliphs is known to have enjoyed watching chess tournaments. For the amusement of the court there were the jesters, clowns and fools and the promoters of cock-fights and ram-fights. These were all paid a regular salary. Many other people were also paid solely to amuse the Caliph by keeping him company and eating with him at table.

The feasts of the Nauruz and the Mihragan were celebrated in Baghdad as they had been in the past in the courts of the Sassanians and the Achaemenians. They were always accompanied by audiences and the exchange of gifts. The custom of exhibiting wild animals during receptions at court was doubtless also copied from the Sassanians. It was customary to exhibit lions at official audiences also. In 966 two Byzantine envoys came to offer peace terms to Caliph Muktadir. An account of the reception ceremony tells how they arrived bearing precious gifts and were welcomed with great pomp. The

[1] Translated by A. von Kremer, op. cit.

palace halls and galleries were full of soldiers and all the walls were hung with precious tapestry. Muktadir received the envoys seated on his throne with the vizier and the grand eunuch standing at his side. Along the route from the city gate to the palace was stationed the whole army, consisting of 160,000 men, then, from the palace entrance, the way was lined with 700 white slaves and 700 chamberlains. In the palace itself were a hundred chained lions and all along the corridors were displayed 10,000 gilt suits of armour and many other rare objects. The envoys were first led to the "Hall of the Golden Tree". This had a marble pond in the middle, out of which rose a golden tree with eighteen branches. On the branches were perched artificial birds. Then they were taken to the Firdus, or Paradise Hall, the floor of which was completely covered by a rich carpet.

The marriage of Caliph Mamun to Buran, the daughter of the vizier Hassan Ibn Sahl, was described by a certain Taalibi. This gives us an idea of the magnificence of royal weddings. The vizier entertained the Caliph and all his suite for a fortnight on his estate on the Lower Euphrates. On the wedding night the bridal chamber was covered with carpets of gold thread and baskets of pearls were hung over the heads of the assembled ladies-in-waiting. The chamber was lit by great amber torches. During the festival organised for the grandees and army officers paper streamers were thrown, each bearing the name of some estate. Anyone catching a streamer before it fell became there and then the owner of the land and property named on it. Other streamers carried the names of slaves, horses or mules. To compensate his father-in-law for all this expense the Caliph gave him a year's revenue from the provinces of Fars and Ahwaz.

Taalibi also described the feast held to celebrate the circumcision of a son of Caliph Mutawakkil in the palace of Balkuwara in Samarra. This was a newly-built residence, a day's journey up the Tigris. After the feast gold-threaded carpets set with precious stones were spread on the ground to form two long rows. On these were placed many different figures made of a paste of amber, aloes and musk. The guests sat opposite each other in two rows and before them were placed great plates of massive gold set with precious stones. On these the chamberlains emptied deep baskets full of gold and silver coins. The guests were then invited to empty their goblets and to take three handfuls of gold and silver. As soon as the pile of coins had disappeared the plates were refilled. Finally a proclamation was made: "The Prince of the Believers commands each one to take as much as he pleases." At the end of the feast each guest received a robe of honour. To celebrate the event the prince freed a thousand slaves.

Let us return to the palaces and gardens which were the setting for this sumptuous court life. For a century the favourite residence of the Princes of the Believers in the City of Peace was a large mansion originally intended for Djafar, the brother-in-law, close companion and later the vizier of Rashid. This had been built at the end of the eighth century in the then undeveloped and still rural district to the east of the Round City on the other side of the Tigris. It formed the nucleus of a new royal quarter which grew rapidly and became known as the Dar-el-Khalifat, or Residence of the Caliph. The historian Yakut, writing about 1225, described this palace. He tells how Djafar liked listening to poets and minstrels as he drank deeply of the wines. This led to frequent remonstrations from his father Yashya, Rashid's vizier, as Mohammedans are forbidden to drink alcohol. Djafar therefore decided to build himself a residence outside Baghdad so that he could indulge his pleasures, without the risk of scandalising the population. The young Caliph, who was often a willing guest at Djafar's banquets, showed great interest in the building of this pleasure-house. A prudent friend advised Djafar to forestall the Caliph's jealousy by saying that the building was intended for the monarch's son, Mamun, the heir to the throne. The prince willingly accepted this gift on behalf of his son. The mansion, first named Djafari, was then called Mamuni and later Hassani. Until the fall of the Barkemides, however, it remained the property of Djafar, and it was only after Djafar's tragic death that Mamun came to live in it and made it one of his favourite residences. He enlarged it, added grounds for polo and horse-racing, and built a zoo which later became very famous.

When Mustadid (A.D. 892–902) came to the throne, the new royal quarter on the site of the present East Baghdad became the permanent residence of the Caliphs. This was the beginning of much new building. The Hassani palace was enlarged, Mutamid drew up the plans for the Tadsh palace and built for himself the two residences called Firdus ("Paradise") and Thuraya ("The Pleiads"). The latter was connected to the Hassani palace by an underground passage over twenty miles long. It was used especially by the women of the harem.

The Kasr-at-Tadsh ("Palace of the Crown") was the principal residence of later caliphs. Muktadir (908–932) also built Daresh-Sharadsh ("The Palace of the Tree"), so called from the silver tree which stood in the middle of it in a circular pond. The tree had eighteen main branches on which were perched all kinds of golden mechanical birds. Most of the branches were of silver, but some were of gold and they had leaves of varied colours which quivered in the wind. The birds whistled and sang and were worked by a hidden mechanism. Two groups each of fifteen equestrian statues faced each other across the pond. Both the horsemen and their mounts were dressed in brocade and the riders were armed with long lances as if about to engage in battle.

Near the Firdus, and surrounded by gardens, stood another palace, the New Summer House. In the middle was an ornamental pond of tin. Around this ran a little stream, also in a channel of polished tin which shone more brightly than silver. Around the pond were four summer-houses furnished with gilt chairs with gold-embroidered cushions. On the lawns of the garden were some four hundred dwarf palm-trees. Their trunks were ornamented from top to bottom with carved panels of teak. They yielded normal-sized dates and were carefully trained to produce fruit all the year round. All kinds of delicious melons were grown also.

There was another garden within the walls of the Tadsh palace described by Masudi in his *Golden Meadows*. This was planted with orange-trees from Basra and Oman, originally brought from India. They were still a novelty amongst the flora of the Near East at this time and were greatly admired. Their branches were intertwined and their red and yellow fruit, says Masudi, hung amongst the foliage like so many stars. There were shrubs and scented plants everywhere and flocks of exotic birds.

None of the palaces in Baghdad has been described by contemporary historians in sufficient detail for us to picture their outward appearance or interior decoration. Our only knowledge of this type of building comes from the German archaeologists' excavations at Samarra, where Caliph Mutasim (A.D. 833–842), Harun al-Rashid's third son, transferred his residence from Baghdad in A.D. 836. This was over sixty miles upstream on the Tigris, and thus at a safe distance from the capital, where the excesses of his Turkish bodyguard amongst the local population had caused the Caliph continual embarrassment. He built the Jausak palace in Samarra and had it richly decorated with frescoes. His seven successors built other palaces and mosques there but the court returned to Baghdad in 892. Samarra was the new capital, therefore, for a mere fifty-six years. All that survives of it dates from this period, which is a great advantage from the archaeological point of view. The excavations revealed two large mosques, several palaces and large houses and a number of private dwellings which had belonged to high officials and courtiers.

The plan of the Balkuwara palace excavated at Samarra is different from any in Baghdad. Its outer walls formed an approximate square with each side over half a mile long, and along the central axis there were three courts of honour. There was an *iwan* and a cruciform throne-room from which a second *iwan* led into gardens along the banks of the Tigris. The gardens had ornamental ponds and a landing-stage. On two sides of the third court and of the throne-room, the prince's apartments, the harem and the servants' quarters were built symmetrically around a number of inner courtyards. This plan was copied from al-Hira, the palace-camp of the Lakhmides, a pre-Islam Arab dynasty formerly ruling in Iran. The inner walls of the hall and the rooms, both in the palace and in the private houses, were decorated with stucco friezes. These reached up to a height of three feet or more, after the manner of the plaques found in Assyrian temples. The design of the plaques consisted of so-called "endless" motifs which could be continued in any direction or interrupted at will. Numerous variants in the design will indicate to the art historian the transition from the ancient lotus leaf to the newer "arabesques". Above the friezes the walls were often decorated with figurative paintings or covered with carpets and brocades. Some of the designs of the carpets show human figures and even towns, especially Mecca and Medina, the two holy cities. The floor of the *divan*, where the rich received their guests, was often covered with a rich carpet. A chronicler of the time describes a visit to one of the Samarra palaces:

"I went one day into the upper rooms of the Caliph's palace and found myself in an apartment furnished with a great Persian carpet from Susanjir. In front of the couch was a smaller carpet and against the walls were arranged cushions with red and blue patterns. The large carpet had a wide border and in each section were portraits with inscriptions in Persian which I was able to read. On the right of the place of honour of the *divan* the carpet bore the design of a man wearing a crown. When I read the inscription I saw that it was a portrait of Siroes who murdered his father Parviz ('The Victorious').[1] Other pictures followed and under one portrait, on the left of the place of honour, I read 'This is the portrait of Yazid-ibn-Walid, the murderer of his cousin Walid-ibn-Yazid. On this very carpet Mutawakkil, the father of Muntasir, was killed and the carpet had to be washed to remove the bloodstains.'"

This is a sad commentary on the family chronicles of the Sassanians and the Abbasids.

But, the reader will say, what about the Koran's prohibition of the portrayal of the human figure? The question is justified,

[1] Chosroes II (A.D. 590–628).

but this prohibition, like that of adultery, was often ignored. Statues and portraits were not allowed in mosques, for scientific and theological reasons which are too complex to be gone into here. The fact remains, however, that there were enough portraits and statues in Baghdad and other Iraq towns in the time of the Caliphs to stock a museum. The founder of the capital, Al Mansur, had set the example himself by placing an equestrian statue on the dome of his palace in the Round City and his successors followed suit. The two ranks of fighting horsemen in Muktadir's palace were mentioned above. In a grandee's house there was a bath with silver taps shaped like birds at the ends. When the water ran the birds sang. The entrance-hall of the house was paved with designs in red, green and gilt mosaic which deceptively imitated still-life. Caliph Al Amin had pleasure-boats built in the shape of lions, elephants, vultures, a snake and a horse. These were constructed at great expense and were celebrated by a poet of the time. Tents were decorated with figures of humans and animals. Several writers acknowledged the good that mural paintings could do to a man's nature, and advised their use in bathroom decoration:

"Here there must be masterpieces of art, pictures exceptional for their beauty, such as might portray loving couples, hunting scenes with wild animals and horses in full pursuit, landscapes with meadows and gardens, for such pictures wonderfully increase a man's animal, natural and moral vigour."

Or again:

"All doctors, learned and wise men agree that beautiful paintings rejoice and refresh the soul, drive away dark thoughts and insinuations and admirably fortify the heart by the banishment of evil thoughts."

The following passage reveals an astonishing knowledge of the laws of optics:

"When, in a pretty picture, harmonic colours such as yellow, red, green and white are combined in the right proportions, they cure melancholy and drive away the care and sadness which attend the human soul, and the soul is refined and ennobled by the contemplation of them. Remember the wise men of old who invented the use of the bath. They realised with their keen and healthy minds that bathing takes away one's strength and so, to counteract this, they ordered that bathrooms should be decorated with fine paintings which rejoice the heart with their beautiful colours. These paintings are of three kinds, according to the animal, moral or natural strength which they affect. For animal strength there are scenes of battle, hunting and horse-racing; for moral strength scenes of love and of lovers sulking; for natural strength gardens, fine trees, flowers of all colours and so on."

This scheme was adhered to, as we can see from the only surviving ancient bathroom in the East. This is in Qocair Amra's hunting-lodge, built for the Omayyad Caliphs in the eighth century in a *wadi* (valley) east of Damascus. The *wadi*, which is out in the desert, is covered with verdure in the rainy season. The bathroom is decorated with bathing and hunting scenes, athletic contests, pairs of lovers, trees, flowers and a portrait of the owner of these many splendours, Caliph Walid. He is shown seated on his throne in the midst of the sky, the earth and the waters, and is surrounded by the monarchs then in subjection to the Omayyads. This scheme had been drawn up in detail by a wise man of the court and very accurately carried out by the painters. After this digression to give us an idea of the painting in palaces and baths in Baghdad, Samarra, Kufa, Basra and many other cities in the Kingdom of the Caliphs, let us return once more to Samarra.

The many private houses excavated in this Pompeii of Islam give us a very clear idea of domestic architecture. They were all built to similar plans. A covered entrance led from the street into a spacious rectangular court. On one of the shorter sides of the court was a T-shaped main room with two small rooms in the corners for the storing of mats, carpets and cushions. Large houses had a second court where a similar room was reserved for the women when seraglio and harem were separate. Some houses had two of these main rooms on the opposite sides of the same courtyard, one being used in winter and the other in summer, an arrangement still to be found in eastern Iran. Around the court were other living-rooms and servants' quarters. All these houses had baths and a water system, often also fountains and basement living-rooms with ventilation pipes such as are still found today.

This general description can be rounded off with commentaries and descriptions by contemporary writers. One of these, for example, describes the way of life of a rich man in Baghdad:

"I visited Mohammed-Ibn-Nasr on a cold winter's day. He received me in a great vaulted hall the walls of which were covered with Armenian earth and were so smooth that they shone like mirrors. . . . In the middle of the domed hall, easily twenty cubits wide and the same distance long, stood an immense metal grate, eleven cubits in circumference which burnt wood from the ghada tree.[1] In the upper corner of this hall sat the master of the house, dressed in a long garment of Persian cloth from Tostar. The floor was covered with a silken carpet. He bade me sit near him, but I was almost fainting from the heat and endeavoured, therefore, to get outside again into the cold as soon as possible. Some time later I had occasion to pay him another visit. This time I was shown into another room in the centre of which was a pretty ornamental pond. At the end of the room there was a couch on raised tiles, and from it, through the open window, could be enjoyed a pleasant view over the park, with its antelopes and an aviary with its turtle-doves and other birds. I could not help remarking that it must have been like living in paradise. My host replied by asking me to stay until the morrow. I consented, and soon servants set before me an onyx table more beautiful than anything I had ever seen. In the middle of it stood a many-coloured onyx bottle with a gold rim and filled with rose-water. By

[1] A desert shrub giving a pleasant-smelling charcoal.

the side of this was a dish containing a sort of paste made from breast of chicken. Also on the table were onyx dishes containing sauces and various delicacies. I was then served with *sanbuses*[1] and, to end the meal, cups of almond milk. We then rose and passed through the curtain dividing the dining-room from the reception-room. Here a great bowl of China porcelain was set before us full of violets and gilly-flowers. In the middle of the bowl was a pile of magnificent sweet-smelling Syrian apples. 'This,' said the master of the house, 'is our light morning meal.'"

So much for the life of the rich. The Caliphs did even better, if that were possible. They were literally surfeited. Muktafi, for instance, ate ten dishes a day, plus a young goat and three sweet dishes on Fridays, a feast-day in Islam. On festive occasions the Caliph's table was decorated with figures made of amber and camphor, costly materials in those days. They were fashioned into the shape of animals, human beings and fruits and their strong perfume filled the room. The table was also decorated with flowers and rose-petals were strewn over the floor and the clothing of the guests. The food was served in an unbelievable variety of shapes, particularly the sweetmeats. Sugar towers and palaces were a feast for the eyes as well as for the palate. Any feast without sweetmeats was considered a failure.

It is evident that life could be very refined in Baghdad. All the applied arts flourished: ceramics, glassmaking, textiles, metal-work and wood-carving. Nothing of this has survived in the city itself, but there are examples elsewhere. The pulpit in the Friday Mosque at Kairuan, for example, has very richly carved panels. In the same building the *mihrab* wall is dressed with ceramic tiles of a metallic lustre which were made in Baghdad, showing that the art of glazed pottery was known there as early as the ninth century. It spread from Baghdad to Iran, where it flourished in Rhai and other towns, then to the West, where it flourished magnificently in Spain, spreading from there to Italy.

The progressive decline of Baghdad set in in the tenth century with the appearance of minor dynasties in the distant

[1] Carps.

provinces. One of these, the Buides, captured the capital in 945 and seized temporal power. They built several palaces but the city suffered from the continual struggles between the two Islamic factions of the Sunnites and Shiites, not to mention the rivalry between the various members of the Buides family. Caliph Al Kaim's vizier had to appeal for help to Toghrul Beg, the leader of the Seljuk Turks, who occupied the town in 1055 and three years later was proclaimed Sultan by the Caliph. The Seljuk Sultans never lived in the Caliphs' city which consequently lost its character of the capital of the Persian Empire. It acquired, however, a number of new buildings. Sultan Melik Shah's famous vizier Nizam-el-Mulk built a *madrasah* (Koran University) in 1065. This became well known throughout the world and its walls are still standing. The Caliphs had now only spiritual power but they continued to build palaces. Mustaz-hir (1094–1118) surrounded the eastern part of the town, including the royal quarter, by a wall which still enclosed Baghdad in the nineteenth century and is still partly standing. One of the monumental gateways in this wall, the Bal-el-talisman ("Talisman Gate"), was decorated during the restoration of the city under Caliph Al Nazar in 1221. Above the entrance arch of the gateway is a representation of a human figure, seated and grasping two dragons, one in each hand. The dragons are arranged symmetrically and their tails are decoratively intertwined. This cosmo-magic group was copied hundreds of times all over Asia and it occurs again and again in Western medieval art. As the name of the gateway shows, it was supposed to have some magical power of protection.

In January 1259 the Mongol Khan Hulagu captured Baghdad and the last Caliph, Mustazim, was assassinated with all the members of his family. The city was pillaged and set on fire but Hulagu did what he could to mitigate the destructive frenzy of his hordes as he did not wish Baghdad to be destroyed completely, as so many other cities had been. He even restored several important monuments, and so Baghdad escaped complete ruin. The "City of Peace", with its troubled and often tragic history, is today the capital of Iraq.

8

ISFAHAN: "HALF THE WORLD"

The inhabitants of Isfahan, proud of their city's splendour, used to call it "Half the World". Today their claim seems exaggerated, but the city is still proudly called Nispe Iran ("Half Iran") although it is no longer the capital. Persia's history is indissolubly linked with Isfahan and no other Iranian town, nor any other city of Islam, has so faithfully retained its original character. It is the last monument extant to an oriental monarch who knew how to build, a late but still living example of the many towns described by Arab and Persian historians.

The watercourse to which the great oasis of Isfahan owes its existence is the Zende, or river of youth, river of life. This flows down from the mountains in the west of the Baktiares country. Over the centuries it has brought down a deposit of marl, from which its waters have washed away the salt, making it extremely fertile, and feeding the sub-soil and irrigating the surrounding plain. But the supply of water, only plentiful in the spring, was insufficient and so the Sefuwa Shahs of the sixteenth and seventeenth centuries, Tahmasp, Abbas the Great and Abbas II, tried to divert the Karun, a tributary of the Tigris, across the mountains in order to increase the flow of the Zende. This was to be done by a tunnel or a water-gap, but the means at their disposal turned out to be insufficient. This ambitious project would have turned the Karun valley in Mesopotamia into a desert, but would have doubled the area of the Isfahan oasis. It shows a breadth of vision which was not unusual amongst the rulers of this dynasty. Another watercourse was, in fact, diverted to the

Zende. This was the Mahmud Ker and the work was executed under the orders of Abbas I. All the cereals and fruits which grow on the Iranian plateau were cultivated in this oasis, but Isfahan is famous especially for its melons. Its soil is particularly suitable for them as it is well manured with pigeon-dung.

Ptolemy mentions the city under the name of Aspadana. Isfahan means "military camp". The town arose out of the growth of two very ancient villages, originally a mile or more apart, on the north bank of the Zende. The more easterly of these was called Shai and the other Al-Yahudiyah ("Jews' Town"). According to Mukkadasi (tenth century) the latter was originally a Jewish community settled there by Nebuchad-nezzar. Another more likely version of the origin of the "Jews' Town" is the founding of the colony by the Sassanian king Yazdgard I (A.D. 399–421) at the instance of his wife, herself a Jewess. The site seems to have pleased the Jews as it was said to resemble the outskirts of Jerusalem. The site of Shai, also called Shahristan, is still marked today by an ancient minaret in the middle of a small village on the north bank of the river some two and a half miles from modern Isfahan. This minaret is all that survives of the ancient town which was not rebuilt after its destruction by the Mongols. Yahudiyah, later called Jubareh, is today the oldest and largest district of Isfahan and still a partly Jewish quarter. In the Middle Ages, when Shahristan declined, it became the centre of Isfahan and has many ruined buildings with minarets as well as the Friday Mosque, which was continually restored. It was formerly quite important, but was overshadowed by the Sefuwas' new buildings. Today it is a very poor quarter.

When Shah Abbas I, the Great, came to the throne in 1585 he abandoned the Sefuwas' traditional residence, Tabriz, for Isfahan, which then became the first city in Iran. Although the Shah had many traits of character common to oriental despots, such as a morbid distrust of his fellow men, he was nevertheless one of the most valiant, active and contented of Iran's monarchs. He reigned for forty-five years. During the whole of this time he was well prepared to defend his country

and careful of the well-being of his subjects. Isfahan is mainly
his creation. Pietro della Valle, who stayed at Abbas's court
in 1617, describes it thus in a letter:

"I shall stay here to see Isfahan and to rejoice in the sight
of it, for it is a large, beautiful and populous city, in a word,
a more beautiful city than any I have ever seen in the
Levant, so much so that one may say that apart from the
extraordinary site of Constantinople, Isfahan is not only
the equal of this city but in many respects excels it. With
regard to the extent of this city, the part which is called
Isfahan proper is probably as large as Naples. But other
towns have been built round Isfahan by the present king.
One of these is New Tabriz, inhabited mainly by people
brought from this town. This the king has named Abbas
Abad. Another is Julfa, inhabited exclusively by Armenian
Christians brought here from Julfa in Armenia. All of them
are much given to trade and are very industrious. The third
is inhabited by the Guebres who worship fire. The king's
design would appear to be, so far as one can judge, the
unification of these three townships with Isfahan, to form
one city. The people here labour with great zeal, and so far
advanced is the work that little remains for its completion.
The king himself gives money and land to anyone in need of
it for building. When all is finished Isfahan will be bigger
than Constantinople or Rome."

A story told by Chardin shows how Abbas succeeded in
making the rich and the middle classes collaborate with him
in his town-planning schemes:

"When the great king set up his court in Isfahan and conceived the idea of making this city as great as it has since
become, he made not only all the grandees but also all the
wealthy citizens promise to contribute by the erection of
some public building which should be at once ornamental
and useful. He learnt that a certain grocer was one of the
wealthiest and so he went to see him in his shop, and, with

the familiarity which came naturally to him, said: 'For a long time I have known that you have the reputation of a good and wealthy man. It is doubtless due to your honesty that God has blessed you so abundantly. I should be very pleased to be adopted by an old man who is so virtuous. I take you now for my father; your sons are my brothers. Make me your heir along with them; I shall see to it that they lose nothing. If you prefer it, however, you may erect during your lifetime some building in the city which shall both adorn it and be useful to its citizens.' "

The merchant decided for the second proposal and built a caravanserai which he presented to the king. The king "duly recompensed his children".

There were six types of building in which Persian life evolved: the house, the baths, the bazaar, the tea-house, the caravanserai and the mosque. Three of these reached monumental proportions: the caravanserai, the mosque and the bazaar. The number of these, their artistic value and, in the case of the bazaar, their commercial prosperity, denoted a city's importance. Ancient Arab and Persian travellers' tales always spoke of them with the greatest respect.

Just as our town halls and churches, the two most important public buildings, are usually separated from their surroundings by a public square, so the bazaar, the royal palace and the mosque in Isfahan were built round an open space known as a Meidan. This enabled caravans to make a halt without obstructing ordinary traffic and allowed the greatest freedom of circulation. In a word it was the hub of a great city. It fulfilled these conditions both practically and aesthetically, it was popular and representative and it was used as a market, a polo-ground and a festival-ground by the king and his people.

The Meidan-i-Shah ("Royal Square") can still be seen today in its original design but it has lost certain decorative features. These have, however, been described for us by travellers who saw it in its original form. It is a rectangle, four hundred and twenty-two yards by one hundred and fifty-three yards, running north to south, and is surrounded by a line of regular arcaded façades broken by the Ali Kapu and by the monumental gateways leading to the mosque and the bazaar. Formerly there was a walled-in canal all the way round, some sixteen feet from the buildings, this intervening space being filled with pleasantly shady plane-trees. The canal has been choked up for a long time now and of the plane-trees standing today very few can have survived since the building of the square.

The north side of the Meidan contains the high gateway leading to the bazaar and has galleries over its arcades. The gateway is called Kaisarieh, from the name of the tailors' bazaar behind it. Its vault is decorated with the painting of a battle scene, of which, unfortunately, very little remains. The galleries are used as Negar eh Chane, or musicians' galleries. At certain times of the day and even at night during festivals and rejoicings, Persian and Turkish orchestras of trumpets accompanied by enormous drums can be heard playing here. The eastern side of the square is dominated by the gateway and the magnificent ceramic dome of the Sheik Luft Ullah mosque. The western side contains the monumental doorway leading to the coppersmiths' bazaar and also the Ali Kapu ("High Gate"). In the middle of the south side stands the entrance to the Great Mosque whose brightly-coloured domes and minarets rise high into the sky.

In the centre of the esplanade there once stood a one-hundred-and-thirty-foot-high mast. This has now disappeared. Two wide marble columns over eight feet apart at each end of the square were once used for polo. These are still standing. The Meidan was also the market-place and was crowded with small traders, dealers and jugglers who mingled with the passers-by and the caravaneers who had stopped in the town. In the evening the square was the haunt of mountebanks, puppet-players, dice-players, fortune-tellers and tale-tellers. This motley crowd was cleared from the square on solemn feast-days and for big receptions.

The bazaars of Isfahan are still today the loveliest and the most characteristic in Iran. The bazaar at Tehran is probably better stocked with merchandise, but it cannot equal any in

Isfahan either architecturally or in the originality of its décor.
A bazaar consists of two long vaulted halls which intersect at
right-angles. The point of intersection is topped by a dome.
This basic plan, which is also that of the bazaar at Isfahan, is
extended in the larger bazaars to several parallel and intersecting halls. The main point of intersection often has an
ornamental pond and the dome is covered externally with
ceramic tiles. The Isfahan bazaar has ponds and fountains
and is outstanding architecturally. The caravanserai and the
banks are usually adjacent to the bazaar. The coppersmiths'
bazaars, crowded and noisy, are the most interesting to the
visitor.

There are three main types of religious buildings in Islam:
the mosque with columns or pillars and a flat roof, the Persian
mosque-madrasah and the Turkish domed mosque. The first
has a pillared court, the side pointing to Mecca being pro-
longed by several rows of pillars into a covered hall, often very
long, which is used as a prayer-room by the assembled faithful.
During the first few centuries of Islam, this type, the oldest,
spread through Mesopotamia, Syria and Egypt into Morocco
and Spain, the western extremities of the Islam world. The
pillared mosque also came into Iran with the Arab conquest,
but was completely absorbed into a local form of architecture.
It eventually gave way to the second type, the *madrasah*. This
means "school", but particularly the Koran University. Its
architecture developed from the eastern Iranian house, with
its rooms grouped around an open courtyard. This type of
house was regular and symmetrical, the middle of each side
having a vaulted room, called an *iwan*, which opened through
an arch on to the courtyard. This was the plan adopted for
the *madrasah*, but on a much bigger scale. One of the *iwans* of
the *madrasah* is oriented towards Mecca; this is called the
kiblaiwan and behind it there is usually a domed hall. In
Arab and Turkish countries the mosque also came to be used
as a *madrasah*. In Persia it was the other way round: the *madrasah* came first and eventually came to be used as a mosque.
In most mosques there were schools of theology and some of
these are still in existence today. The third type of religious

building, the Turkish mosque, originated in the Byzantine domed church. Saint Sophia in Byzantium was the model for all the great mosques of the Turkish Empire.

After this brief introduction let us return to the mosques oı Isfahan. Like all the great mosques in Persia, they are of the second type, the mosque-*madrasah*. The oldest is the Masjid-i-Jum'a, or Friday Mosque, in the old Jubareh quarter. Its foundation is said to date back to Caliph Mansur (745). It is very large and contains traces of older pillared mosques. The great court, with the *iwans* opening onto it, was built under the Sefuwas. The largest and most magnificent mosque in Isfahan, however, is the Masjid-i-Shah, or Royal Mosque, built by Abbas the Great from 1590 onwards. It stands in the middle of the south side of the Meidan-i-Shah. Only its monumental entrance-gate is built on a north-south axis, parallel to the main axis of the square. The mosque itself is built on a northwest-southeast axis so that its *mihrab*, the recess set in the wall at the far end, shall point, according to ritual, to Mecca. The bold conception and ingenious solution of this plan is an illustration on a grandiose scale of the Gospel's precept "Render unto Caesar that which is Caesar's and unto God that which is God's". The problem was to site the mosque in harmony with the design of the square and yet respect the ritual requirement of the *mihrab*. It was solved by building a high entrance-gate flanked by two minarets and leading into the courtyard. The mosque thus fits into the Royal Square with suitable majesty, yet without breaking the unity of design, as its buildings are half-hidden behind the façades of the houses. The Royal Mosque has a great open courtyard with four *iwans* and three adjacent domed halls. The largest of these halls, the one in the south-east, is the main prayer-hall and has a huge dome which can be seen from far away.

The Persian mosque excels all others in Islam by the splendour of its wall decoration. The basis of this is the ceramic tile which we can, it is true, admire in our museums. Seen in isolation, however, this can give no idea of the splendour and the infinite variety of the whole pattern of these walls. Dressing walls with bricks and ceramic tiles is an ancient oriental tradition. We have seen how the walls of the ancient palaces at Babylon, Assur and Susa were decorated with brilliantly coloured glazed bricks. The tradition was handed down until it reached its peak of perfection under the Timurids in the fifteenth century and the Sefuwas. The Royal Mosque at Isfahan is one of the finest examples of this art. Every wall, both inside and out, the vaults, domes and minarets are all dressed with ceramic tiles with, mainly, a light or deep blue background. The designs on these blue surfaces seem to be of infinite variety. Certain motifs are repeated, vases, palms, rosettes, stylised flowers and leaves, but their combination is always different as also is that of the scrolls joining them, which often cunningly emphasise the architectural function of the surfaces they decorate. There are four minarets, two on the main gateway and two on the main *iwan*. They could not have been intended for their proper use, as they overlook the gardens of the royal harem and of neighbouring houses. Here a religious custom has had to give way to the proverbial jealousy of the Persians.

The second mosque in the Meidan, on the east side, the Luft Ullah, is much smaller, but its richly decorated ceramic domes are in keeping with the truly royal setting of the square.

Opposite this mosque stands the Ali Kapu ("High Gate"), formerly the entrance to the royal seraglio, a huge park containing a palace, houses and shops and said to be nearly four miles in circumference. This "High Gate" has a very original structure with three storeys facing the square and five at the back, so that it looks like a huge throne with its terrace as the base. The terrace has eighteen columns of wood supporting a flat roof and was used by the monarchs as a *talar*, or throne room, for solemn receptions. It was also used for watching polo and other shows in the Meidan. The building is of porphyry, the two façades are dressed with porcelain plaques and the apartments decorated with rich paintwork. The ceramic work of the Sefuwa period, the murals and the cloth and carpet decoration all show a distinct Chinese influence. This is evident both in certain motifs such as streamers (used in Chinese decoration to represent clouds), dragons and phoenixes and in the design and combination of the scrolls. This mixture of Chinese and Persian styles is the great attraction of the Ali Kapu murals. There are "endless" motifs enlivened by paintings of people, including pairs of lovers. These are flat, highly chromatic and astonishingly like some modern paintings.

The upper floors contain certain rooms with strangely panelled walls. The panels are of wood and contain hundreds of vase-shaped recesses. These were intended to hold specially shaped vases in the most varied colours, but mainly the bluish-white vases of the Ming period and Persian flask-shaped vessels made by the Chinese in the Chinese style. Vases were even fixed, almost horizontally, into recesses in the ceiling. Chardin describes this strange method of decoration:

> "There is nothing more cheerful or more gay than this infinite number of vases, cups, bottles of all shapes and materials, of crystal, cornelian, agate, onyx, jasper, amber, coral, porcelain, gold, silver, enamel, all apparently set haphazardly into the walls and even the vaults, so delicately that they seem about to fall at any moment."

Ali Kapu is a Turkish name, and not Persian, as most Iranian names are. This is explained by the origin of the Sefuwas who came from Ardebil in Azerbaijan in the north-east of the Empire, a province with a mainly Turkish population. Turkish was spoken in the Sefuwas' court in Isfahan, although the dynasty was really Iranian in origin. The Arab word for "gate" is "bab". The name "High Gate" is in keeping with the symbolical meaning attached to all names of gates from time immemorial in the Orient. Babylon simply meant "Gate of God" ("bab-ilon" in Assyrian, "bab-el" in Hebrew). A hundred or so years ago the founder of a Persian religious sect called himself, metaphorically, "The Gate". It is because of their symbolical value that most of the gateways to Persian mosques are of such huge proportions. Their mighty vertical walls rise up to thirty or even fifty feet and are often topped by two small minaret-like towers. Their majesty and grandeur impressed the believer with a sense of his own insignificance. They have no practical use, but are simply an expression in stone of the Oriental mind. They are a huge illustration of the "Bismillahi rahmani rahim" ("in the name of the merciful god"), the invocation called *Basmala* which begins each one of the *surates* of the Koran and which the believer murmurs piously before doing anything out of the ordinary. In everyday life the gateway was also a public monument. In many places, and according to a very ancient custom, it was here that justice was dispensed. It was a meeting-place and an observatory from which one could look out over the far countryside. The ancient monumental gateways in Asia were decorated with winged genii. They were venerable monuments with steps to keep out chariots and horsemen. Even the king could only cross them on foot. It is not surprising, therefore, to find a chain across the Ali Kapu to keep out vehicles and horsemen. Ali Kapu was also an asylum for criminals and fugitives and had two separate gardens, each with a summer-house, for men and women separately to find refuge. Only the sovereign could drive the fugitive out, and then only indirectly by forbidding food to be taken to him.

In the middle of the seraglio to which Ali Kapu formed the entrance is the Shehel Sutun, or "Palace of the Forty Columns". This stands in a great park and was rebuilt by Sultan Hussein (A.D. 1694–1722) to replace Shah Abbas's palace which had been destroyed by fire. It has a terrace with eighteen wooden columns supporting a wooden roof (the "forty" is the conventional oriental exaggeration) with a throne-room behind. This opens on to the terrace through a doorway with two columns. The throne-room is flanked by two cradle-vaulted oblong rooms. Diagonally to its principal axis there is a large hall with three flat wooden domes. This has open terraces on the north and south sides and on the north side there is an entrance-hall flanked by two rectangular rooms. The plan of this building seems to have been copied from that of the Achaemenian palaces at Pasargadae and

Persepolis. In spite of the apparently straight-forward arrangement of the rooms the visitor has a curious sense, as he passes
from one to the other, of losing his direction. This is because
the rooms are juxtaposed along diagonal axes, whereas the
interior decoration and the decoration of the terraces are
perfectly symmetrical. Phenomena of this kind are found not
only in the architecture of palaces and private houses, but also
in ornamentation, literature and many other phases of Persian
life. There are Persian proverbs so abounding in puns as to be
virtually incomprehensible without a very close analysis of
the language. The Shehel Sutun had a purely representative
function: it was used for audiences and solemn assemblies and
was a setting for the appearance of royalty. The palace was
approximately in the centre of the park and the throne-room,
the *iwan-i-nichin*, or *shah-nichin*, was in the centre of the
building, excluding the columned terrace.

The interior decoration of the palace uses what was then and
is still considered the loveliest and richest material: the
mirror-mosaic. The base of the walls is dressed to a height
of nearly five feet with Yezd marble plaques, painted with
diamond-shapes and bouquets of flowers. Above this is laid on
the *ainehkari*, or mirror-mosaic which is still in a good state of
preservation. It consists of faceted mirrors set in gilt stucco borders and juxtaposed like mosaic. The ceiling of the throne-
room has similar mirrors with polychrome borders. The cof-
fered ceiling of the terrace is painted with geometrical designs.
The ceiling of the great hall has an equally magnificent decoration of lacquered paintwork on paper, a process highly esteemed
in Iran. Flowers resembling peonies joined together with
scrolls, vases, streamers and animals are painted against a blue
and green background. Each of the two long sides of the hall
has three panels illustrating scenes from Persian history. One
of them shows the Indian prince Humayun, a refugee at the
Sefuwa court at Tabriz, feasting in company with Shah
Tahmasp. The two princes are sitting on a dais in front of
metal plates and piles of fruit, whilst around them stand body-
guards, falconers, musicians and guests. In the centre foreground two girls are dancing.

The originality of the Shehel Sutun does not lie in its sumptuous decoration, however, as this can be equalled in many rich men's houses, but in its magnificent setting and the delightful way in which the columned terraces effect the transition from garden to interior. It is small in comparison with the garden, to which its design is subordinated. It must also be remembered that this building was once surrounded by a narrow canal. This supplied water to fountains and a pool both in the columned entrance-hall and the throne room. The garden was thus brought into the palace itself, right up to the sovereign's throne. This kind of scheme can be found today in certain modern buildings designed by Le Corbusier, Mies van Rohe and other contemporary architects. The throne, set in front of a huge mirrored recess, stood at the end of a long perspective of gardens, whilst the hall, running diagonally to this axis, might be considered as leading from one side of the garden to the other. To this happy combination of two elements can be added a third: the splendour of the Shah enthroned amidst his court. The spectacle of a royal audience never failed to impress by its grandeur, as Chardin relates:

> "No more stately ceremony can be seen than that which the King of Persia gives in this hall. The King's throne, which is like a small rest-bed, is furnished with four thick cushions embroidered with pearls and precious stones. White eunuchs, small in stature and of great beauty, stand behind him in a semicircle, with four or five other taller eunuchs behind, holding his shining and richly ornamented weapons. The greatest nobles of the state stand on the sides of the dais which bears the throne. The lesser nobles stand on the second dais. The high-born youths and those not admitted to the inner circle close to the king stand at the end of the hallway with the musicians. The serving officers stand in the garden within sight of the king."

Of the remaining buildings of the royal court, summer-houses, harem, private houses and shops, only a few remain and these are of little interest. There were, however, buildings outside the perimeter of the palace which were also connected with Shehel Sutun and inspired by the same spirit. These are still standing, and amongst them is the summer residence of Abbass II on the south bank of the Zenderhud. This was called the Sadetabad ("House of Happiness") and was supplied with water over a fourteen-arch brick aqueduct called the Pul-i-Juba. It had two main buildings, the Aineh Chane ("Pavilion of the Mirror") and the Heft Dest ("Seven Compartments"), or royal harem. Gardens ran along the banks of the river and by closing the sluice-gates of the nearest bridge, the Pul-i-Shatshu, the Shah could bring the waters of the river up to the steps of the Pavilion of the Mirror and go boating with his wives in the magic light of a night-festival. Today only a few shapeless walls remain of this fairy setting. Old prints show a striking resemblance between Aineh Shane and Shehel Sutun. In both buildings the audience-room was a pillared hall.

A summer-house of the same kind has been preserved for us. This is the Hasht Behesht ("The Eight Paradises") built by Shah Suleiman in about 1670. Architecturally this is the most perfect summer-house imaginable. Its dome stands at the intersection of two avenues of poplars. One of these, running east-west, contains ornamental ponds and the stairways leading to the terrace. The living-rooms, reserved at that time for the Shah's wives, are at the four corners and on two storeys. The domed hall originally had friezes picturing historical scenes. Chardin was entranced by this place and admired the two canals with their pelicans and swans, the summer-house built entirely of polished marble and the gilt dome with the silver pond underneath it. Chardin's calm, unbiased opinion is worth having. Although used to the architectural grandeur and the pomp of Versailles, he recognised that these buildings, in some respects mere playing-card houses, have their own peculiar charm and are, in their own way, as lovely as the most magnificent palaces in his own country.

From the royal quarter on the opposite bank of the river, an avenue some two or three miles in length ran due north-south, crossed the Zenderhud on a splendid bridge and led to the centre of the town. It was a Royal Way and was called Shahar Bag ("The Four Gardens"), but only the northern half, between the bridge and the city-centre, has survived. A degenerate descendant of the Kajars, the eldest son of Shah Nasr-eddin, jealous of the splendour of the former Sefuwa residence, destroyed everything on the opposite bank of the river, and, in the town itself, had many plane-trees along the avenue cut down. Chardin has preserved for us some of these lost beauties:

"The canal running right through the middle of the town has walls on either side of carved stone some nine inches high and wide enough for two horsemen to ride abreast on them. The edges of the ornamental pools are just as wide. . . . Alongside this charming avenue are fine spacious gardens, each with two summer-houses, a very large one in the middle with an open hall in the centre and rooms at the corners, and another one built over the gateway leading to the garden, open in front and at the sides to allow an easy view of passers-by in the avenue. These summer-houses are of different shape and construction, but mostly of the same size, all richly painted and gilded. They are a most vivid and agreeable spectacle."

The finest of these buildings along the Shahar Bag is the *madrasah* of Shah Hussein (1694–1722), the last of the Sefuwas. He was better at building than at governing his country and was too feeble to make a stand against the Afghans who invaded Iran in 1722, took Isfahan and laid it waste. The plan of his *madrasah* is similar to that of all Persian *madrasahs*. Around an oblong courtyard with an ornamental pond runs a two-stage gallery. Behind this are the students' rooms and the façade is broken by four *iwans*. This is one of the loveliest and most harmonious of all Iranian mosque courtyards. No other has such well-matched and well-preserved mosaic tiles or such magnificent old plane trees whose rich foliage makes the blue enamel of the wall-tiles look even lovelier. The play of light and colours is quite enchanting. A canal with running water goes along the whole length of the courtyard. At the entrance-gate there are the usual sellers of food and fruit and the tea-merchant serves the national drink which goes so well with the simple meal of rice, cheese, *mast* (yoghourt), bread and fruit. Next to the *madrasah* is the great Mader-i-Shah caravanserai built at the expense of the Shah's mother. Its main entrance opens on to the bazaar, and not on to the Shahar Bag. It has two courtyards, one containing living-apartments and the other stables. Both have ponds with running water. A raised plat-form in the middle of the larger courtyard was used by the merchants as a kind of stock exchange.

The Shahar Bag crosses the wide Zenderhud river on the magnificent Allah-werdi bridge. This connects Isfahan to Julfa, the Armenian town, and was built by Abbas the Great's close friend and Commander-in-Chief. It is over three hundred yards long, is built of brick on a limestone base and has thirty-three ogival arches each six yards wide. Ramps lead from the road to the bridge at both ends and at the Isfahan end the bridge has a monumental gateway. The roadway over it is ten yards wide and has high covered galleries along both sides for pedestrians. These have flat roofs which are reached by stairways inside the corner towers. Other stairways lead down to a vaulted passage-way which runs between the pillars and walls of the arches. The total height of the bridge is nearly twenty-eight feet. The towers at both ends have stone walls. This is the finest ancient bridge in the world and it is equalled in beauty only by the second Sefuwa bridge in Isfahan, the Pul-i-Shatshu, a mile or two downstream, although this is shorter and architecturally much simpler. The part of the avenue on the other side of the bridge, the Hesar Jerib ("The Thousand Fields") has disappeared except for part of the terrace. Ferahabad, Shah Hussein's pleasure mansion, famous for its terraced gardens and fountains, once stood there, but this, too, has gone.

Julfa, the Armenian town, is a little farther on to the south-west of the Allah-werdi bridge. This town owes its origin to one of the many transfers of population forcibly imposed upon a people who suffered so much affliction and unhappiness.

This policy began with the Sassanians. The settlement in Isfahan of the Jewish colony of Yehudiya from Armenia was mentioned above. When Shah Abbas I realised that he could not defend Armenia against the Turks, who were superior both in number and strength, he decided that he would leave the enemy only waste land to occupy. Twenty-four thousand Armenian families were therefore forcibly transported to Persia and divided up amongst the various provinces of the Empire. The majority of them merged with the Musulman population so that before long they forgot their own language, religion and traditions. Abbas destroyed the then flourishing town of Julfa on the Araxes near Nakhitshevan and transferred the whole population to New Julfa, a name imposed on the resulting settlement near Isfahan. By 1650 the new town had a population of thirty thousand who had adapted themselves well to their new life, had built up an active trade and were flourishing. A European visitor will find little to interest him in Julfa's narrow, shady, silent streets except perhaps its own particular type of people, with women and girls in traditional costume and its Armenian cathedral with a half-Persian, half-Italian style of interior decoration.

Before leaving Isfahan and Iran to travel deeper into the world of Asia, let us consider briefly one characteristic of the Iranian people which, it must be added, has only preserved its purity in certain parts of the country. There has always been, alongside the Iranian, a strong Turkish element, which has come to be known as Turanian.

The name Turanian is less an ethnic reality than a mythological concept covering all the enemies of Iran. It was used in this latter sense by the Iranian national poets of old and constantly recurs in the *Shahnama* ("History of the King") of Firdousi. These Turanians were nomad tribes who threatened and ravaged Iran with their invasions. They were mainly Turkish tribes, certain of which, the Seljuks, the Mongols and the Timurids, conquered Iran at various times. All these invasions came from the north-east across the river Oxus. Following the period of the Caliphs, Iran was, in fact, more often under Turanian than Iranian rulers and the last dynasty, the Kajars, was Turanian, or, more exactly Turkmenian. The Turkish element of the population today has settled north of the Elbruz mountains and in the west of the country. The Persians inhabit the centre, the east and certain regions of the south. In the south there are also Semitic Arabs. All these three races are to be found in Isfahan, which is a kind of link between desert and mountain and which contains also a very old-established Jewish colony. The Iranian is a scholar, merchant or artist, the Turanian an official or a warrior.

Both the Iranian and the Turk share a common religion, Islam, but within this there is a division between the Sunnites and the Shiites. The Sunnites remained faithful to tradition ("sunna") and to the first three Caliphs Abu Bekr, Omar and Othman. They were principally the Turkish minority. The Persians were mainly Shiites, although this sect was Arabic and not Persian in origin, and spread over Iraq and North Africa. The Shiites refused to recognise the first three Caliphs as the legitimate representatives of Allah on earth and recognised as *imams* the fourth Caliph, Ali, the Prophet's cousin and son-in-law, and his successors. After the assassination of Ali in A.D. 661, the Syrian Moawiya, an Omayyad, usurped the Caliphate. The *shiah* ("sect") of Ali was contained within Iran by Siyad, the energetic governor appointed by the first Omayyad. When Moawiya died, Hussein, Ali's son and the grandson of the prophet, hastened to Kufa to have himself proclaimed Caliph. He was massacred, together with a group of his followers, at Kerbela by the troops of Yesid, Moawiya's successor. The fury of Hussein's adherents knew no bounds and the "shiah" gained such a following that it became the religious community of the nation. Ali and his two sons Hassan and Hussein became national martyrs and are still invoked today in Iran as frequently as we evoke the name of Jesus and Mary. They are worshipped as the first three *imams*, or successors of Mahomet. They themselves had nine successors, and the return of the twelfth is awaited today as marking the end of all time. This *imam* is held to have disappeared in a cave near Samarra. The funeral mosques of Ali at Nejef, of Hussein at Kerbela, of the seventh *imam* Musa and his daughter Fatima at Kum and of the eighth *imam* Risa at Meshed are venerated by the Shiites as their most important sanctuaries and places of pilgrimage. Risa, who was poisoned on the orders of Caliph Imum, is also worshipped as a martyr and the devotions of the faithful around his tomb reach fanatical proportions. The mosques where the other *imams* are buried are also places of frequent pilgrimages and the parents of the *imams* are also worshipped in a large number of domed mausoleums throughout the ancient Persian Empire.

The worship of *imams* is connected, in the popular mind, with the veneration of the legitimate rulers of Iran. Religious worship is thus an expression of the national conscience. The Persians know and love their history and in the remotest mountain villages the heroes and the great events of history are still the favourite reading. It is quite common to see, in public squares, story-tellers evoking the past and praising in particular the Sofuwa dynasty. The Persians are well aware that they spring from one of the oldest civilisations in the world and this is the basis of their sense of superiority over the European.

This deeply-rooted national spirit and this fidelity to tradition also find expression in the principles of Persian architecture which all spring from a native origin. The typical Arab mosque with columns became in Persia the *madrasah*, based on the plan of Khorassan dwelling-houses. The caravanserai also had its origin in a very old type of village which has survived to the present day in the Khorassan oases. This was a very simple arrangement of rows of houses with domes, grouped around a large square and surrounded by a defensive wall. The origin of baths, in their simplest form two adjacent vaulted rooms, is obvious in this country whose people first built the vault and the dome. Sassanian ruins show that these types of building were traditional in Iran long before Islam. They also show the very conservative nature of Persian architecture. Islam emphasised the equality of all men before God. This is reflected in the architecture of the mosque, where the *imam* faces the same direction as the worshippers. The latter take their places side by side in long rows. The halls of prayer extend sideways and not lengthways. The concept of the procession, the slow and solemn approach to God whose presence must of necessity be manifest, is quite foreign to Islam, where it would be considered idolatrous.

This admirable spirit of equality before God, the basic principle of Islam, is the spirit of its creator, the Arab, the free man. He was never in sympathy with the spirit of the Persian, who always allowed himself to be ruled by despots. Thus a surprising interchange took place: the Persians gave up their ancient ceremonial, lay and not religious in origin, to early Christianity and themselves took up an essentially simple form of religious worship. Their religious architecture thus reflected a spirit of equality quite contrary to their despotic traditions and very different from the civil architecture of the Empire. The adapting of Mohammedanism to the Persian national character did not come through architecture. It was left to Arab Islam to create, in Persia, a religious architecture which, with its typically Iranian forms, its characteristic *iwans* and its brilliant coloured domes, succeeded in conveying its idea of God with grandeur and nobility.

9

BUDDHIST GROTTO TEMPLES

In A.D. 632, the year Mahomet died, the Chinese pilgrim Hsuan-tsang reached the land of Bamiyan on his way to India. This is a valley in Afghanistan, some 8,200 feet up in the mountains, at the intersection of two migration routes, one from China to Iran through the Pamir and Hindu-Kush mountains and the other from the Indus valley to Balkh through Kabul. It was already known to Strabo who called it the frontier of languages, civilisations and religions and the cross-roads of Central Asia, and the route from India he called the Great Royal Way. These were trade routes, but they were also followed by the conquerors with their hordes and armies: Cyrus, Alexander, the Seleucids, the Getae, the Chinese, the Caliphs, Jenghiz Khan, Timur, Babar and Nadir Shah.

The valley of Bamiyan experienced its first upheaval with the coming of Islam in the second half of the seventh century A.D. Islam drove out the two previous religions, Zoroastrian-ism and Buddhism, which had managed to co-exist for several centuries. The invasion by Jenghiz Khan in 1221 finally destroyed the valley and its towns. The Mongol hordes, showing no mercy, exterminated the men, razed the towns and wiped out their civilisation. The innumerable monasteries and stupas were reduced to ruins.

In several places on both sides of the valley (it takes three hours to ride through it) rise vertical cliffs of conglomerate, an easily-worked stone which facilitated the excavation of cave-dwellings. These cliffs contain caverns and grottoes, many of which were made into shrines. Colossal figures of the Buddha were carved out of blocks of isolated rock. Only the bare outline of these remains today. Statues of the Buddha

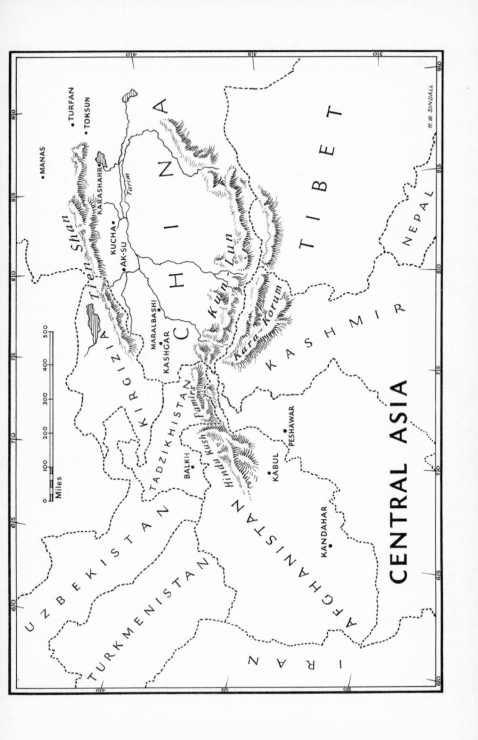

CENTRAL ASIA

and reliefs of all sizes were carved into the natural rock recesses. Some traces of them can still be seen today. Two statues have been particularly admired by travellers on account of their colossal size and several descriptions of them have come down to us. A complete archaeological survey of these figures was made by the Frenchmen Godard and Hackin. The oldest account of them is by Hsuan-tsang[1] mentioned above. He describes the valley, its buildings and Buddhist monuments such as they appeared to the traveller before the Islam conquest. This is how he describes Bamiyan, or, as he calls it, Fanyen-na:

"This kingdom, some two thousand *lis* from east to west by some three hundred *lis* from north to south, is surrounded by snow-capped mountains. The people live in towns, in the mountains or in the valleys. The capital lies on the steep slope of a valley some six or seven *lis* long. To the north it is defended by sheer rocks. The land produces late corn and a few fruits and flowers. It is suitable for cattle-raising and many horses and sheep graze on its pastures. The climate is harsh and the manners of its people are uncouth and primitive. Their clothing is principally of wool and animal skins. The literature, money and customs are the same as those in the land of the Tokharians. Their language is somewhat different, but they resemble the Tokharians very closely in physical appearance. These tribes are distinguished from all neighbouring peoples by their love of religion; from the highest form of the adoration of the 'three jewels'[2] to that of the hundred spirits they show in their worship great seriousness and extreme humility. The merchants regulate their activities by the omens given by the celestial spirits. If these are favourable,

[1] Hsuan-tsang was one of the Chinese pilgrims who travelled to India to visit Buddhist holy places and to study Sanscrit sacred texts which they then took back to China and translated. The accounts they wrote of their travels are a very valuable source of information on Buddhism. Hsuan-tsang was born in A.D. 599 or 603 in Honan, brought up under Confucianism but converted to Buddhism, and became a monk at the age of thirteen. He left China in 629 for a long journey to India through Central Asia and did not return until 645.
[2] The three jewels are Buddha (enlightenment), Dharma (doctrine) and Shanga (communion).

they act accordingly; if unfavourable they endeavour to placate the gods. There are ten monasteries and about a thousand priests who profess the religion of the 'Little Vehicle'[1] and belong to the school of the Lokotta-ravadinas.

North-west of the town, where the king lives, there is a Buddha on the sheer mountain-side. He is standing and is one hundred and forty to one hundred and fifty feet high. He wears shining gold raiment and dazzling precious jewels. To the east of this place a former lord of the land built a monastery. Further east still stands the statue of Sakya Buddha. This is in metal, cast in different pieces then assembled together, and is one hundred feet high. Twelve or thirteen *lis* to the east of the town is a monastery which has a Buddha sleeping apparently as if he had entered Nirvana. This statue is very elongated."

Hsuan-tsang is wrong in saying that the statue of the historical Buddha was made of metal. It was, in fact, carved out of the rock, but was subsequently dressed in metal and then gilded. The other statue he mentions, that of the Maitreya Buddha which is over one hundred and sixty feet high, wore a *sanghati* (monk's gown) of stucco, originally polychrome and decorated with gold and jewels. This statue was almost twice the height of the Colossus of Rhodes and nearly half as high as the towers of Chartres Cathedral. The upper part of the face of both statues was damaged by Moslem fanatics. On both sides of the recesses in which these statues stand there are stairs cut out of the rock. These go up as high as the statues' heads and lead to rooms formerly lavishly decorated with gold and lapis-lazuli. The walls of both recesses are decorated with paintings. Opposite the Sakya Buddha's head there is a picture of the moon-god standing in a four-horse chariot. Underneath, and running round the wall of the recess, is a painted balustrade, with a seated Buddha in the middle flanked by gift-bearers. On the vault of the recess of the Maitreya, the future Buddha, and the predecessors of Sakyamuni and their Dhyani Buddhas are pictured in medallions.

[1] See below, p. 150.

Above them are genii throwing flowers. These two statues are thought to have been carved between the second and the fourth centuries A.D. Between the Maitreya's legs, galleries cut out of the rock lead to vast grottoes with dome-shaped roofs, whose fillets and pilasters, imitating a lost method of construction in wood, are of the greatest archaeological interest. There are many grottoes and caves all over the cliff face. These, too, had recesses for other Buddhas of various sizes, but they are all now empty. The grottoes, used as shrines or meeting-places for *viharas* (monks), were doubtless decorated originally like those of the basins of Tarim and Tun-huang on the western frontier of Kansu which we will now visit.

The road past the cols of the Hindu-Kush and the Pamir mountains reaches a basin of gigantic size, shut in on all sides by high mountains, in the north the Tien-Shan chain, in the south-east the Kara-Korum and in the south the Kun-Lun. This is the Tarim basin, and it takes its name from the main river rising in the Pamir and fed for many months of the year by tributaries from the high valleys in the north and the south. As in Iran, these mountain valleys and their outlets make fertile oases, whilst the inner basin remains a desert of sand and salt. There have always been two important routes through this area: the northerly one along the slopes of the Tien-Shan, the southerly one along the last foothills of the Kara-Korum and the Kun-Lun. They were used for trade between China, Persia, India, Asia Minor and Europe. Two arms of this silk route linked the Han Empire and the Roman Empire. It was along these routes that Buddhism spread from India to China, and with it Buddhist art. Along the thousand or so miles from Kashgar to the Chinese province of Kansu there are, or there were, many oases. Some of these were staging-places and also Buddhist religious centres. There, in the soft walls of the loess cliffs at the end of the valleys, were dug, at varying heights, thousands of caves and grottoes, most of which were painted inside. Grünwedel and von Lecoq removed a number of these mural paintings and sent them to the Museum of Ethnology in Berlin. They illustrate scenes and legends in the lives of the Buddha and Buddhist saints. We see also the pious donors of these sanctuaries; they are fair-haired, blue-eyed men dressed like Western knights and they are Tokharians, an Indo-Aryan people.

The Tokharians, called Yue-Chi by the Chinese, were in Kansu, a western province of China, in the third century B.C. They were driven out in 166 B.C. by the Turkish Huns and withdrew westwards to the north-east border of Tien-Shan. In 135 B.C. they penetrated into the Graeco-Bactrian Empire and settled in Gandhara (Kandahar) on the Kabul river, and at the Himend springs. They made their capital at Puru-shapura, the present Peshawar. In about A.D. 120, under their king Kanishka, they extended their rule over eastern Turkestan. Here the donors' portraits in the Buddhist grotto temples, which date from a later period, show us their physical appearance. This tribe, called Tokharians by Lecoq after the discoveries he made in the Tarim oases, and Kushans by the Indians, seems to be identical with the Scythian people whose funeral-mounds, called Kurgans in Southern Russia, are found along the northern Tien-Shan as far as Dzungaria. These mounds have a rough stone statue on top and contain objects belonging to a bronze civilisation comparable to those found in Scythian funeral-mounds in the Crimea. They doubtless mark out the route followed by the Scythian knights into China. After their defeat they settled in Bactria and Gandhara. In the lands they conquered, these knights adopted, as well as the Buddhist religion, the Hellenic civilisation of the mixed Graeco-Iranian peoples. This is one explanation of the rise of a "Graeco-Buddhist" art in Gandhara in the early years of the Christian era. It emerged from the combination of a Hellenic art, introduced previously by Greek settlers, and a new faith. The birth of ancient Christian art in Europe was somewhat similar. In Graeco-Buddhist art the characters of classical mythology, Apollo and Diana, the figure of the rhetorician and the philosopher, the goddess with the cornucopia, Nike and Ganymede carried off by the eagle, all reappear under new names and in a Buddhist interpretation. The central figure of all Buddhist art, the seated Buddha, is a purely Indian creation. He is the Indian yogi, seated in meditation, to which Buddhism has given a monumental form of great purity. But the Hellenic impulse was necessary before the artist would dare to represent the Enlightened One. This followed after centuries of hesitation, as is shown by those rare Buddhist monuments, the stupas of the second and the first centuries B.C.

The day when, in the middle of Central Asia, Professor A. von Lecoq discovered these vestiges of elaborate art in the sacred grottoes of the Kush oasis was without doubt the happiest of his life:

"I shall never forget," he writes, "the impression made on me by the figures of the donors of the Tokharian princes when I first penetrated into one of the collapsed temples of the Kush oasis. In the temples of the Turfan oasis, the portraits of the knights and princes are predominantly Asiatic in their faces and dress, but here I found myself gazing on pictures which recall, in an extraordinarily vivid way, the period of European chivalry. In the uncertain light of our lamps, the knights, dressed in their rich armour, were standing gracefully on the tips of their toes, with their long cross-hilted swords attached to their metal belts. Beside them were ladies in sumptuous dresses, with low-cut bodices hung with little bells and long skirts with a train; they were leaning slightly forwards in that characteristic attitude found in women's portraits in Europe down to the present day.

"How did they live, these Tokharians of so noble a bearing, these fair-haired, blue-eyed men, in the Tarim oases? There is no literature which can tell us, but the land they lived in makes it possible for us to guess their way of life and the mural paintings show us their physical appearance. The portraits are all of one type only, and not of individuals, and the people were only distinguishable by the inscriptions of their names. Most of these paintings show us the representatives of these conquering peoples as Buddhist faithfuls, founders of temples and worshippers of sacred images. They also appear as armed warriors. The lands their vassals cultivated have scarcely changed since those days, and Lecoq's description of them gives us an idea of the fertile oases of the Tokharians which were similar to those of northern Iran on the other side of the Pamir mountains.

"At the edge of the desert the land rises. Here it is principally fertile loess. The river Tarim, bringing life to all eastern Turkestan, along with its tributaries, traces a vast arc in this loess earth. The skilful industrious peasants have cut innumerable irrigation canals which transform, as if by magic, this desperately bare land into a wonderful garden. There are groves of eleagnaceae which, in springtime, give off a heavy sweet perfume from their sulphur-yellow umbels, wonderful orchards of plum-trees, apricot-trees, peach-trees, mulberry-bushes and pomegranate-trees, with occasionally walnut-trees and pear-trees with their tasty fruit. In the huge well-tended fields are harvests of unbelievable abundance: millet, maize, excellent wheat, madder, cotton, potatoes, turnips, garlic and onions.

"Vines are grown where suitable. These produce many kinds of grape which are delicious and often very large. As the winters, though short, are often severe, the vines are planted along ditches in which the plant is buried when the weather is very cold. The commonest fruit, however, is the melon. This is grown in unbelievable quantities and different varieties all of which are sweet both to taste and to smell. It is the main food of the people all the year round. The water-melon is less tasty. This is grown in two varieties, one with pink flesh, the other with yellow.

"The commonest trees are the willow, the poplar and the mulberry. The stately round-topped elm, offering its pleasant shade to the sun-weary traveller, is more rare. The fuller, nobler shape achieved by these trees is due to grafting.

"In the oases, these enchanted gardens, towns and villages have been built and an occasional isolated farmstead. Most of the houses are poor, but the well-to-do have comfortable rooms built in the Persian style, with good chimney-pieces and often decorated with fine paintings. These oases are separated by tracts of desert. As well as the desolate and dangerous dunes and the ordinary tree-less steppes, there are three other kinds of wilderness. Firstly the endless jungles of tamarisk, where stretches of level or undulating land are covered with these isolated shrubs with their lovely pinnated foliage. But when the land is invaded by moving sand-dunes, the sand and loess-dust pile up against the shrub until only the top is showing, struggling for life, out of a conical heap of sand. In many places the land is covered by these little hillocks and, offering no visibility, is very difficult to cross. Secondly there are the forests of poplar-trees. This is a delightful variety, the *populus euphratica*, with a slender trunk and, depending on the branches, differently-shaped leaves. These trees are found mostly near watercourses. One can, however, ride for hours through a forest of dead trees, where the river has changed its course and the vegetation has perished. Finally there are the deserts of stone, covering vast areas in the mountains and the lower slopes of the foot-hills. In certain places, between Toksun and Karashar, for example, the road is entirely covered with stones, from enormous rocks to smaller boulders, stones, gravel and pebbles. Horses are easily hurt by them and, according to local people, the dust, containing salt, gives them swellings and other complaints which make them unfit to travel. Mirages are very common and the unwary traveller is easily misled by them. The commonest mirages are of stretches of water surrounded by isolated shady trees.

"The foothills of the great mountain chains are terribly desolate. The rocks, torn by frequent earthquakes, are piled up in fantastic shapes. There is not a single tree or shrub, no water, and in many places, not an animal to be seen.

"As to bird-life, magpies, crows and several kinds of shrike are quite common; so also are vultures, peregrine, sacred or stone falcons, sparrow-hawks and eagles. In some areas, between Kashgar and Aksu, for instance, there are great quantities of sparrows closely resembling our own. The pheasant is common around Maralbashi; the beautiful feather-legged partridge is found in considerable quantities in the steppes, the stone-ptarmigan lives on the fringes of the mountains, as also does the bustard, but we never saw this bird, which is very wild.

"The typical animal of the plain is the gazelle, graceful and fairly small with lyre-shaped horns. It is found in large herds. The lynx, wild cat, fox and marten are common. We saw rabbits but no hares.

"Around Maralbashi, Shisho and Manas and in the Lob-Nor great thickets of reed shelter pheasants and tigers and the ground occasionally looks as though it had been ploughed over. This is the work of the wild boar. Although he is well protected, he is often killed by tigers and wolves, the latter being very numerous but cowardly and not very dangerous." [1]

The people who live in these lands today are not the descendants of these Indo-Aryan Tokharians. They are Eastern Turks, a mixed race with an often strikingly European appearance, with clear, even blue eyes which they probably inherit from Indo-European ancestors with whom the Turks must have mixed. Here again Buddhism, formerly widespread, yielded in the tenth century to Islam and the Islamic civilisation of Asia Minor. The country is famous for its white felt carpets with their borders of embroidered scrolls and its "Samarkands" or carpets with characteristic polygonal and circular motifs, mainly in brown, yellow and blue. These are very different from Persian carpets. The old family industries which produced them are gradually disappearing under the impact of Western civilisation.

Before visiting the grotto temples we must consider briefly the religion of Buddhism and its founder. In Nepal, at the foot of the Himalayas, amongst monotonous rice-fields and swampy forests, there exists an important inscription by King Asoka who died about 232 B.C. and was mainly responsible for the spread of Buddhism. The inscription records that the king went on a pilgrimage to Lumbini, the Bethlehem of Buddhism and the birthplace of the Buddha, the sage of the Sakya family. Shortly after the birth of the Buddha his mother died and he was left in the care of an aunt. He married and had a son, Rahula, but at the age of twenty-nine he left home to seek

[1] A. von Lecoq: *Auf Hellas Spuren in Ost-Turkistan* (Leipzig, 1926).

salvation and enlightenment in asceticism. After years of patient striving, Gautama (the Buddha's clan name), seated under a tree—the nyagrodha (*Ficus religiosa*)—in the deepest meditation, attained perfect wisdom and the knowledge of fulfilment which preserved him from a new incarnation. Henceforth Gautama Sakya knew himself to be the Buddha, the Enlightened One. For many years he travelled the country, going from town to town dressed as a monk. In the rainy seasons he sheltered with his disciples in parks outside the towns. As was the custom amongst monks, he begged his food every day and taught those who wished to hear. Most of his disciples, like himself, came from the cultured classes, as it was a tradition amongst the Brahmans, on reaching maturity, to give up their active business life in order to devote themselves to asceticism. When Buddha, at the age of eighty, felt his end approaching he summed up his teaching in these words: "All form is fleeting; fight on unceasingly."

This simple story of Gautama Buddha's life soon became embroidered with legends which became the subject of much literature and art. The Buddha's doctrine was not new in India, but was connected with the Brahman religious philosophy as formulated in the Upanishads. This sought an answer to the perpetual questions about life on earth and the transmigration of souls, that inevitable consequence of the merits and demerits of a past life. Originally Buddhism aimed at answering these questions rigorously and methodically, and the way to salvation was traced out with the same logic. The doctrine was summed up in the "four sacred truths":

"This is the sacred truth of suffering: birth is suffering, old age is suffering, sickness is suffering, death is suffering. To be conjoined with what one loves not is suffering; to be separated from what one does love is suffering; not to be able to attain one's desires is suffering. In a word, the five objects of apprehension [1] are suffering.

---

[1] The five constituents of personality: (1) form = body, (2) feelings, (3) perceptions, (4) volitional impulses, (5) consciousness. (E. Conze: *Buddhist Scriptures*, Penguin, 1959, p. 248)—translator's note.

"This is the sacred truth of the origin of suffering: it is craving that leads from rebirth to rebirth, with joy and desire which find satisfaction here and there; the craving for enjoyment, craving for the future, craving for the past.

"This is the sacred truth of the suppression of suffering: this craving will cease at the complete annihilation of all desire: renounce desire, break away from it, rid yourself of it, give it no place in your life.

"This is the sacred truth of the way leading to the suppression of suffering: it is the sacred way of which the eight parts are named right belief, right will, right speech, right actions, right existence, right effort, right attention, right meditation."

The Buddha's doctrine took no account of a God. It did not entrust man's deliverance to an imaginary divinity. It was a religion of reason. Religious conscience did not rest on faith but sprang from a well-directed reason. The irreligious man thus came to be not an unbeliever but an unreasonable person.

The end of suffering is the Nirvana. This again was not a Buddhist invention, but it became the central point of Buddhist doctrine and, through it, known all over the world. The word means "to fade away". Did this fading away from earthly existence mean a resultant state of non-being or an entry into the supremely happy existence beyond the reach of desire and death? When asked questions of this nature by his disciples the Buddha would reply that he did not teach anything which did not lead to peace and enlightenment:

"There are, my disciples, things not created, not born, not made, not formed. If this non-bornness did not exist, my disciples, there would be no outcome for what is born, created, made and formed."

Nirvana is:

"Neither coming nor departing, neither staying nor dying, nor being born. It is without beginning, without evolution, without ceasing: it is the end of suffering." [1]

[1] H. Oldenberg.

However tempting it might be to linger over this the wisest and most consoling of doctrines offered to man, we must pass on from this wisdom offered to the elect and consider the true Buddhist "religion". This arose from the doctrines outlined above and was intended for the ordinary people. We find its imagery in the sacred grottoes in the Tarim basin and in many other cave monasteries in China. This philosophy of salvation by one's own efforts was not suitable for the ordinary people and could never have become a universal religion. This must stem not from reason but from non-reason, not from knowledge but from faith, from faith in invisible powers and in their supernatural help to man. This is the kind of religion that spread through India and Eastern Asia with Mahayana Buddhism whose many divinities, specialising in all kinds of trades and conditions of man, dispensed their consolation to those in need of help.

Whereas historical Buddhism taught that deliverance, reincarnation and entry into Nirvana could only be attained through a monastic life and a renunciation of the world, the new doctrine offered consolation to everyone with an assurance that all could be granted salvation, if not in Nirvana, at least in the Heavenly Kingdom which most people preferred anyway. The only requirement was the faithful worship of one of the many Buddhas who had been created in the meantime. This new doctrine, embracing all men, is called the "Great Vehicle" (Mahayana) as opposed to the "Small Vehicle" (Hinayana) which is reserved for the few. The vehicle is the means whereby one may cross the river of rebirth and suffering and reach the life beyond, either Nirvana or one of the Promised Heavens.

There is no doubt that Mahayana Buddhism sprang from the original doctrine of Gautama Buddha. In fact, the idea of pity, at first self-centred, spread to the whole of humankind and became an idea of salvation. Mahayana Buddhism, however, also opened the way to hypocritical selfish pity and to vain superstition. Its greatest innovation was the introduction of the Bodhisattvas who help mankind to attain salvation. The altruistic doctrine whereby deliverance from reincarnation is not the supreme end but, on the contrary, having achieved this end a man must give up Nirvana to continue to live on earth, gave rise to the idea of a band of saviours known as the Bodhisattvas whose aim was to achieve the condition of Buddha. They may, if they wish, enter Nirvana after one of their reincarnations. It was just about as difficult to become a Bodhisattva as it was to become a Catholic Saint. Just as, within the Church, there are popular saints whose powers of assistance have been well tested, there are in the Buddhist religion favourite patron-saints in addition to innumerable unknown Bodhisattvas. This, however, was not all. Gautama Buddha was not the only Buddha to appear on earth. He is supposed to have had three, or even six (and sometimes more), predecessors and to have a successor who will be the last Buddha, the present Bodhisattva Maitreya. All these Buddhas correspond to mystical Dhyanabuddhas, each of whom reigns over one of the many Dhyana heavens and has a Bodhisattva as successor. Gautama's Dhyanabuddha is Amitabha, whose Dhyanabodhisattva is Avalokiteshvara (iteshvara = the Lord, he who looks down from on high; similarly Padmapani the lotus-bearer and Kwan-yin or Kwannon in China and Japan). The statues of the Buddha, therefore, represent not only Gautama, the historical Buddha, but often also Amitabha, or Avalokiteshvara who is easily recognisable as he carries a seated image of Amitabha in his hair. Maitreya is shown as often standing as seated. These few simple ideas on Buddhism will help us in our visit to the temples of the Tarim basin.

The grottoes are carved out of the steep slopes of conglomerate or loess, fairly high above the valley bottom. They were once connected by galleries cut out of the rock. The halls used for worship are of different sizes, from fifty to sixty-five feet deep and from thirty-three to fifty feet high. Workshops, living-rooms for the monks and larders are adjoining. There is usually an entrance-hall, followed by a rectangular sanctuary at the end of which stands the sacred image, the statue of the Buddha, together with painted terra-cotta figures of lesser importance. A gallery runs all the way round so that processions may pass right round the altar. This processional ritual is found in all Indian religions and has its parallel in the Catholic Church. The walls are painted with scenes from the life of the Buddha and from Buddhist legends. The ceiling is usually vaulted and decorated with stylised mountain scenes.

In the summer of 1905 Lecoq found at Ming Hoi, near Qizil, the "Painters' Grotto". This lies along a road cut out of the rock up a very steep slope in the vicinity of the town of Kucha which Lecoq considered the loveliest in East Turkestan. The roof of the sanctuary has imitation beams cut out of the rock and arranged in corbels, imitating the wooden roofs often found in Central Asian houses and in those we have already seen in Bamiyan. The highest central section was decorated with lotus flowers and the lower triangular sections with devaputras ("sons of God"). The lotus flower, sacred already in ancient Egyptian art, where it gave rise to the palmette motif still used today, is also the sacred plant of India. It brought the first Being to the surface of the waters. As a fully opened flower it becomes the throne of the Gods. Stylised in its different phases of growth it has served as a model, both in India and Egypt, for decorations with a vegetation motif. At the end of the "Painters' Grotto" there is a high, arched recess in the wall. This formerly held the sacred image which was surrounded by mountain shapes in relief. The image is now in ruins.

The grotto was painted to illustrate a very frequent theme, the Indrashailaguha, in which Indra and other gods visit the Buddha as he sits in meditation in a mountain cave. The mountain is inhabited by all kinds of wild animals. Divinities, bearing garlands and scattering flowers, fly around, and at the entrance to the cave stand Indra and other gods who have come to greet them. Some of the decoration is in painted stucco relief, but this is wearing away until in places only the background shows. The lateral walls of the sanctuary are separated from the walls of the ambulatory by decorated strips representing two painters, one above the other. They are richly attired, carry a dagger in their belts and have a very elegant bearing. They are at work, with a brush in their right hands and a goblet in the other, and are standing on tip-toe, a stylised attitude, against a red background. An inscription at their feet tells us their names. They have Syrio-Persian features and wear black wigs, like the Egyptians. The side walls of the grotto are decorated with paintings representing the sermons of the Buddha who is shown, in all these pictures, seated on a throne with flames coming out of his shoulders. In most of the pictures, the Buddha's constant companion, Vajrapani, the bearer of thunderbolts, is shown sitting by his side. Monks stand at his feet and above him fly Devas holding garlands and scattering flowers. The place of the sermon is shown in the foreground and the background. A gazelle, for instance, indicates the gazelle wood near Benares. The walls around the altar are decorated with different scenes, one of which shows the Brahman Drona sharing out the relics of the Buddha after the Buddha's entry into Nirvana. We see Indian princes, armed and on horseback, excitedly laying claim to their share of the relics whilst Drona, standing on the ramparts of the town, tries to calm them down. The next scene shows us the venerable Brahman with plaited beard and hair, amongst the now pacified princes. He is presenting a funeral urn whilst the princes, each holding a casket, are waiting to receive from him their share of the ashes. Another painting shows a monk, larger than life-size, preaching to the royal family.

During the thousand years of the great migrations, Eastern Turkestan had a troubled history. Conquering tribes came one after the other—Huns, Tokharians, Hephtalites, Turks, Tibetans, Uigurs—but in every case their expansion was halted by the Chinese. Tokharian art belongs to the first half of this period. Some centuries later, another artistic style appears in the eastern part of the Tarim basin, in the oases around Turfan, amongst the Uigurs. These were a Turkish people who reached the height of their powers in the eighth century and ruled the country for a long time afterwards. In Hinayana Buddhist art at Kucha, the single subject is the person of Gautama Buddha. In Turfan, however, the content is Mahayana, the figures are Eastern Turkish and the style is strongly Chinese. Indian Buddhist art had by then long ceased to influence China and the Uigurs' art shows a renewal of the Chinese influence which reached its height in the seventh to the ninth centuries under the Tang dynasty. In Turfan it shows itself in traces of large-scale paintings of a surprising character. The Mahayana desires the salvation of all men, and so thousands of Buddha figures are to be found, lined up against the walls of the grotto temples. The Buddhas all sit in the same position with legs folded, amidst rainbow-coloured clouds and under jewelled parasol-shaped canopies hung with little bells.

A new type of picture, unknown to Hinayana art, occupies a central position in Mahayanist religious painting in China and Tibet. This is the *mandala*, which shows a Buddha or a Bodhisattva, surrounded by his friends and helpers, in a characteristic setting. Thus Amitabha, Gautama's Dhyana-buddha, always appears in his "Western Paradise", Sukhavati Maitreya, the future Buddha, in his heaven Tushita. These pictures correspond to certain religious paintings in the Catholic Church, for example, Raphael's "Dispute" in the Vatican. The importance of the *mandala* to Buddhist ritual is, however, much greater, as we shall see.

Similar Mahayanist paintings have also been found in a temple at Bezeklik, in the neighbourhood of Murtuk near Turfan. This temple, built of sun-dried brick, stands with its back against a mountain wall. It consists of an entrance hall extending into an ambulatory around a cella, or enclosed sanctuary. The cella had a dome and the entrance and the ambulatory were roofed with cradle-vaulting. There were paintings on the walls, but these are now in the Museum of Ethnology in Berlin. Two steps led from the entrance hall to the cella. Here the sacred image, which had disappeared before the temple was discovered, stood on a pedestal facing the entrance. The *mandala* on the west wall, although partly destroyed, established that the temple had been dedicated to Avalokiteshvara. The walls adjacent to this one were decorated with scenes from Buddhist legends. On each side of the entrance hall were figures of three gift-bearers, men or possibly women, and in the embrasures of the doorways stood Panchika and Hariti, the guardian spirits of little children. The walls of the ambulatory were decorated with fifteen big scenes from the Pranhidi (adoration) and there were further paintings showing twelve monks, three on each side of the entrance to the ambulatory and of the exit from it.

In the centre of the *mandala* is an ornamental pond whose deep blue waters are lined with tiny waves. Two dragons with intertwined tails are rising from the water and trying to seize with their fore-paws the green flame-decorated jewel lying in a stemmed glass which rests on a lotus-flower. A stylised flowering tree carries in its branches the great lotus, the throne of the sacred image, only a trace of which remains, as the top part of the temple walls is damaged. On the right of the pond stand two Brahmans, one old and the other young. The older one is carrying a stick; he is dressed in a tiger-skin and wears stockings which reach up to his knees; he has a beard and his long hair is knotted into a chignon. His right hand is raised and he looks angry. The younger one, his disciple, stands on a lotus flower at his side and is holding the old man's left arm with his two hands. He is dressed in the same way as the old man. He, too, seems angry and is looking in front of him. On the other side of the pond are two women who could be Chinese. One, in the foreground, is carrying a sacrificial glass containing three green jewels. The other, a servant, stands behind her, her hands joined in an act of prayer. Above each of these two groups there is a dragon kneeling, with pointed ears and three eyes and completely covered with armour. In each of the lower corners a *dharmapala* (dharma = doctrine, pala = guardian) looks threateningly at the visitor. These *dharmapalas* have six arms. With one hand they are holding in check an animal-demon and with the others they are carrying symbolic weapons. Above, on each side of Avalokiteshvara, stand the Gods. We will not deal with the paintings on the lateral walls of the cella, as there is very little left of them. They told the story of Garuda, the mythical bird, the enemy and killer of snakes.

The Pranhidi scenes which were all removed to Berlin told the story of the previous lives of Gautama Buddha, also called Sakyamuni (the silent sage from the family of the

Sakya). During the hundreds of years of his earthly life he had witnessed many events, of which more than five hundred are related in the *Jatakam*, the great collection of *jatakas*, or stories of his different incarnations. The Buddha had incarnated all possible forms, not only man, the son of both rich and poor, but also animal, the stag and the elephant. In all his incarnations he had been distinguished by his good deeds which foretold his future state of Buddha. He had also met the Buddhas of former times, had worshipped them and made the vow (*pranidhana*) to become a Buddha himself. Then he had received the message that his wish had been granted.

Let us consider one of these *jatakas* as an example. It is the Dipankara-jakata, or the story of the Buddha's meeting with the Buddha Dipankara. An inscription above the scene says:

> "When I perceived the great radiant Dipankara, I, who at that time was a young Brahman, made him a tribute of seven blue lotus flowers. End of the second Asankhyeya period."

The legends relate how one day Buddha Dipankara made a solemn entry into the town of Dipavati. The king of the country had all the flowers picked to decorate the town and to cover the way the Buddha was to follow. The young Brahman Sumati was unable, therefore, to find a single one for himself, but he obtained some lotuses from a girl on a promise to marry her in a future reincarnation. Then Sumati went to meet the Buddha and threw his flowers before him. Instead of falling to the ground, however, the lotuses formed themselves into a halo around the Buddha's head. At the sight of this miracle the young man prostrated himself, spreading his long hair over the ground so that the Buddha might walk on it, and pronouncing at the same time his solemn vow to become an Enlightened One himself one day. On the mural painting, Dipankara, with a halo around his head and a lotus flower in his hand, is predicting to a Brahman, prostrate before him on the ground, that he will be a Buddha. The same young man reappears above in another scene showing him standing and throwing a lotus flower before the Buddha. The figure on the left, which has been given a beard by mistake, is actually the girl who gave Sumati the lotus flowers. The other figures are the Buddha's companions amongst whom we see Vajrapani (vajra = thunderbolt, pani = bearer), the Buddha's tutelary genius, wearing a demonic expression and carrying a brush to ward off flies. High up on the right there is a Chinese house with a curved roof. The paintings in the cella and the ambulatory date from different periods and are therefore in different styles.

If we continue eastwards from Turfan across the southern part of the Gobi desert, a journey of several weeks by caravan will bring us to the oasis of Tun Huang on the frontier of the Chinese province of Kansu. Here there is the great cave monastery of Ch'ien Fo Tung, or the "Grottoes of the thousand Buddhas". This was a flourishing religious centre under the Wei dynasty in the fifth century A.D. and later under the T'ang dynasty (618–906). The paintings here show the rich variety of Chinese Buddhist art. Coming from Turfan we see clearly the transition from an Indian to a Chinese inspiration which, however, is still influenced here by a nomad tent-life civilisation and expresses itself exclusively in the medium of textiles. At Kucha and Turfan the grotto temples conformed with the local unbaked brick architecture of the surrounding countryside. They had vaulted roofs cut out of the rock or ceilings imitating the wooden roofs of Central Asia. Their plan was a slightly modified version of the Indian *stupa* with an ambulatory. At Tun Huang, where the influence of Chinese art is evident, the ambulatory disappears and the halls of worship, which are also smaller, are carved out to represent a tent with the tops of the walls sloping inwards and a flat roof. The paintings add to this effect; they have carpet motifs and fringed borders. The image of the principal deity, amidst his *parivara* (escort of Gods), stands against the back wall. Everywhere polychrome sculptures in the round gradually give way to relief then to painting, the transition occurring most frequently in a line of figures, which gradually develop from two-dimensional painted to relief on the lateral walls. The principal deity's haloes are also painted; some of them are magnificent, made of flames which rise to the heavens where knights and *gandharvas* throng together amidst stylised clouds. The lateral walls are also frequently decorated with *mandalas*. We shall pause to look at one of these in detail. This is a representation of the *Sukhavati* ("The Paradise in the West"), the residence of Amitabha, a supreme deity and the one most frequently worshipped in Eastern Asia.

Amidst a fine group of terraces overlooking Lake Sukhavati, Amitabha is majestically seated on a lotus flower and surrounded by the Bodhisattvas Avalokiteshvara and Mahastamaprapa and lesser deities. All the Gods are resplendent with brilliantly coloured circular haloes. From these terraces a carpeted bridge leads to a smaller one where, between two rows of musicians, an *aspara*, or heavenly dancer, is exhibiting her art. From this another bridge leads to other lateral terraces on each of which a Buddha is enthroned, surrounded by Bodhisattvas. Finally a bridge, reaching down to the lower edge of the painting, leads to the lotus pond where Bodhisattvas are sitting on lotus flowers and where they will stay for eternity. The five great deities are sheltered by richly decorated canopies. In the background the celestial hosts are flying on clouds over the "Palaces of Joy". This is typical of all Sino-Tibetan *mandalas* of the period. By their structure, based on a series of overlapping triangles, in accordance with the permanent laws of optics and perspective, like the great compositions of the Italian Renaissance, and by their wonderful harmony of colours, these hieratic paintings produce, like the counterpoint of a Bach fugue, a compelling and everlasting impression, whatever one's individual artistic tastes.

In addition to a wealth of Buddhist images and decorations the "Grottoes of the thousand Buddhas" contain hundreds of historical compositions some of which, although only indirectly connected with the Church of the Mahayana, are nevertheless of priceless documentary value in the study of landscape and historical paintings of the T'ang period. Very few of these paintings have survived.

Buddhist Grotto Temples

Reproductions of the Tun Huang grottoes give only a faint idea of their brilliant colouring. An American archaeologist has said:

"No book reproduction of these sanctuaries can compare with a first-hand view. The brilliance of the colours, the enchanting forms and the grandeur of these majestically enthroned trinities in their paradise make such a powerful impression on the visitor as might only be compared with that experienced by a Christian as he enters a great Cathedral."

Three days' journey east from Ch'ien Fo Tung, where there were more than a thousand grottoes in the T'ang period, there is a more modest sanctuary, the grotto of Wan-fo-hsia ("The myriads of images of the Buddha"). Most of the Buddhist caves in China are decorated chiefly with statues or reliefs. The most famous of these are Yun Kang, near Ta't'ungfu on the northern frontier of Shansi province and Lung-men ("Dragons' Gate"), south of the ancient capital of Lo-yang in Honan province. There are many others all over China.

10

MERU, THE MOUNTAIN OF THE GODS

In our chapter on the Tower of Babel we spoke of Babylonian cosmology and of its continued influence on Sumero-Babylonian civilisation and later on all the civilisations our planet has so far known. In India and amongst Far-Eastern Indo-Buddhist peoples this cosmology set the pattern their civilisation was to follow, even in the smallest detail, and it finds its monumental expression in their architecture.

The point of departure of Asiatic cosmologies was the doctrine of correspondence, the belief in a mystical link between the microcosm and the macrocosm, between man and the universe.

"According to this belief, the elements, the colours, the animals, plants, stones and metals, the parts of the body and the qualities of character, every event in one's life, age, sex, continence and indulgence in love-making, life, death, everything corresponded to the different stars and the cardinal points and these determined one's destiny. Everything has its 'mystical link' defined in relationship to the structure of the universe, and its 'mystical time' in its relationship to the course of the planets. Thus humanity is for ever under the influence of cosmic forces which may cause healing or death according to whether man has or has not ordered his life in conformity with their laws. This applies even more to large communities than to individuals: states, towns, monasteries can only prosper in so far as they respect these laws. Ancient peoples endeavoured, therefore, to attain this conformity, this harmony with the cosmic

7. Isfahan: "Half the World".

8.&9. The Borobudur in Java. *Above*, a bas-relief showing the entry of a prince.
Below, bell-shaped dagobas on the top terrace.

forces, by giving their empires, capitals, palaces, temples and monasteries the form of a microcosm, by creating them in the image of the mythical structure of the universe and organising within this framework, and in accordance with the cosmic laws, the civil service, the administrative divisions of the country, the weights, measures, money and, in fact, every state enterprise. The interpretation of these cosmo-magic forces naturally varied according to time and place." [1]

The Babylonian map of the world showed a disc surrounded by a chain of mountains in the middle of an ocean. At its centre was the mountain of the universe which rose right up to the heavens. In Buddhist cosmology the cosmic mountain—called Meru—is also the centre, the pivot, the axis of the universe. It is surrounded by seven golden circular mountains which are divided by seven circular seas. The whole is surrounded by the ocean of the universe, having at the four cardinal points the four continents. The southern continent, Jambudvipa, is the world of man. The earth's end is an enormous rampart of rock, the Cacravala. At the summit of Meru lies the heaven of the thirty-three Gods, Trayastrimsha, dominated by Indra, with the divine city of Suddharkana. Higher still rise sixteen other heavens. The cosmology of the other great Hindu religion Brahmanism is similar. A town built in the image of one of these systems would therefore be understood by both groups of people. A fortified town with a royal palace at its centre and a water-filled moat around it rose high into the heavens. Such was Jambudvipa, surrounded by a rampart of mountains and the ocean.

An example of an ancient city built on these principles is to be found in Cambodia. It is the group of buildings at Angkor Thom, the former residence of the Khmers. It is not circular, like the earth in ancient Hindu cosmology, but square, like all the other ancient cities built on this principle. It was evidently intended that these towns should bear an analogy to the supposed structure of the universe, but not imitate it exactly. That

---

[1] *Weltbild und Bauform in Südostasien* (Wiener Beiträge zur Kunst und Kultur Asiens, IV, 1930).

this analogy was intentional is borne out by inscriptions. At the centre of the town, founded about A.D. 900 by King Yasovarman, stood the temple of Phimeanakas. This was called the "central mountain" or the "queen of mountains" and was evidently intended to represent Meru. It is a fairly steep truncated pyramid on the top of which stood a small temple on a stepped platform. The whole building was gilded. It was a mountain of the world and of the gods in the manner of the Babylonian ziggurats. In the temple the "Lord of the Gods", Siva, was worshipped in the form of the *linga*, or phallic symbol. Siva became incarnate in every King of Cambodia who drew his mystical royal powers from the Lord of the Gods present in the *linga* and also in a mystical union with the earth. We learn from a Chinese visitor who came to Angkor Thom in 1296 that in the palace there was a golden tower at the top of which the king lay sleeping:

"All the natives maintain that the tower is inhabited by the spirit of a nine-headed serpent which rules over all the land in the kingdom. It appears every night in the form of a woman. The king lies with her before any of his wives or concubines. Not even the most distinguished of these would dare to enter the room. Then the king arises and leaves in the second watch. He may then sleep with his wives and concubines. If the spirit of the serpent fails to appear one night, this is taken to mean that the death of the king is imminent. If the king misses one night with the serpent, he is struck with misfortune."

Thus the king, uniting with the serpent-goddess, renewed nightly his mystical union with the earth and his kingdom.

The temple was therefore not only the symbol of the mountain Meru, but, by the cult of the force of the original god incarnate in the *linga* and the nightly union of the king and the earth-deity, it became the mystical centre of the kingdom, a centre of forces which, like a burning-glass, concentrated all the divine powers of heaven and earth and transmitted them to the king and the empire.

The centre of the town of Angkor Thom, enlarged in the eleventh century, became a Buddhist sanctuary, the temple of Bayon, and was no longer dedicated to the cult of Siva. The Bayon, like the Phimeanakas, became a symbol of the cosmic mountain. The town itself was square-shaped with five gates, one in the middle of each side and the fifth opening on to a road running parallel to one of the sides and leading from the east to the palace and the Phimeanakas. The Bayon stood in the centre. The gates were topped by pyramidal towers. At each corner of the square stood a small temple crowned with figures in relief. The Bayon and the gates were decorated with huge masques of Avalokiteshvara, the "Lord of the World," to whom the temple and the town were dedicated. The temple later became once more a centre for the worship of Siva. For this only slight modifications were required, for, as a Javanese poet of the fourteenth century put it: "The Buddha is not different from Siva. The persons of Siva and of Dshina are one." (Dshina, an attribute of the Buddha, was the conqueror of earthly bonds.) The huge four-fold heads of the Bodhisattva Lokeshvara, facing the four quarters of the earth, over the gateways, meant that the town was under his protection.

Each of the gates of Angkor is reached from the outside by a carriage-way spanning the one hundred and thirty-foot-wide moat and bordered with balustrades of fifty-four stone statues of *devas* (gods) and *asuras* (demons) each carrying a long nine-headed *naga* (sacred cobra). These statues represented the churning of the Sea of Milk by the *devas* to extract the essence of immortality. The temple symbolised Meru and the moat the Sea of Milk. The town walls, and therefore the town itself, were associated with the Bayon which was itself an image of the cosmos. The Khmer empire and its capital were under the protection of the Lord of the World and guardian of universal order, the Bodhisattva Lokeshvara (loka = world, eshvara = master) "and from the top of forty towers his four-headed image looked down upon the inhabitants".

Another town, of very recent foundation, was also built in accordance with cosmo-mystical beliefs. This is Mandalay, in Upper Burma. All ancient Burmese towns were built on these lines, but Mandalay, the last capital of the Empire, was founded as recently as 1857 and is naturally the best preserved. Its fortified walls formed a square with sides a mile and a quarter long and running in the direction of the cardinal points. The total length of the wall, two thousand four hundred *ta*, corresponds with the date of its foundation, two thousand four hundred years after the death of the Buddha. There are three gates in each wall, making twelve in all, and each is decorated with the signs of the zodiac.

There is a surrounding moat, nearly three hundred and fifty feet across, and on this the king made a circuit of the town in solemn procession at his coronation, to symbolise his taking possession of the town. Four bridges cross the moat, leading to four main gates, from which roads lead to the royal palace in the centre. There is a fifth bridge, with its gateway, at the southern end of the wall. This was used principally to take corpses out of the town, and the road leading to it was held to be unlucky. The eastern entrance, however, was considered to be very favourable, as the whole town, like all towns and palaces in Indo-China, faced east and this entrance was used for all official processions. Mandalay was a royal city and most of the population lived outside it, only court officials and civil servants being allowed to reside within the perimeter. The same thing applied to the Round City in Baghdad and to the Forbidden City in Peking. The Royal Palace, in the centre, faced east, as also did the most important official rooms in it; the private suites faced west. At the western end of the palace was the throne-room of the first queen. It was her custom to receive here the wives and daughters of visiting dignitaries. The ruling planet in the west is Venus, and also in the west dwelt the race of the *nagas*, the sacred cobras which played an important part in Indian and Indonesian mythology. They could appear in human form, particularly as women. The daughters of the serpent-king were held to be the most beautiful and the most knowledgeable in love-making. The temptation of the Buddha by the daughters of Mara, the devil, also took place in the west. This part of the world thus came to assume an erotic significance.

Meru, the Mountain of the Gods

The eastern part of the palace, which contained the audience-chamber, was called the "Palace of the Earth" because, like Meru, it was at the centre of the world. It was topped by a seven-stage wooden tower. The "Lions' Throne", under its protecting tower, was held to be the mystical centre of the city and the empire. The Burmese name "Centre of the World" for their throne, and the Chinese "Empire of the Centre" for the Chinese Empire sound presumptuous to European ears, but they are obviously both a part of Far Eastern cosmology.

In Burma, court and government officials were rigidly divided into classes according to this same cosmology. The basis was the number four—the number of the cardinal points. There were four first-class ministers, four second-class ministers, four privy counsellors, four chief tax-collectors who raised taxes in the four parts of the kingdom, four royal aides-de-camp, four royal messengers, four royal scribes, four heralds, and so on. This corresponded also to the four mythological *lokapala*, the guardians of the world. Each one was responsible for one side of the mountain Meru, and for one side of the heaven of the thirty-three gods at its summit. They were also the guardians of the temples in the Mahayana religion, and were represented under different forms in Indo-China, Tibet, China and Japan. Their four terrifying faces are to be found at the entrance to most Buddhist temples in the Far East. In Burma the four gates of the palace were guarded by four platoons of troops each under a captain who represented one of the *lokapala* and whose flag was coloured to represent the orientation of the gateway: white for the east, green for the south, red for the west and yellow for the north.[1]

The queens were divided into strict classes on the same system. Officially there were eight: four principal and four secondary. They were named after the quarter of the palace they occupied: the queen of the central palace, the queen of the western palace, and so on. The division into eight corresponded to the eight directions of the winds.

[1] *Gazette of Upper Burma*, part I, vol. ii.

The "Lions' Throne", the cosmo-mystical centre of the Empire, was, of course, decorated as befitted its importance. It carried representations of Indra, the principal god of Hindu mythology, the other thirty-two official deities, the four guardians of the world and a peacock and a hare, the symbols respectively of the sun and the moon. Royal power and dignity were linked in Burmese eyes with the actual possession of the throne and the palace. The king, seated on Indra's holy chair, in the microcosm of the Burmese Empire, was the Indra of this small universe and its legitimate ruler.

Since very ancient times seven-stage towers like the Pyatthad tower over the Lions' Throne in Mandalay have been identified with the mountain of Meru. This would seem to be confirmed by the name of Meru which is given in Bali to a certain kind of wooden temple with staged towers. These are held to be the seats of deities who thus reside, as it were, on the summit of Meru, as they do in the Suddharcana, the city of the gods.

The buildings mentioned so far show how frequently the mountain of Meru was represented in the form of towers of various shapes built either of stone or wood. A well-known archaeologist who has studied the problem reached the conclusion that the mountain-temple is the basis of all major Indo-Chinese architecture, so much so that it is doubtful if there is any important building where it is not found. It almost certainly appeared first in India, in the Hindu civilisation, and spread through the Brahman and the Buddhist countries of the Far East. All Hindu religious buildings in India have towers; whether these represent Siva on the top of the Himalayas or on Meru, the symbol is the same.

The oldest form of Indian building, however, is the *stupa*. It was originally a kind of mausoleum but, like the bell-tower on Catholic churches, it attained a diversity of shape and decoration which had little to do with its original function. In its simplest form it consisted of a circular tower a few yards high supporting a huge flat-topped hemispherical dome topped by a symbolical stone umbrella with a stone balustrade around it. The top of the tower was reached by an external staircase and it was possible to walk round it along a terrace protected by coping-stones. There was a similar circular walk at the base of the tower which also had four gateways set between pillars. This was the most representative Buddhist building and the focal point of Buddhist worship. For the first three centuries B.C. it took this simple shape, but later it assumed gigantic proportions. The tower grew higher and the dome became taller and pointed and supported on round and polygonal shafts and topped with a more imposing and complicated roof. In the second century A.D. King Kanishka built a *stupa* nearly two hundred feet high of which fantastic descriptions have come down to us. The Burmese *zedi*, the Siamese *prangs* and *chedi*, rising to over three hundred feet, and the buildings which go by the name of Chinese pagodas all descend from this ancient Hindu memorial, the *stupa* or *dagoba*. Even today the Royal Way from Peshawar to Kabul is littered with their mighty ruins, and there are hundreds of them in the ruined villages of the Tarim basin whose grottoes we visited in the preceding chapter. There are hundreds of monumental *stupas* also in Tibet and Nepal and a dozen or so in Ceylon, but the less important *dagobas* are numbered in their thousands. In Indo-Chinese countries these *stupas* with towers all represent the mountain Meru and are oriented towards the four corners of the earth. In Siam they are decorated with the figures of the four *lokapala*. Most of these buildings hold a deity enthroned in a cella at the top of the sacred tower, like the god in the Babylonian ziggurat of three thousand years ago.

Just as the outward appearance of these temples represented a mountain, so also the interior, with its dark rooms, was intended to simulate caves. A good example of this type of building is the temple of Ananda in Pagan, the ancient capital of Burma. This was built in the eleventh century A.D. It is square and of brick, with four entrance-halls built on to the middle of each of the sides. The centre is a solid block with four niches carved out of it for the idols and surrounded by a vaulted gallery, nearly forty feet high and enclosed on the outside by walls with a double row of windows. The entrance-halls are slightly lower than the gallery. The central block is topped by six terraces of decreasing size, the highest having a *stupa*-like tower with a gilded point. At the corners of the terraces are lions and seated Buddhas. There are also lions on the pediments of the entrance-hall, apparently to guard the temple, and seated Buddhas in recesses at each side of the doorways and on the tower. The pediments, the doorways and the windows are also richly decorated. Each one of the four cellas, enclosed by large teak doors, contains an enormous statue, over thirty feet in height, of one of the four Buddhas who appeared on earth during this period: Krakuchanda, Kanakamuni, Kasyapa and Gautama with his two disciples. Kasyapa's statue is in bronze, the others are in different kinds of wood, the material having apparently been chosen for cosmomystical reasons. The head and shoulders of these enormous Buddhas are illuminated by light from an invisible source which, in the shadowy interior, gives them a supernatural appearance. The corridors are decorated with many stone and wooden reliefs of deities, demons, scenes from Hell, warriors, dancers, mythical birds and animals. The inner gallery has eighty high reliefs illustrating the life of Gautama Buddha.

The temple of Ananda is only one example of these stepped pyramids topped by a *stupa*, or brick mountain-temples. At the centre, instead of a hall, there is a compact mass of brick with corridors, staircases and recesses similar to the grottoes and galleries of a cave temple. It was intended to represent a mountain with caves. This is shown by the following account in a Burmese Chronicle of the Palace of Glass:

"One day eight venerable saints were standing in front of the king's palace, awaiting alms. The king took a bowl, gave them food and asked 'where do you come from?' and they replied 'From the Gandhamadana mountain.' Now King Htilaingshin (the surname of King Kyanzittha, 1084–1112) was a pious man. He built a monastery and offered them the use of it during the rainy season. He invited them to his palace and supplied their wants for three months. One day he asked them to summon up, by their holy power, an image of the cave of Nandamula in the

Gandhamadana mountain. This they did. King Htilaing-shin then built a great *Ku* (literally "cave" then "temple") on the model of the cave of Nandamula and called it Nanda."

This is the story of the temple of Ananda, whose name is that of the favourite disciple of Gautama Buddha.

These buildings were erected under powerful Buddhist empires in a period corresponding to our Middle Ages. The true grotto-temples, however, are as old as Buddhism itself and go back to the third century B.C. All the open-air temples and monasteries dating from this earlier period in India have long since disappeared, but the great cave *chaityas*, Buddhist churches built into the rock, and the *viharas*, meeting-halls and monasteries attached to these churches, such as those at Kondani, Bedsa, Nasik, Karli and particularly the famous grotto temples at Adshanta with their fine paintings, are still there to prove the very early custom of situating places for meditation and prayer in mountain caves.

There was another way of creating a mountain-dwelling for a god: the converse method of carving the mountain into the shape of a temple. The exterior was cut out of the rock, complete with *stupas* and *shikaras* on the top, as if it were a real building constructed on the strictest architectural plan. The most famous buildings of this kind are the Siva temples at Ellora, east of Bombay and not far from Ajanta on the high Deccan plateau, and those at Mamallapuram on the Coromandel coast near Madras. They were all built in imitation of open-air temples, long since disappeared, and included prayer-halls which were hewn out of the rock.

Let us return to the symbolic architecture of the mountain and look at the vertical organisation of the earth as represented by the mountain Meru in Brahman and Buddhist cosmology. Meru is imagined as a five- or six-staged tower, the penultimate stage containing the first of the six divine heavens, the abode of the four *lokapala*, or guardians of the world. The summit is the second heaven of the thirty-three gods and was considered to be eighty-four-thousand *yodchanas* high (a yodchana varied, according to the country, from nearly four and a half to nearly twelve and a half miles). Above Meru there rose into infinite space four holy abodes, and, above these, the sixteen Brahman heavens of the "world of form" whose inhabitants, freed from the hold of all senses and desires, have only pure form. Higher still are four *arupa* heavens, formless worlds, whose inhabitants are invisible. These twenty-six heavens lead, according to popular Buddhist tradition in Indo-China, to a twenty-seventh, Nirvana. The distances between the heavens correspond to our astronomical distances.[1]

The Buddhist universe, therefore, rises to infinity like a tower with an endless number of stages. Buddhist architecture, with its tendency towards the vertical, is a clear representation of this. These staged buildings with their umbrella roofs could correspond either to the terraces of the mountain Meru, as in South-east Asia, or to the different stages of the heavens, gliding about in space, as in China. They form a striking contrast with the religious buildings in the Mediterranean countries and in Asia Minor and with Egyptian temples or domed churches and mosques in Syria and Iran. They reflect the different conceptions of the world in the East and the West. The Western world, created by God, lies between heaven and earth. The Eastern world is much closer to the true cosmos and extends into infinite space. It is a remarkable thing, however, that the Sumerians, as we have seen, reached and expressed in their architecture both of these widely-differing concepts of enclosed space on the one hand and on the other of the vertical representation of the world in the staged temple.

The umbrella roofs found over the earliest Indian *stupas* and later on Chinese and Siamese pagodas, some of which had ten, twenty or even thirty of them, were intended to represent not only the mountain Meru but also the most distant heavens above it. There is in Indonesia a building which goes even further and seems to achieve the impossible by representing the "heavens of formlessness" yet without violating these mystical concepts. This is the Borobudur in Java. It was built in the eighth century A.D. and has eight stages, the lower five being

[1] Cf. C. F. Koeppen: *Die Religion des Buddha.*

square and the remainder circular. On the top is a *dagoba*. The base of the temple is square, with its sides oriented towards the four cardinal points. Steps lead from the middle of each side from the base to the circular platforms. The vertical walls of each terrace are decorated with bas-reliefs and the balustrades surrounding them have statues of Buddhas in recesses. This rich ornamentation ceases on the fifth terrace, however. This has bell-shaped *dagobas*, which, though not large, are nevertheless not empty and out of one of them a Buddha can be seen emerging. There was also a sitting Buddha in the large *dagoba* on the top of the temple, but he was removed at some time and set down at the base of the building. Thus he who more than a thousand years ago had entered the "dark world of formlessness" was revealed by sacrilegious hands for the benefit of the modern sightseer.

What, then, is the meaning of the Borobudur, this temple of the "Innumerable Buddhas" which seems like a vision from another world? Much has been written and discussed about it since 1814 when it was first discovered buried under jungle vegetation and work was begun on its restoration. This work continued spasmodically and with very long intervals until 1907, nearly a hundred years after its first discovery, when the Dutch government ordered the restoration of the reliefs which, when put together, cover over three miles in length, and the five hundred or so Buddhas, seventy-two of which have, however, been left inside the *dagobas*. A detailed description of the temple would take too long. We will simply indicate its significance, which has only become clear after very recent research.

The many Buddhas decorating the building are all of exactly the same shape, tending towards the abstraction of reality, a classical form established in India in the Gupta period (A.D. 320–470). They are all seated with crossed legs, yogi-fashion, the normal position for all Buddha statues. They only differ in the position of their hands. These hand-positions, called *mudras*, indicate the varying degrees of concentration and the mystical phases which the Buddhas have attained. The Dhyani-Buddhas also have corresponding *mudras*. These are said to have originated in certain hand-gestures made by Gautama Buddha at certain phases of his spiritual career. They are:

The Bhumisparshamudra, or the gesture of touching (sparsha) the earth (bhumi) made by Gautama when, tempted by the daughters of Mara, he took the earth as witness to his vow of continence until he achieved enlightenment. The gesture consisted of moving the right hand from its position of meditation (flat on the left hand, both hands reposing on the lap) down over the thigh until the finger-tips touch the ground.

The Varapradamudra, or solemn promise to heaven to accomplish one's vows. As before, but with the hand turned palm upwards.

The Dhyanimudra, or gesture of profound meditation by which Gautama attained enlightenment. Both hands flat, one on top of the other, with the tips of the thumbs touching.

The Abhayamudra, or absence of fear, by which Gautama showed the consolation that meditation had brought him. The right hand is held vertical, palm outwards, with the thumb-joint touching the big toe joint (for seated statues) or the fore-arm is held vertical (for standing statues). This is the usual *mudra* for standing statues of the Buddha. Gautama and Maitreya are shown thus as a *guru* (master, prophet and protector).

The Dharmachakramudra, or *mudra* of the rotation of the wheel (chakra) of the doctrine (dharma). This was the position of Gautama's hands when, after attaining the quality of Buddha, he taught the four sacred truths. The position of the two hands symbolises the rotation of a wheel.

These are the five most important sacred *mudras* of Buddhism and they are the most frequently represented in Buddhist art. The sacred ritual of the Brahmans has a hundred more. The five Dhyani-Buddhas are also distinguished from each other by these *mudras*. They correspond, in the higher spheres, to the five human Buddhas. On the Borobudur they are on the four sides and in the *dagobas* of the circular terraces. Each cardinal point is under the protection of one Dhyani-Buddha, whose figure, a hundred times repeated, rules over the corresponding side of the Borobudur: Akshobya, the Dhyani-Buddha of the second Manushi- or human-Buddha Kanakamuni, seated in Bhumisparshamudra, occupies the niches of the eastern façade. Ratnasambhava, the Dhyani-Buddha of the third human-Buddha Kashiapa, appears in the Varapradamudra on the southern side. Amitabha, the Dhyani-Buddha of the fourth human-Buddha Gautama Sakyamuni, the only historical Buddha, reigns in Dhyanimudra on the western side. On the north side Amoghasiddha, the Dhyani-Buddha of the fifth human-Buddha Maitreya, the awaited saviour, is consoling the pilgrims with the Abhayamudra. Vairochana, the highest Dhyani-Buddha of the first human-Buddha Krakuchanda, seated in Dharmachakramudra, is hidden in the *dagoba* of the circular terraces. The supreme Buddha, Adhi-Buddha, was seated in the great *dagoba* at the top of the building. He is now shown in the open air at the foot of the Borobudur in the position of the Bhumisparshamudra.

The series of bas-reliefs on the base take the visitor beyond the *samsara* (the world of the transmigration of souls) and the *kama* (the world of senses and desires). They unfold before his gaze all the earthly life of the Buddha and the work of the first Bodhisattvas, and lead him into the regions of the future Buddha Maitreya and the Dhyani-Bodhisattva Samantabhadra and finally into the empire of formlessness of the heaven Arupa. The Dhyani-Buddhas of the four cardinal points on the square terraces symbolise the Rupadhatu, or the world of pure form. Here the bas-reliefs appear only visions of the former worldly life. The empty circular terraces, with their seventy-two *dagobas* behind which one senses rather than sees the mysterious effigy of the supreme Dhyani-Buddha, seem to solve this almost impossible task of representing the heavens of formlessness.

The Borobudur, therefore, is not a symbol of the Mountain of the Gods. It represents the upper heavens and the doctrine of the Mahayana and shows a conception of the spiritual life very different from that of Angkor Thom.

EXCAVATIONS IN CHINA

In no other country of the world has there been so consistent an interest in and veneration for antiquity as in China. Archaeological and art historical collections have been gathered by Chinese emperors and members of the learned class since the Sung dynasty, more than four hundred years before the Renaissance in Europe led to a similar enthusiasm in the West. Yet no other great treasure-store of ancient art has been so slow to feel the spade of the scientific excavator. A very few—though very significant—excavations of prehistoric man were made during the nineteen-twenties and thirties, and one government-sponsored dig was carried out in Honan Province in the nineteen-thirties. It is only in the last ten years that popular antagonism to disturbing the hallowed ground where ancestors were buried has been overcome, and extensive excavations have taken place. In 1929 a palaeolithic skeleton was discovered thirty miles south-west of Peking. This came to be called "Peking man" or *Sinanthropus Pekinensis*, estimated to date back to about 500,000 B.C. This discovery put China on the archaeological map, for she was now known to have possessed the equivalent of the Western "palaeolithic series". This skeleton was seen to be typically Chinese and not Mongol. Previously the proto-Chinese had been thought to spring from the most varied origins. Stone tools were also found beside the Peking man which conferred on him a distinct advantage over other palaeolithic types such as the "Homo Heidelbergensis".

Since then traces of palaeolithic man, including weapons and hearth-stones, have been found in other parts of China, in the Ordos district and on the Yellow River between the provinces

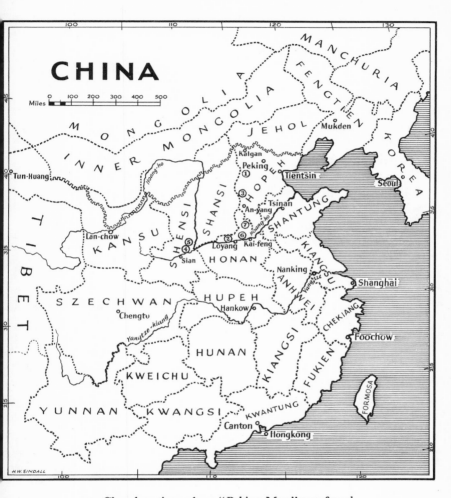

1. Chou-kou-tien, where "Peking Man" was found.
2. Yang Shao, neolithic decorated pottery site.
3. An-yang, the Shang capital.
4. Hao, the Chou capital.
5. Tombs of the first Chou kings.
6. Lo-yang, the Eastern capital.
7. The tombs of Siun-hien.

of Shansi and Shensi. In 1933–34 several skeletons were found in a cave near the site of Peking man from the last palaeolithic period, nearer to that of European palaeolithic man. A year later, the remains of Gigantopithecus, a giant man which some have believed to be a remote ancestor of both the Java and Peking skeletons, were discovered in the extreme south of China in Kwangsi Province.

Six years before the Peking man came to light, an equally sensational discovery of objects from the neolithic period was made by the Swedish archaeologist J. G. Andersson in the provinces of Kansu and Honan. Andersson found a piece of hard painted pottery as beautiful in shape and colour as the famous ceramics of Susa. There are nowadays many examples of vases from this period in well-known museums all over the world as well as in private collections. Some of them are very similar to Western neolithic pottery, whilst others show the distinctive design we have come to associate with the oldest Chinese bronze vases.

In about 1898, odd pieces of inscribed bone and tortoise-shell were discovered in Honan Province which soon attracted the eager interest of Chinese and foreign language specialists. Ancient jades and marvellously patinated ritual bronze vessels, together with the inscribed bones, began in following decades to appear in increasing numbers in the Peking curio shops. Any enquiry about the origins of these antiquities was met with the same evasive reply: they had simply appeared on the Peking market but no one knew from where. Further enquiries revealed that in a village in the An-yang district in northern Honan, some eighty miles north of the Yellow River, peasants ploughing their fields had turned up fragments of inscribed bone. One peasant, evidently more cunning than his fellows, had explained that they were pieces of dragon-bone which, when powdered, made a wonderful drug. The bones were then sold to the drug-sellers. Archaeologists found that, together with the tortoise-shell, they had been used by soothsayers of the Shang period before 1000 B.C. who put them in the fire to make them crack, the cracks being interpreted as answers to questions sometimes inscribed on them. Several years passed before it

11. Bronze ritual wine-vessel in the form of a double-headed ram. Shang-yin or early Chou.

10. *Ting* with oblong rectangular body and two high loop handles. Shang-yin period.

12. Inscribed bronze vessel. Shang-yin or early Chou.

13. Bronze ritual wine-vessel, inscribed. Early Chou.

was possible to decipher the characters of the inscriptions and to proceed to a systematic investigation of the site, which ultimately revealed thousands of these bones.

Even the Chinese themselves have found it no light undertaking to conduct scientific excavations in their own country, and immense treasure still lies buried under Chinese soil. Not only archaeological excavation, but every kind of unusual work carried out on the land has always been regarded with suspicion by the inhabitants who consider that these operations might disturb prevailing magical influences. Engineers who built the first railways had to contend with these superstitions. The cutting of trenches across a fairly wide area of land in order to locate the site of some ancient buried city and to trace the layout of the walls inevitably brings to light certain tombs. Tombs are sacred and no one may touch them. Studies in cosmology and magic and all kinds of considerations are required before the site of a tomb can be chosen and if the choice is propitious it can bring good fortune to the whole family for generations. A site which is favourable to one family, however, may not be so to another. The tombs, therefore, are dispersed over the countryside and can be seen everywhere, in the middle of fields of corn and maize, for example, and the funeral mounds are left intact even when the field is being cultivated.

The Chinese are a patient people and capable of great endurance, but they will brook no interference with their ancestor-cult. History tells us, for instance, of a city besieged by enemies and in a desperate plight. No help could be expected from outside and the inhabitants were without food or water. The general in command confided to a man he suspected was a spy: "I hope the enemy will not think of opening the tombs of our ancestors, for that would force us to surrender." This information duly reached the enemy on the following night. When, on the next day, the attacking troops began, in front of the gates of the town, to open up the tombs, the besieged citizens were seized with such fury that they made a victorious sortie and annihilated the enemy.

In China, however, as in Egypt and in many other countries, the robbing of tombs had for a long time been a very lucrative occupation. Neither traps, poison nor terrifying curses inscribed on the coffin could keep back the thieves. As the Chinese love of the past is as strong as his veneration for his ancestors and their tombs, there had long been a flourishing trade in antiques in Peking, where there was as much rivalry between private excavators as between the makers of faked relics.

Excavations on the site of the Shang residence in An-yang were started in 1931 by the National Institute of Historical and Philological Research, but there were great difficulties to be faced. Because of the climate excavating had to be limited to four months in the year, two in the spring and two in the autumn. The winter is too cold and the summer too hot. But these four months fall partly in the very windy season when sand-storms are frequent and these raise the yellow sand into a thick dust which settles into the deep layers of loess found in these north-western provinces. The winds are strong enough to blow a man over and carry him along for several feet. It is under these difficult conditions, with their faces protected by masks and goggles, that the Chinese archaeologists uncovered, layer by layer, at An-yang, the principal city of the oldest known civilisation in China.

A further danger which the excavators had to face, at least in the early stages, was that of bands of brigands. The province of Honan, and particularly the district of An-yang, were unsafe areas because of the wretched poverty of the peasants whose only source of livelihood was often theft and pillaging. When a landowner had been lucky enough to make an important find, he ran the risk of being carried off by brigands and held to ransom. The robbers of tombs had evolved their own method. As they could only work by night they spent the daytime sounding the ground by driving in long, hollow sticks where they considered the site favourable. The nature of the soil brought up inside the stick indicated whether or not there might be an ancient tomb under the surface. If the soundings were favourable, a gang of fifty or sixty men, armed with pistols, returned to the site at nightfall. Some dug a trench whilst others formed a defensive ring round them. Work proceeded quickly as it was necessary to finish before dawn. Anyone intruding upon the operation was killed off without mercy and only a detachment of well-trained soldiers could break up the gang.

When official excavations were begun on the site of the ancient Shang residence the mound was already pitted with holes made by clandestine diggers. The damage done to scientific investigation by this kind of pilfering can be judged by one example. Seven large tortoise-shells, covered with inscriptions, were found deeply buried. They gave very full information on near-by buildings, including the date of their construction. Six inches away was a shaft dug by a peasant. If he had found them and removed them they would have been virtually useless.

Up to 1934 not a single inviolate Shang tomb had been discovered. None could be dated accurately and no precise information could be deduced about Shang burial customs or religion. No ritual bronze vessel had been unearthed under anything approaching scientific conditions. The most important link of all was still missing—a skeleton which would give us an idea of what the Shang people looked like. The pillagers had indeed found hundreds of skeletons, but they had scattered their bones far and wide so that the spirit of the dead would not seek its revenge on the living. Now the gaps are being filled in by many excavations, though summarizing reports are not yet available.

12

THE GREAT SHANG CITY

Officially the first Chinese dynasty was the Hsia (2205–1766 B.C.). This was followed by the Shang dynasty (1766–1122 B.C.). Such records of these as exist in ancient literature, however, have been doubted and Chinese history proper was held to have begun with the Chou dynasty. This was assumed, though not with certainty, to have followed the Shang in 1122 B.C. Recent excavations at An-yang put back the known history of China some 250 years and it is now possible to date it as early as the fourteenth century B.C.

According to Chinese tradition a powerful tribal chief Pan-Keng settled with his people shortly after 1400 B.C. in the region of An-yang. Here he built, on the banks of the Huan river, the "great Shang city". Archaeological discoveries have confirmed this. The inhabitants of this city were therefore the oldest known to Chinese history and the kingdom of which the city was the capital was that of the Shang dynasty.

The site was remarkably apt for a capital city. Loess soil, a mixture of disintegrated clay and vegetable particles, is considered to be one of the most fertile in the world. It does not commonly carry trees or shrubs and does not, therefore, need clearing. The river at this spot forms an ample curve and it protected the town on three sides and brought water for the crops and the cattle. The fourth side of the town, facing west, was protected by a chain of mountains running north-south, some of whose foothills projected eastwards towards the town and provided the necessary wood for building. Everything required for the development of a lasting civilisation was therefore at hand. This had not, apparently, gone unnoticed by previous tribes, as traces of neolithic habitation were found in another curve of the river, and it is probable both that they were still in occupation when the Shang peoples came and that they were subdued by them.

These neolithic dwellings were dug out of the ground in a circular trench some ten or twelve feet in diameter and piled up in the centre to resemble a bee-hive about the height of a man. The roof consisted of wooden beams covered with straw and earth. The entrance was through a hole in the roof. Loess is firm enough to make good vertical walls, so these dugouts were very habitable. There are many thousands of similar dwellings in China today, especially in the loess mountains of Honan, Shensi and Shansi provinces, where they are a greater protection than surface buildings against sand-storms, the burning heat of the summer and the freezing cold of the winter. They are even provided with the rudiments of modern comfort and with doors, windows and several rooms they are scarcely distinguishable inside from ordinary houses. The neolithic habitation was by comparison a very primitive affair and later came to be used either as a store-place or a slave's house.

The houses of the Shang people were very different and were so far advanced that they have become the typical Chinese dwellings ever since. This is built on an earth platform with a brick facing. Kiln-baked brick was unknown in the Shang period and the earth was poured into a wooden framework and rammed down layer by layer—a technique which has been used from the neolithic period to today. The result was a wall so firm that, in the case of the Shang terraces, for instance, it has resisted the rains of thirty centuries. The earth platform was a little wider than the house and jutted out in front of the entrance. The gable-ended roof was carried on three rows of pillars resting on stones in the earth. The only important difference between the Shang house and the modern Chinese house is that now the centre row of pillars which went right up to the ridge has been done away with. The walls of a Chinese house, whether ancient or modern, do not support the roof. They are simply partitions between the pillars. Formerly they were made of rammed clay, now they are usually one thickness of brick.

The following lines from the *Shih Ching*, or Book of Odes, the oldest collection of poetry preserved in China, dating from the seventh century B.C. or earlier, gives an accurate picture of the construction of a Shang house:

"He called upon his overseer of public works,
He called upon his Minister of Education,
And charged them to build dwellings.
They levelled all the land by skilful measuring,
They built wooden frames which rose straight and high.
The temple of our ancestors grew mightily.
Armies of men brought earth in baskets
And, shouting joyfully, poured it into the frames.
They rammed it in with great ringing blows,
They levelled off the walls and these resounded mightily,
They built up five thousand cubits at once,
And so well did they labour
That the rolling of the great drum
Would not cover the noise thereof."

Another poem from the same book shows how the logs for the framework of the building were brought down from the forests:

"We have climbed the King mountain
Where pine and cypress grow in symmetry;
We have cut them down and brought them hither;
We have squared off their trunks with deference,
For the trunk of the pine is mighty
And rises high above all other.
High are the many pillars.
The temple was finished—the abode of peace."

This pride in great projecting beams and tall pillars is found again in modern China. When the "Temple of the Happy Year", the main building in the Temple of Heaven in Peking, was destroyed by lightning in 1889, the problem arose of finding tree-trunks tall enough to replace those which had supported the roof. The old ones had been eighty-two feet high, but there were no more trees of this size in the country. They were eventually imported at considerable expense from Oregon. The framework of Chinese houses and temples is still painted today, especially on the outside, with lucky emblems, particularly peaches, the ancient symbol of longevity, books, old-style vases and even landscapes. Similar motifs are found also on vases. We have it on the authority of Confucius and other writers that this exterior decoration was practised at least as early as the Shang period. Little is known of interior decoration, but it was almost certainly of a similar kind. Wood-carving must have reached a high level of artistry before the Shang period. This art has been practised in China since time immemorial.

The principal occupation of the Shang people was agriculture, but they also hunted. We have information about this from bone-inscriptions which mention hunting "bags" of up to three hundred and fifty beasts. They hunted the tiger, panther, stag, gazelle, bear, hare, pheasant and even the elephant which seems still to have been extant in these parts. The hunting of the tiger and other wild animals seems to have been enjoyed as a dangerous sport. A poem from the Book of Odes describes one of these hunts:

"Chou has gone off to the hunt,
Standing in his four-horse chariot.
The reins are like streamers in his hands
And the horses bound on the left and the right like
    dancers.
Chou is in the marshland.
The fire blazes out everywhere at once
And he with his bare arms seizes the tiger
And presents it to the Duke.
Oh, Chou, do not begin again!
Take care no harm comes to thee!"

The Shang people fed on domestic animals, especially the pig. Pork was the most commonly eaten meat in the neolithic period, not only in North China but all over the world, and particularly in Europe. Beef, mutton, dog-meat and fowl were also eaten. Although they raised cattle, the Chinese never ate dairy produce and even today they look down on it, with the notable exception of American-imported ice-cream. This is rather surprising, as their neighbours, the nomad Mongols, live on dairy-produce. The American anthropologist and sinologist Berthold Laufer maintained that Europe and Asia can be divided into two according to milk-consumption. Diary-produce is not eaten in China, Korea, Japan, Indo-China or Malaya, whereas all Indo-Europeans, Scythians, Semites, Turks, Mongols and Tibetans have always eaten it. Laufer goes even further and says that epic poetry has flourished widely amongst milk-consuming peoples and hardly at all amongst the others. He does not, however, explain why this should be so.

The sinologist H. G. Creel tells a story which illustrates the Chinese dislike of dairy-produce. A Chinese who had lived for many years on the Mongol frontier of Tibet came to Peking. As he spoke Mongolian well and was well acquainted with the customs of these people he decided, as a joke, to pass himself off as a Mongol prince. In this guise he received many invitations. Some of his hosts soon began to doubt his identity, however, and decided to put the matter to the test. One day he was invited to a feast at which, instead of the usual Chinese delicacies he was offered only milk, butter and cheese, the favourite food of the Mongols. At the sight of this food the false prince fled in terror; nothing could induce him to touch it.[1]

This fact is also a very solid argument against the Chinese ever having been a race of nomads. Nor is there anything in ancient Chinese literature, as Creel points out, to support this once widely-held theory. On the contrary, agriculture has always been, from the earliest times, an almost sacred occupation to the Chinese. In ancient Chinese script the pictogram for "masculine" was a sign representing work in the fields. The rites and sacrifices attached to agriculture were also just as sacred. The bone-inscriptions give us detailed information

[1] H. G. Creel: *The Birth of China* (London, 1936).

about these also. The annual sacrifice celebrated by the Emperor in the Temple of Heaven right up to the end of the Chinese Empire in 1911, as well as the ceremonies held in the Temple of Agriculture, go back to the Shang period and possibly even further. In the second and third months of the year the oracle was consulted about future harvests. Sacrifices were made to the ancestors and prayers offered up for good crops. The king made an occasional personal inspection of the fields. An essential condition for a good harvest was, of course, sufficient rain. The climate of North China is dry in autumn, winter and most of the spring. The bone-inscriptions consulting the oracle thus contain questions such as: "Will there be enough rain for the millet-harvest?" or "Will Ti grant us sufficient rain this year?" or simply "We beg for rain." Sometimes there is an anxious "Will there be a disastrous rainfall this year?" This evidently referred to the sometimes calamitous flooding in the summer which destroyed crops and washed away the earth, undoing the patient work of many years.

The most important cereals were corn, millet and rice. Corn seeds found in neolithic sites seem to indicate that they came originally from the West, but the principal cereal of the stone age, and still the basis of most poor people's food the world over, was millet. In the Shang period a kind of beer was brewed from it and used in sacrificial rites. Rice seems to have been grown in neolithic times in North China, as is shown by imprints of rice seeds on vases. A kind of flax was grown also. Work in the fields was done by the men; the women prepared the meals and took them out to their menfolk. Silkworm breeding, however, was done by women. The Book of Odes describes this as follows:

"With the coming of spring the heat begins,
And the golden oriole sings his song.
The young women take their hollow baskets
And go along the narrow paths,
Looking for the tender leaves of the mulberry-tree.
In the month of the silk-worm they strip off the leaves
And cut down the high branches

Whose leaves are out of their reach.
They only pick the leaves of the young trees.
In the seventh month is heard the shrike.
In the eighth month the women begin to spin.
They make the dark-coloured and yellow cloth.
Our red silk is renowned
And is used for clothes for the young prince."

In the Shang period the ownership of land and property and the comfort and wealth that went with it was attained by farming, cattle-raising and hunting. There was a certain amount of trading, but this was limited by poor communications. Goods were bartered, although there was also payment by money, which consisted of cowrie shells.

Certain discoveries showed that there had been a considerable degree of skilled craftsmanship. Clay spindles and cloth remains proved that weaving had been practised. Spear- and arrow-heads in stone and bone and figurines of men and animals testified that carving had reached a high degree of skill. A great number of ladles and hairpins with bone decoration had survived, but objects of wood had, of course, disintegrated. Like a number of other Bronze Age peoples, they did not paint their pottery, but decorated it by engraving the earthenware whilst it was still soft. Some vases show signs of glazing. There were more than fifteen different shapes of vases, many of which recur in later ritual vessels.

The subject of vases brings us into the realm of fine art. These have always been highly appreciated in China and in the twentieth century in Europe and America where Chinese objets d'art have fetched record prices. This is no mere snob value, either, as many of these ancient vases are far superior to any other examples of ancient fine art whether in the East or the West. To appreciate them fully, however, a certain aesthetic and archaeological training is necessary. These ancient vases, the true forerunners of a whole section of Chinese art, do not appeal immediately to the unpractised eye as a Sung vase, for example, does by the beauty of its shape or the delicacy of its colours.

The Great Shang City

"It is only gradually that we realise that these animals and other motifs, apparently so strange to us, had a precise meaning and a particular significance to the mind which created them. When we see a lot of them, when we become familiar with them, we begin to realise and then to appreciate the incomparable art which combined these varied motifs into such delicately balanced designs in the tiniest corners of the surface and so skilfully interdependent that they never appear excessive. People who admire these vases soon conceive a passion, nay, an obsession, for them. Foreigners are said to have ruined themselves almost through not having been able to resist 'another beautiful piece . . . just one more'."[1]

There are three main reasons for the popularity of Shang bronzes: their age, their aristocratic nature and their aesthetic effect. In ancient collections of canonical writings, particularly in the *Li-Chi*, or Book of Rites, the vases are mentioned, with their names and dimensions. Illustrated descriptions of them and catalogues of the Imperial Collection have been in existence since the tenth century and the last was edited in 1751 by the Manchu Emperor Ch'ien Lung, a great art lover. Because of their very great value they have been copied since very ancient times and copies of vases from the Sung period have even been found in the Imperial Collection in Peking. It is only within the last forty or fifty years that it has been possible to date them with any accuracy by excavating them scientifically and deciphering their inscriptions. This has revealed two main types: the Shang (fourteenth to twelfth centuries B.C.) and the Chou (eleventh to fourth centuries B.C.). Within each of these there are several different styles and periods.

The aristocratic nature of these vases, outstanding both as vases in themselves and as examples of fine art, is due to their use in the ancestor-cult, the most authentic of Chinese religions. They are sacred vessels, comparable to our chalices. Their decoration is symbolical and mystical, and it declined to become

[1] H. G. Creel, op. cit.

conventional and purely formal as the ancestor-cult itself declined, in the last Chou period, into a convention. Each act in the sacrifice to the ancestors required its own type of vase and each vase had its family-name. The ancient Greeks, as well as modern peoples, used different words for different vessels such as an amphora, a cup, a pitcher, a flask, and so on, but the naming of Chinese vases was different. The *li* vase, for example, has the shape of the primitive earthenware tripod pot, such as was made by hand for thousands of years, and hollow, curiously bulbous feet. It came into ritual use as a bronze vase in the second millennium B.C. Its name has the ring of that of a very ancient and distinguished family. The *ting* vase, which has a rectangular bottom and stands on four legs, shows by its shape that it was originally wooden. Like the *li* it was a pot, but more slender and had many variants. Its greatest period was in the feudal empire of the Chou dynasty, when nine gigantic examples were made to represent the Empire's nine provinces. They disappeared during a crossing of the Ssu river in 333 B.C., when the boat transporting them was shipwrecked. The attempts made to save one of them became a favourite theme of mural decoration in the Han period. Although called upon to serve the Empire, the *ting* vessels did not thereby cease to serve the people also, and millions of Chinese continued to prepare their daily food in them, as is shown by the popular saying "Chung ming ting shih" or "The bell is ringing, the meal is ready in the *ting*".

The *hsien* vase had also seen service on the domestic hearth before its use in the ancestor-cult. There was no better cooking-vessel than this. It was divided into two sections, the lower, similar to the *li*, for water, and the upper, like a kettle, for the food.

Many vases used for drink-offerings, however, were not taken from types of domestic vessels. Examples of these are the family vase, the *ho*, used to mix the water and the wine, and the drink-offering vases *chia* and *chüeh*.

The *ting* vase in the Musée Guimet shows the motifs most commonly found on the outside of this type of vessel. The bottom part has a face of a monster against a background of stylised scrolls and spirals. The monster is called the *t'ao-t'ieh*, but research has so far failed to reveal either its origin or the symbolism of the motif. It appears to be a combination of elements taken from different animals, dragons and other fantastic creatures. Its large protruding lidded eyes were doubtless taken from older vases where they were used as ornamental knobs. These are the very oldest examples of a basic tendency of Chinese art which was to make nature resemble the animal kingdom by giving it animal forms. The aesthetic impression given by these vases can certainly be analysed, but their strange power can only be experienced if they are seen in the original. The amateur needs a certain amount of preparation if he is to appreciate them fully. To the ordinary person they will simply seem exotic, but the connoisseur or the artist will not fail to be impressed, particularly by the finer pieces. The symbolism of their decoration, of course, cannot affect us as it must have done the Chinese of the Shang or the Chou periods. We are affected almost entirely by their shape alone, their plastic form in which is expressed all the great vitality of a new art. Another factor which contributes greatly to their appeal, though it has nothing to do with their original appearance, is their patina, a noble malachite green which, when polished, takes on a soft velvety sheen. This is peculiar to these bronzes and recalls the appearance of jade. It is the result of a slow chemical process which has been going on for three thousand years.

The vases were used in the ancestor-cult, as practised in every house, whether rich or poor. The ordinary people used earthenware vessels, of course, and not objects as precious as these. The royal family's sacrifices are described in the bone inscriptions. Sacrifices were made to the father, his brother, the grandfather and his forefathers. "Forty-two male ancestors and brothers of male ancestors belonging to six generations are mentioned on the bones as having received sacrifices." [1] During the ceremonies the ancestors' names were never spoken. The personal name of the Emperor was never to be spoken or written either. Each of the ancestors was mentioned by the day

[1] H. G. Creel, op. cit.

of the week (there were ten of these) on which he was born or died: hence Father Monday, Mother Tuesday, Elder Brother Friday, and so on. Sacrifices were also made to divine powers such as the wind, invoked also under the name of "Envoy of Ti". Ti, or Shang-Ti (that is "Highest Ti") was the supreme deity of China, but his origin is unknown. Perhaps he was the oldest ancestor of the Shang people. "In fact," says Creel, "authors who recognise in Ti a deified ancestor or the father of the first Shang king may possibly be right and thus all important Shang deities may have been ancestors."[1]

The ancestors, Shang-Ti and other spirits were questioned by writings on the bone and the tortoise-shell tablets. But how were their answers made known? The tablets were heated on burning embers until they began to crack (Mongol fortune-tellers use the same procedure) and the shape of the cracks denoted the answer which was interpreted by soothsayers. The cracks were roughly T-shaped but varied greatly in design and size, the two strokes rarely forming a right-angle, and they could really only indicate "yes" or "no", "lucky" or "un-lucky". Varying degrees of good or evil omen were, however, read into the signs and a question about prospects for the harvest might be answered by "very good". Sometimes an event was confirmed: "Will it rain tonight?" was answered by "There has been virtually no rain". The soothsayer was, of course, liable to interpret the signs to suit himself, just as a king did not feel himself obliged to obey an oracle if it was unfavourable. Ling, the king of the Chou state from 540 to 529 B.C., asked if he would conquer the world. The reply was "No", so he threw the tortoise-shell to the ground, saying, "What? You will not grant me such a little thing? Very well, then, I'll conquer it by myself."[2] One tortoise-shell sufficed for a whole series of questions and was frequently used when the king was travelling. It is natural that enquiries

---

[1] Op. cit.

[2] Until the voyage of Chang Ch'ien (138–126 B.C.) the Chinese thought that the world scarcely extended beyond the frontiers of their Middle Empire, which ended at the Tibetan border and was, according to them, surrounded only by a narrow area inhabited by barbarians. The world to them was a square with sides some 10,000 *li* long (a *li* was about five hundred yards). (From A. Herrmann: *Lou-lan*, Leipzig, 1931.)

should be made about the weather and travelling conditions, just as we consult our weather-forecasts and guides.

When the oracle answered, the replies were inscribed on used bones as a kind of attestation. These have provided much information about the Shang civilisation. Later, questions and answers were recorded in books, but these have not been preserved. Chinese scholars have listed the most important questions put to the celestial powers. One of these lists is given by Creel:

1. Sacrifices: To which spirits should sacrifices be made? When, what animals, of what colour and how many?

2. Information to be laid before the spirits: The enemy's misdeeds, the number he has killed and taken prisoner so that the spirits might intervene and punish him.

3. Concerning official banquets(?)

4. Journeys and the stages thereof: If the date is favourable and where halts should be made.

5. Hunting and fishing: If the date is favourable and where this should be done. As the oracle could only answer "yes" or "no" the places had to be named one after the other (rather like our table-rapping procedure).

6. War: When should an army be sent out and at what strength? Must the enemy be sought out in open country or must the army remain on the defensive?

7. The crops: What quantity of the various cereals could be expected? What amount of alcohol? General harvest forecasts.

8. Rain, snow and wind.

9. Fine weather, especially when would the weather improve again after a storm?

10. Sickness and its remedies.

11. The ten-day week: Will it be favourable or unfavourable?

12. Miscellaneous.

This list does not claim to be complete, of course, and questions such as "If the king goes out hunting today, will he not encounter violent rain?" would come under two headings, "hunting" and "weather". The spirits were not always trusted and sometimes they were accused of tormenting the living. "Will grandmother Chi's spirit persecute the son of Hao?" or "Does the spirit of grandfather Hsin wish me evil?"

The Chinese realised, naturally, that the food and drink they offered up in sacrifice to the ancestors were not really consumed. They explained this very logically by saying that since the dead person had left his body behind him he could have no need of actual food, and that all a spirit required was the essence of nourishment. Sacrificial meals, therefore, were partaken of also by the living assembled together for the sacrifice. These ceremonies are often reproduced later in wall-paintings in the Chou period. Mainly animals were sacrificed: oxen, sheep, pigs and dogs, sometimes in considerable quantities. One sacrifice to three dead kings is said to have comprised one hundred cups of alcohol (or beer?), one hundred sheep and three hundred oxen. The animals were burnt, drowned or buried alive. Humans were sacrificed also and, if the bone inscriptions are to be believed, by the hundred. About a thousand headless human skeletons were found in An-yang in 1935, buried in graves ten at a time. The heads had been buried separately. For massacres such as these prisoners of war were used generally, from barbarian nomad tribes with whom the agricultural Shang people were constantly at war, like the sedentary Iranians and the Turanian pillagers.

Amongst these human victims must also be included the royal wives and the members of the court who, as under the Sumerians, Indians and other peoples, were buried alive with the monarch. The barbarous practice was abandoned under the Chou dynasty, but did not completely disappear.

13

THE CHOU CIVILISATION

Any comparison between the civilisations of Asia Minor and Eastern Asia is misleading. Different lands bear different fruits. If, however, to make a comparison which will be familiar to us, the Shang civilisation may be said to resemble the Sumerian, then the Chou is like the Babylonian. We have indicated Europe's debt to the latter in the chapter on the Tower of Babel. This debt was no less than the very basis of civilisation: the law, the measurement of time, the calendar, weights and measures and many other things. These gave a common start to European and Near Eastern civilisations, but here the influence of Babylon stopped, unless we count the evil legacy of superstition. It was left to the Ionian Greeks to found the moral sciences and Plato (fourth century B.C.) was the first great thinker who is still today one of the fundamental philosophers. Measured on this scale the Chou civilisation cannot fail to impress. Creel likens its rate of development to a train which, after a long journey at moderate speeds, goes faster and faster as it approaches its destination. The progress made by the Chou civilisation in the five hundred years or so from its beginnings until the time of the two philosophers Lao-tsu and Confucius is as great as that attained in the West over a period of two thousand years. The Shang civilisation was scarcely more advanced at the end than the Sumerians had been in 2500 B.C. In the history of the Mediterranean over two thousand years elapsed between the Sumerians and the Greece of Heraclitus and Plato. Lao-tsu and Confucius are more widely read in the West today than Plato. The former is as obscure to us as Heraclitus, but the message of Confucius is as fresh today as it was in the beginning and as clearly understandable. Philosophy and literature did not end with Confucius either. They continued with Mo-ti, Mencius, Li-tse and Chuang-tsu, so that in the third century B.C., when the Chou dynasty came to an end, they had left behind them a store-house of artistic and spiritual treasure which was to inspire future generations in China throughout the long course of her history.

In the *Chia Yü*, the "Dialogues" of Confucius, the assumption of power by the Chou dynasty is related as follows:

"When King Wu had triumphed over the house of Yin (the dynastic name assumed by the Shang) and restored the good government of former times, then, even before alighting from his chariot, he gave as fief to the descendants of Huang-ti the land of Ki and to the descendants of the monarch Shun he gave the land of Chen. When he had alighted from his chariot, he gave as fief to the descendants of the ruler of Hia the land of Ki and the land of Sung he gave to the descendants of the house of Yin (Shang). He caused a mound to be erected over the tomb of Prince Pi Kan, and released Count Ki from bondage. He summoned the master of ceremonies Shang-yang and reappointed him in office. He lightened the burdens which had been placed upon the people.

"On the way home, travelling westwards, when he had crossed the Yellow River he set the war-horses free on the southern slopes of the Hua Shan and had the draught oxen set to pasture on the steppes of the Peach Forest. They were never to be harnessed again. He had the chariots and armour daubed with ox-blood and stored away in arsenals to show that they would never be used again. He had the bucklers and the javelins reversed, wrapped in tiger-skins and put away. He made his army leaders and generals vassal princes and commanded them to put away their bows and store their arrows in their quivers.

"By these acts the world recognised that King Wu would no more have recourse to arms. The armies were then stood down and bow-shooting was organised in the meadows. In the east they shot their arrows to the tune of "The Wild Cat's Head" and in the west to the songs of the *k'i-lin*. War-like competitions, in which the arrows had to pierce all the thicknesses of leather of the targets, were abandoned. Court dress was worn and festive headgear as well as wide belts on which was carried the audience-tablet. Heroes as strong as tigers laid down their arms. During the sacrifices to the god of harvests the king gave his ancestor Hou Tsi a place beside the supreme deity and the people learnt filial piety. He held audience and went on tours of inspection. Then the princes knew the master they had to serve. He tilled the field of sacrifice. Then the people learnt to know their parents. These six acts teach the most important things on earth. He gave food to the three classes of old men and to the five classes of men of experience in the Great Hall of Instruction. Then the Son of Heaven made sacrifice himself with bare breast. He offered them food and made them eat, he held out goblets to them when they rinsed out their mouths after eating. Wearing the royal cap and with his buckler in his hand he himself joined the dancers who were performing before them. . . . Thus did the institutions of the house of Chou spread throughout the land and customs and music went hand in hand."

This colourful account gives a picture of the new organisation of the kingdom and of the rules concerning official feasts. Former dynasties were wisely preserved and endowed with fiefs to forestall any possible future revolts. Everything was done according to exact rules and a precise ceremonial, thus laying a durable foundation on which the Chou dynasty was to prosper for centuries to come. The centre of this system, and its regularly-repeated confirmation, established according to divine law, was the annual Feast of Heaven. To this the Chinese remained faithful right up to the end of the Empire in 1911. It is unique in the history of civilisations that a sacrifice, or rather an official celebration, should be held yearly for more than thirty centuries as this one was in the successive capitals of the Empire.

"This sacrifice, held in the meadows outside the gates of the capital of the Lord of Heaven at midday, expressed not only the communion of man and heaven, but the communion of man with man. Participation in the sacrifice was regulated strictly according to law. The ceremony comprised the worship of heavenly and earthly spirits and the cult of nature and the ancestors. It constituted, therefore, the religious basis of the whole moral order and it is not surprising that Confucius said that he who understood the meaning of the great sacrifice understood also the order of the universe as clearly as if he could see it written on the palm of his hand. This sacrifice was, as it were, the metaphysical centre of the Chou civilisation. It comprised both moral and music. The sacred mimes, accompanied by impressive music, portrayed, in a mysterious symbolism, the bonds between the cosmic powers and the lives of men. . . . The sacrifice offered to the supreme Lord of Heaven and to the ancestors of the dynasty whom King Wen had placed beside the Lord (an innovation which gave the patriarchal system its supreme sanction) was the culminating point of a series of ceremonies. The role of high priest in this sacrifice to God, the all-powerful Lord, was a prerogative of the King. He alone was entitled to command this display of splendour due to the Lord of Heaven. For the vassal princes and the nobles, the sacrifice was the religious act which betokened their power. Each vassal state had its deities which it worshipped. Each prince had to honour the gods of the mountains and rivers in his own part of the country. Thus the sacrifice was a duty and a right for all men, even for the ordinary people who worshipped their ancestors in their own homes. The ancestors were classed by generations. The eldest was enthroned in the hindermost temple, the others in temples orientated alternately north and south. Only the King could worship his ancestors with royal honours. Other descendants of the King who were only princes sacrificed according to their rank. From this time dates the custom of burying a man according to the rites corresponding to the rank of his ancestors."[1]

The figures of King Wen, his son King Wu, whose seizure of power was related above, and his brother the Duke of Chou have come down in the traditions of the Chinese people as patriarchs whose deeds have always been quoted as examples in Confucian morals. In the political dialogues between the philosopher Meng-tzu (Mencius) and several princes of the late Chou period in the fourth century B.C. we find, for example, the following conversation:

King Hsuan of Ts'i questioned Meng-tzu: "It is said that the park of King Wen was seventy *lis* long. Is that so?"

Meng-tzu answered: "Tradition has it so."

The King: "Was it in truth so large?"

Meng-tzu: "Yes, and even so it was too small for the people."

The King: "My park is only forty *lis* long and yet it is too large for my people. How can this be?"

Meng-tzu: "The park of King Wen was seventy *lis* long, but anyone wishing to pick grass in it or gather up dead wood had permission to enter; anyone wishing to shoot a pheasant or a hare also had permission to enter. Thus the king possessed his park in common with his people, so that for the people it was too small. When I arrived at the frontier of your kingdom I made enquiries about the most important official interdictions before I dared enter. Anyone who killed a stag or a deer in this park received the same punishment as a murderer. So it is that the park is like a great man-trap in the midst of your kingdom. Is it not just that the people find it too large?"[2]

The new kingdom set up by King Wu would soon have crumbled had it not been for the energetic intervention of Duke Tan of Chou, who thus became the second founder of the Chou dynasty. Shortly after he took over the Regency of the Empire on behalf of the heir to the throne Prince Cheng, who

---

[1] Richard Wilhelm: *Geschichte der chinesischen Kultur.*
[2] From R. Wilhelm: *Mong Dsi* (E. Diederichs, Jena).

was still a minor, two of his brothers and the son of the last Shang ruler made a concerted uprising. The Chou capital was in the valley of the Wei, whereas the Shang still had their residence, as in the past, in North Honan. The Duke of Chou led out a punitive expedition to the east and spent several years in North Honan consolidating the supremacy of his royal house. The Shang ruler and one of the rebel brothers were executed and the Duke's other brother was banished. So as to render the Yin (or Shang) house harmless, their power in the region of their former capital was broken and their suzerainty over the Shang peoples given over by the Duke to a loyal brother who reigned over the state of Wei, north of the great Shang city. A brother of the last Shang ruler, who had quarrelled with the sovereign and seemed for that reason trustworthy, was given the state of Sung in south-west Honan. This state lasted until 286 B.C., and it was here that sacrifices to the Shang ancestors continued. This may perhaps explain why the bronze art of the so-called Huai style came to flourish so late here.

When the young king Cheng reached his majority his uncle the Duke handed over power to him. In accordance with his father's wishes the young sovereign ordered the building of a second residence further east at Lo-yang on the Lo River, not far from where the latter meets the Yellow River. He himself, however, continued to reside at Hao in the valley of the Wei. The Chou court did not finally move to Lo-yang until 770 B.C. The history of the dynasty thus divides into two periods—the Western Chou and the Eastern Chou. We shall not trace the course of this history here. Briefly it was a feudal state whose vassal princes became more powerful and independent as the king's suzerainty became more purely formal, but the slow decay of the central power lasted for more than half a century and this political decadence did not arrest the growth of Chinese civilisation.

The ancient Chou cities Feng and Hao in the region of the Wei have not yet been excavated and so we know less about early Chou archaeology than we do about the Shang. This gap had been partly filled by the excavation of the Chou tombs at Hsün-Hsien in North Honan. It was from Honan that Wu K'ang Shu, a brother of the "Warrior King", governed the new state of Wei after the fall of the last Shang. His capital was Ch'ao Ko, some twenty-nine miles south of the great Shang city.

Eighty-six tombs were discovered at Hsün-Hsien, ten of these, very large and deep and each covering over ten square yards, must certainly have been tombs of royal princes and noblemen. They were covered with rammed earth, like the Shang tombs, and were not marked outwardly by any tumulus. They were approached by inclines from the north and south. The burial chambers were smaller than those in the Shang tombs. They were shored up with wood and measured over six feet wide and nearly thirty feet long. The body was simply laid down in them, together with certain objects each of which had its allotted place. Along the southern wall, on each side of the entrance, were bronze masks of human faces. On the southern side also were the chariots; the armour was on the western side, the weapons on the eastern and the sacrificial vases were on the northern side. Grave-robbers who had pillaged most of these tombs had for the most part simply sunk a shaft on the northern side to get at the bronze vases, the only things of interest to them. Sometimes they discovered more than they had expected. One bronze vase, obviously stolen from a royal tomb at Hsün-Hsien, bears an inscription indicating that it was made for K'ang Chou on the occasion of the foundation of the principality of Wei and also mentions the repression of the Shang rebellion. It is of the Kuei type, shaped like a deep urn with two side-handles. It measures seventeen inches across the top of the handles and dates from about 1100 B.C. It shows the beginning of the heavier Chou style in which the rich decoration of the Shang period gave place to wavy horizontal or straight vertical lines on the widest part of the vase.

The objects unearthed in non-scientific diggings at Lo-yang in the nineteen-thirties brought about a new realization of the superb quality and richness of art produced in China in the second half of the Chou dynasty, particularly from about

500 to 250 B.C. Quantities of silver, gold, jade and richly inlaid bronze vessels and small sculptures reached the art market and collectors and museums all over the world. Recently scientific digging has supplemented the ample inventories known earlier. Many tombs, at Lo-yang and elsewhere, remain to be investigated. These are recognisable by the pyramidal tumuli which cover them to a height of from twenty-six to forty-six feet and are situated on a plateau to the north of the Wei and north-west of the present town of Hienyang. They are the tombs of the first four kings and of the Duke of Chou. In front of the tombs of the first two kings, the "Perfect King" Wen Wang (1169–1134) and the "Warrior King" Wu Wang (1134–1115), the conqueror of the Shangs and the founder of the Chou dynasty, stand temples which have always been places of frequent pilgrimages.

The most famous Chinese texts, including those which form the basis of a Confucian education, were written during the Chou period. One of the distinctive characteristics of this period was a mania for writing. The number of books written on bamboo tablets found in the tomb of a king buried in 296 B.C. made up ten waggon-loads. Records and reports were drawn up for all possible kinds of events. There was even a register of slaves. According to the Book of Annals, however, the supreme book was kept in heaven: "Heaven looks down on men and keeps an account of their just deeds." Orders to civil servants and soldiers were always given in writing, and letters were even written to Shang-Ti and other gods. Members of the privileged classes always carried tablets on their belts so that they could take notes at any given moment. Kings and lords had secretaries to draw up their edicts and to deal with their correspondence. Official documents in the Shang state in the middle of the sixth century B.C. were the responsibility of four ministers. The first composed the draft, the second revised and corrected it, the third polished up the style and the fourth gave it its final form.

The upper-class youth naturally received a literary education. As much practice was given to the writing up of accounts of ceremonial occasions, musical festivities and historical events as to the training in bow shooting and chariot-driving.

Nothing resembling the Book of Annals is to be found in any other literature. It is a collection of ancient documents on the most important historical events, designed to teach the reader what should or should not be done from the example of history. The decadence of certain monarchs is shown to be a result of their inability to use history as a mirror capable of guiding their own times. Everything which passed between the sovereign and the various courts of the great feudal state had to be put in writing. This could not fail to influence policy. "A note must be taken of every act," said a minister reproving the Duke of Shuang of Lu: "if your actions go against the law how will your descendants regard them?" Written material of the early Chou period has only survived in very small quantities, however, and this in many cases has been altered, so the inscriptions on the many bronze vases of the period are particularly valuable if we are to attempt to read the true spirit of the age. These inscriptions were often copied from books, so, in spite of the comparative lack of archaeological material, we have accurate texts going back some three thousand years which are comparable to anything found in the sands of Egypt or to the libraries of clay tablets in Babylon.

The authentic passages of the *Shu Ching*, or Book of Annals, contain speeches made by kings or sovereign princes on certain occasions about acts concerning the foundation of the new state of Lo-yang, about the second Chou residence, exhorting their subjects to be faithful, admonishing new vassals and appealing to members of the Shang family, now in submission, not to foment rebellion. As a sample of these texts we give this appeal by an Emperor to his army chiefs. It is taken from the German translation by Richard Wilhelm:

KAN'S OATH

A great battle was waged under Kan's command.
He summoned his six army leaders.
The Emperor spoke:

To you, men of my six armies
I say under oath:
The man of Hu
Hath shamefully outraged nature
And, in his idleness, hath forgotten all his duties.
That is why heaven hath destroyed his throne
And I am the instrument of celestial punishment.
If you who fight on the left of the chariots
Do not do the duty of the warriors on the left,
You will not be obeying my command!
If you who fight on the right of the chariot
Do not do the duty of the warriors on the right
You will not be obeying my command!
Obey my command
And I shall reward you in the face of my ancestors;
But those who do not obey,
I shall put to death in the face of the gods of the dark land,
I shall kill them all, with their women and their children!

Of all classical Chinese literature the most important to us today, the most richly human collection is the *Shih Ching*, or Book of Odes. The earliest of these date from the Shang period and the latest from the beginning of the sixth century B.C. It is an anthology of three hundred and eleven poems taken from works composed before the time of Confucius. Most of them were intended to be accompanied by music, but this has not survived. The Book of Odes is the richest and most accurate source of information on the Chou period, not only from the insight it affords into the daily life of the Northern Chinese people of the time, but also from the exquisite artistry with which their joys and griefs are expressed. Only through emotion and sympathy can we enter into contact with the soul and mind of the Chinese.

As in poetry of other times and places, the principal theme of these Odes is love. Some of them were popular songs and they have lost nothing of their original freshness through the centuries. Most of them were intended to be sung by women. In this they differ from Western love-poems and are for this reason alone even more charming. The reason doubtless lies in the condition of the women of the time. They were tied to home and farm whereas the men were free to wander abroad. It was probably considered unmanly to sing of one's desire to be loved, unless this led occasionally to brief amatory conquests. Marriages were arranged by parents but there were always secret affairs and furtive rendezvous which form one of the main themes of amorous lyric verse.

> The cricket sings in the grass
> And the grasshopper leaps o'er the green blades,
> Yet I cannot see my beloved.
> My heart is filled with sadness.
> Ah! Could I but see him
> And hold him close to me.
> Then would my grief be cured.

> I have climbed the mountain yonder in the south,
> I have gathered herbs in the woods,
> Yet I cannot see my beloved.
> My heart is filled with sadness.
> Ah! Could I but see him, etc. . . .

> I have climbed the mountain yonder in the south,
> I have gathered the flowers at the edge of the ravine,
> Yet I cannot see my beloved,
> My heart is sick with love.
> Ah! Could I but see him, etc. . . .

> In the field lies a dead deer.
> He is being wrapped with white grasses.
> A young girl has spring in her heart,
> A gallant is asking for her love.
> In the forest are young trees,
> In the field lies the dead deer:
> He is being bound tightly with white grasses.
> A girl is like jade.

Ah! slowly! Ah! gently!
You must not touch my belt.
You must not make my dog bark.[1]

But these arranged marriages, to which the young couple
often consented, also gave rise to mutual lasting love:

My husband has left for the war
And I know not when he will return.
Where will he be at this hour?
The chickens are sleeping in the hollow of the wall
And at the close of the day
The goats and the cows come down from the mountain.
But my husband has left for the war.
How can I help thinking of him?

My husband has left for the war,
Many days and many months ago.
When will he return to my side?
The chickens are sleeping on their roosts
And at the close of day
The goats and the cows come down from the mountain
And return to the farm,
But my husband has left for the war
May he be spared hunger and thirst!

Love took many forms, including the coarser ones of seduc-
tion, prostitution and adultery, but it had its lighter side of
playful mischief:

Sir, if you think kindly of me
I shall hold up my skirts and wade across the Wei;
But if you do not think of me,
There will surely be someone else who does.
Ah, foolish one, poor foolish one!

[1] From Louis Laly: *Choix de poésies chinoises* (Nouvelles Editions Latines).

When young lovers came up against the unyielding opposition of their parents they sometimes eloped and their story had an unhappy ending:

> You were only a boy
> And you came to exchange cloths for silk;
> But you did not come to sell the silk,
> You came to court me.
> I went with you, we crossed the Ts'i.
> I went with you as far as Tuen K'iu.
> "I am not the one," said I
> "Who wants to put things off till later."
> But you had nothing good to propose.
> I begged you not to be angry with me
> And to await the coming of autumn.
>
> I climbed the crumbling wall
> To watch for you coming round the hill;
> And when I did not see you
> My tears flowed unchecked.
> But when I did see you coming
> I laughed and I joked.
> You said that you had asked the tortoise-shells
> And the reed-sticks
> And that their answer was not unfavourable.
> "Come then," said I, "with your cart
> And I will follow you with all I possess."
>
> Before the mulberry loses its leaves
> How beautiful and shiny they are!
> Ah! turtle dove,
> Do not peck at your fruit.
> Ah! young woman,
> Seek not the forbidden pleasure with a man.
> When a man seeks his pleasures
> He can still be regarded with favour
> But when a woman does the same
> Nothing good can be said of her ever more.

When the mulberry loses its leaves
They fall to the ground, all yellow;
Since I have come away with you
Three years have I shared poverty.
Now the swollen waters of the Ts'i
Are flooding round the hangings of my cart.
In my heart nothing has changed,
But you, you have followed the paths of falsehood.
It is you, my master, who have done the injustice
In thus changing your behaviour.

For three years I was your wife
And looked after your house without sparing myself.
Rising early and retiring late.
Not one morning did I neglect my work.
Thus I for my part have kept our bargain.
But you, you have behaved cruelly.
My brothers must know nothing of it
Or they would only laugh.
I keep it to myself, silently,
And weep alone.

I wanted to grow old with you,
To grow old; but because of you I grieve.
The Ts'i, at its edges, has sandbanks
And the marshland its borders.
In the good days when I was young,
With my hair tied simply in a knot,
We could laugh and joke together
And we were joined in trust,
And I never dreamed that trust could be broken,
And now it is all over.

The Book of Odes also shows us the peasant at his daily work:

They pull up the grass and the shrubs
And open up the earth with their ploughs.

In thousands of pairs they go weeding,
Some in the marshy plain, others along the dike.
The master is there with his eldest son,
His younger sons and all their children,
And the strong-armed workmen and their assistants.
Noisily they devour the meal brought out to them
And spare a grateful thought for their wives
Who stand close to their husbands.
Then with their sharp ploughshares
They go off to work in the fields which lie to the south.
They sow all manner of cereals,
Each seed contains a germ of life.
The tender shoots spring up in long rows
And the tender feathery stalks climb higher;
The young crop stands proud
And the weeders go forth in great numbers.
Then comes the host of harvesters
And the corn is heaped up in the fields,
In myriads and hundreds of thousands
And millions of sheaves,
For the beer and the sweet drinks.
Enough to sacrifice to the ancestors both male and female
And to provide for all ceremonies.
It has a pleasant aroma,
It exalts the glory of the state.
It has a scent of pepper
And consoles the old people.
It is not only here that the harvest is abundant,
Nor is it in this season only.
It has been thus for all time.

The last few lines formed a chorus and must have been sung by the harvesters as they worked. There were also, just as there are today, floods and drought with their resultant poor harvests and attendant suffering:

The people can no longer find food
For heaven has struck them down with great evils.

As for the rich, they can manage,
But woe on the weak and the unwanted.

There was poverty even in the best of years and the sight of
rich people caused murmurs of discontent:

You sow not, neither do you reap;
Whence come, then, the harvests of these three hundred
farms?
You hunt not;
Whence come, then, the game we see hanging in your
courtyards?
Ah! the truly noble man
Would not eat of the bread of idleness!

Creel compares this period of Chinese history with our
Middle Ages and thinks that the Chinese aristocrats must have
led a fuller life than our knights and barons. The Chinese were
certainly more cultured and had a well-developed and refined
love of nature. Their religion had ritual ceremonies performed
by the head of the family himself and this must have been a
more joyful affair than medieval Christianity which was too
often austere and celebrated only by the priest. The Chinese
house had welcoming rooms opening on to flowering gardens
and, with its light and airy upper floors, it must have been
more pleasant to live in than the gloomy halls of our medieval
keeps, lit only by narrow slits, or the dark rooms of the small
houses overlooking the narrow streets of our medieval towns.
As in Europe, the aristocrats in China devoted themselves
frequently to their favourite sports of hunting and armed combat. Bow-shooting competitions were the Chinese equivalent
of our tourneys. The Book of Odes describes a feast held on
one of these occasions:

When the guests gather on the floor-mats
They take their places in an orderly manner
On the right and on the left.
Bamboo and wooden plates are arranged in rows

Filled with sauces and almonds.
The beer is good and sweet
And they drink, all equally respectful.
The bowls and goblets are carefully set out;
In turn they raise their glasses
And drink toasts to each other.
Then the great target is set up,
The bows and arrows are made ready,
And the archers are divided into groups.
"Show your skill with the bow."
"I am going to hit that circle."
"Drink up, I beg you."

Official occasions included banquets conducted according to the strictest etiquette, as in modern times. Each guest had his allotted place, according to his rank, and the sacrifice was celebrated. There was musical accompaniment, for which the orchestra played set pieces. After the ceremonial opening came the most enjoyable part of the programme: the consumption of a great abundance of food and drink to a musical accompaniment, the pieces this time being chosen by the guests. Chop-sticks were not used in this period: they were introduced later, in the third century. Food was eaten with the fingers, meat being previously cut up with a knife, and liquids were drunk from wooden spoons. This required constant washing of the hands during the meal and this too was a kind of ceremonial.

Cooking was held in such great respect that in the Book of Odes the king's principal chef is named as one of the most important officials. Amongst the dishes mentioned in the Is-li, or Book of Ceremonies, of the Chou period, there are several made from cereals such as rice balls, rice puddings, millet puddings and cooked flax seeds. There were many vegetables, both fresh and pickled, celery, ferns and various herbs, beans, preserved flowers, various kinds of fish and tortoise-meat, several other kinds of meat and fruits familiar to us except apples and pears which are never mentioned, although they were certainly eaten. The drinks, whether alcoholic or not, were all made from cereals and fruits. At sacrifices and official banquets the drink used was a kind of millet beer. Intemperance was frowned upon in China, as elsewhere. Mention is made of battles lost through the drunkenness of army leaders. The first Chou monarchs introduced prohibition—with about as little success as in the United States some years ago. The following lines, a continuation of the description of the bowmen's feast, show that there was often considerable drinking:

When the guests take their places on their mats
They are all friendly and respectful.
Before they have drunk too much,
Their conduct does not exceed the limits of decency.
But once they have drunk to excess,
Their behaviour becomes light-hearted and frivolous.
They leave their places, come and go
And begin to leap and dance.

When the guests have drunk too much
They shout and quarrel.
They upset the dishes
And dance grotesquely.
Drunk now, they fail to realise their errors.
Their caps awry, they totter
And dance unceasingly.
If they were to leave, once they have drunk too much,
They would not disgrace themselves
And would not bring discontent to their hosts,
But to stay at a feast when one is drunk
Is to cause offence to good breeding.
Drinking is certainly a good thing,
Provided one preserves one's decorum.

At each banquet
Some get drunk, others do not.
An inspector has been summoned,
Assisted by his scribe.

But the drunkards, in their fuddled state,
Grow red with anger at those who do not imitate them.
The sober can say no more
Nor prevent the others from going too far. . . .

In refined circles music was cultivated and it was a sign of good breeding to be able to play a musical instrument. This would almost certainly be a stringed instrument not unlike a guitar or a zither. The melodies played are described as "agreeable and peaceful" and the musical instrument was considered the ideal companion in joy or grief.

Almost every official act, every festival, banquet or sacrifice was celebrated with music, as also was every archery competition, arrows shot out of time with the music not being counted. For banquets and festivals there were two kinds of orchestra: a string quartet and a group of wind instruments consisting of different mouth-organs with several reed pipes. Great sacrifices and other solemn ceremonies were accompanied by a large orchestra of drums, bells, hollow ringing stones of nephrite, and flutes. Each instrument was either suspended from a special stand or laid on a suitable table. The Book of Annals introduces Kui the Great Musician:

"I strike the ringing stone, lightly or heavily. To accompany songs I gently stroke the harp or the zither. Then the fathers and the ancestors approach, take their places at the royal feast and all the princes lend a courteous and attentive ear. In the courtyard in front of the hall flute and drum are heard. They play, then fall silent at the sound of the rattle and clapper. The pipes of Pan and the bells alternate with the singing. Then the birds and beasts flock round at the sound of the sacred music, and the phoenix glides round, beating its wings in time."

By "sacred music" the text implies the nine chants of Shun. According to tradition these were composed by one of the early mythical rulers, Shun, and they are said to have caused such an impression on Confucius that, after hearing them, he refrained from eating meat for three months. This music accompanied a pantomime in dance; in the dances of peace the performers wore pheasant feathers and carried flutes, in war-dances they wore bucklers and carried axes.

The inscriptions on the ritual vases give us very valuable information about the religion of the Chou period, as they tell us exactly what vows the donors made. The first wish of every Chinese was that sacrifices to his memory should be made for as long as possible, as his well-being in the life beyond depended on it. The accomplishment of this vow was, however, conditional upon one's having descendants, and so heaven was asked to bestow the gift of children, grand-children and great-grand-children. One sacrificial vase bore the following inscription: "May my sons and grandsons keep this vase always and use it." Then came the wish for a long life. This is found on more than half the bronze vases of the Eastern Chou peoples who lived at Lo-yang, and it has always been one of the greatest desires of the Chinese. Many symbols represented longevity: the tortoise, stag, crane, butterfly, pine, fir, mushroom, orchid and the peach, the latter being also the symbol of eternal life in mythology. These symbols were found on both vases and silk. They were painted on the silk which was sometimes given to a friend as a gift. One of the main reasons for this wish for a long life, which might perhaps surprise us, was the respect and authority accorded to old age in China. So long as his father was alive, a man was considered a minor, at least by his family, even if he was sixty. Aged grandparents often ruled the roast and tyrannised a whole family. It was only natural that everyone should wish to attain an advanced age and be master himself one day.

The family kept in constant touch with the spirits of its ancestors by oracles and sacrifices. All the family's difficulties were revealed in their prayers and the spirits were begged to help. Offerings were scaled according to rank and fortune, the poor fed their ancestors on fish and the well-to-do on meat, but all classes offered cereal dishes such as millet pudding and cooked vegetables. Under the Chou dynasty the offerings were more markedly vegetarian, the quantity of meat offered being considerably less than in the Shang period. In the previous chapter we spoke of the sacrifice of humans and animals under the Shang dynasty. At Hsu-hsien a large grave, over ten yards square, was found to contain a "chariot sacrifice" of seventy-two horses, eight dogs and twelve chariots. The animals had been buried alive, with the horses still harnessed. The wheels of the chariots had previously been removed and thrown into the grave after the horses and dogs had been buried. The earth of this huge tomb was then levelled off. There had been no human sacrifice.

In the ancestor-cult the most important person was the "Personifier", a descendant of the dead man who was held to be filled with his spirit and who consumed the meat and drink offered at the sacrifice in the ancestor's name. A child could be chosen for this function. The sacrifices took place in the ancestors' room in private houses and in the ancestors' temple in the mansions of the nobility and the kings' palaces. These ancestors' rooms and temples were also the scene of important family gatherings, such as the reception of visitors and the presentation of a new bride. In the ancestors' royal temple official functions were held such as a new monarch's accession to the throne, the ceremony associated with the sovereign's departure to war or his return, the feasting of victory, diplomatic negotiations and royal banquets, the appointment or decoration of high officials and the investment of vassals with their fiefs. Sacrifices were made not only to the ancestors but also to heaven.

The belief in and the worship of spirits gave rise to a class of people who claimed to be in touch with them and even to be possessed by them. These were the sorcerers and magicians. They conjured up spirits, performed all kinds of magic and made prophecies. Superstitious people believed them and yet they were generally not held in any great respect.

The spirits of the dead were believed not to inhabit permanently their rooms or temples, but to visit them only for the sacrifices and on certain other occasions when mats and seats were put out for them. Their permanent abode was heaven. The so-called underground "yellow springs" often said to be their dwelling-place were probably intended to mean their graves. The power of the ancestral spirits was so great in the popular imagination that an enemy sometimes spared whole towns and provinces for fear of the revenge the spirits might take. The spirits have done their country inestimable service adorning it with pagodas, those graceful monuments built all over China, in certain high places in the country, near towns and monasteries, as a protection against the spirits. Pagodas date from later than the Chou period, however.

The belief in spirits and the cult of the ancestors constituted a truly popular religion. There was also Shang-Ti, the supreme God, or the God of heaven, whom we mentioned in connection with the Shang dynasty. He was simply a State God. The king paid him a yearly sacrifice, but there was no longer any link between him and the ordinary people.

14

THE CH'IN EMPIRE

In the year 722 B.C. the Chou king P'ing abandoned his residence at Hao on the river Wei for Ch'eng-chou, near the present Lo-yang in the centre of the kingdom. There was an important reason for this move. In the Wei valley the Chou were exposed to constant incursions by barbarians from the west and north and in abandoning the country they left it to the Ch'in courts who gradually extended their sway eastwards. Soon the Chou were left, like the Caliphs of Baghdad, with only spiritual authority. As a religious leader, the Chou monarch, the son of heaven, was the only person entitled to celebrate the great annual sacrifice to heaven. Their loss of political power was mitigated by the respect paid to their legitimate descent and the memory of the service rendered to the state by the ancient members of the dynasty. They thus lasted for a further five centuries. Chinese history does not, in fact, recognise the new dynasty of the Ch'in until 221 B.C., when the Ch'in king took the title of Emperor. These five centuries are usually divided into two periods—the "Spring and Autumn" (so called from the name of a collection of ancient annals) from 722 to 481 and the "Warring Kingdoms" from 481 to 221. There was, however, continual warfare throughout both periods, both between the various rival states struggling for independence, and between the states and the barbarians from the north and west. There were several attempts to found new political organisations and a federation of states and to elaborate new political and economic systems. The latter were the subject of much propaganda at the various courts by itinerant philosophers, particularly after Confucius. Every political and economic philosophy known in the

215

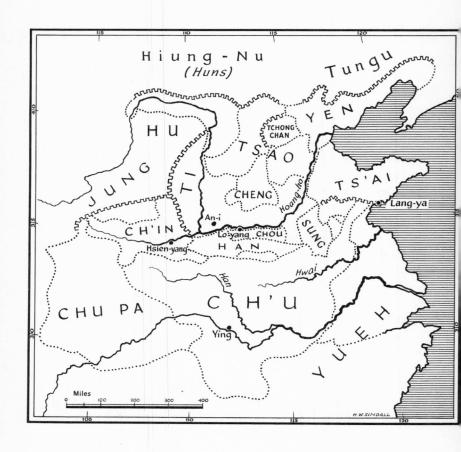

Hiung - Nu
(Huns)

Tungu

HU

JUNG

TI

CH'IN

TSAO

YEN

TCHONG
CHAN

CHENG

TS'AI

Lang-ya

An-i

Hoang-ho

Lo-yang CHOU

Hsien-yang

HAN

SUNG

CHU PA

Han

Hwai

CH'U

YUEH

Ying

Miles

0   100   200   300   400

H.W.SINDALL

Western world, from agrarian communism to mercantilism, was tried out in the China of this period.

If we look at a map of China of the first of these periods, the "Spring and Autumn", the Chou kingdom, with its capital Ch'eng-chou, appears as a narrow strip along the lower reaches of the Ho-fo, a southern tributary of the Hoang-ho. Like Switzerland, this little state, all that remains of the Chou kingdom, is surrounded by states or principalities. There are ten of these: the Ch'in, still small, in the west, the great Ch'in state in the north, the Yen in the north west around the mouth of the Yellow River, and the Ts'ai south of the Yen in the area of the present Chihli. To the south stretches the great state of Ch'u, to beyond the Yang-tse, in the east lies the Wu on the lower reaches of the Yang-tse and finally in the centre are the small states of Cheng, Wei, Sung and Lu. This was the picture from the eighth to the fourth centuries B.C. In about 350 B.C. we find the same group of states, still in conflict, and, in the centre of them, a new one, the Han, the cradle of the fourth dynasty. Before this, however, it was the Ch'in state which gradually extended its power over its neighbours and, having triumphed over its greatest enemy, the great South Chu state, united all these into an Empire which extended from the Great Wall to the region of Canton. The Ch'in became the third dynasty, and their power had been prepared over generations. It was based on a radical reform of the agricultural economy and a strictly centralised state organisation. It put an end to the system under which the peasants cultivated the land for the benefit of their landlords.

"The peasants were grouped in units of five or ten families, mutually responsible and hence constantly watchful of each other. Families with more than two male members had to separate or pay double taxes. The number of fields, houses, servants and even the amount of clothing allowed was strictly regulated. . . . The country was divided into districts, each under an official. Each man was liable to military service for the whole of his life, and this was pitilessly enforced. There were no rewards, only punishments. The military enjoyed privileges and all officials carried arms. In wartime success was generously rewarded and failure equally severely punished. The Ch'in state thus became a faultlessly working machine within which there was obviously no room for any class system. A strong central power had swept all this away." [1]

Ch'in Shih Huang-ti, the first Ch'in Emperor, organised all the conquered states on the model of his own. The Empire was divided into thirty-six, then forty prefectures. This was the origin of the Chinese provinces, and it put an end to the feudal system, replacing it by a centralised power. It was the greatest political and economic reform that China has ever known and the new regime, in spite of all the later temporary setbacks, was preserved or re-established by the great succeeding dynasties.

The title assumed by the new Ch'in sovereign was also new. In place of "Wang" or "King" the title of all preceding monarchs, the Ch'in king Cheng styled himself "Huang-ti" or "August Emperor". The custom of giving dead kings the names of temples, hence passing judgment on their characters and that of their governments, was abolished. Henceforth every Emperor was to be called after the number of his reign in the dynastic succession, "from the first Emperor to the ten thousandth, through all eternity." The new Emperor thus assumed the title of "Shih Huang-ti" or "First August Emperor". *Huang*, meaning "august", corresponded roughly to the Roman "augustus", *ti* to "divus" and so the new Ch'in emperor's name to a certain extent foreshadowed that of the Roman *Imperator*. There is a certain parallel also in the fact that the dynasty came to a lamentable end with Ch'in's successor, for Enh Shih Huang-ti, the "Second August Emperor", was assassinated by his own officers.

The people did not accept this unification without a struggle. Each state had had its own customs, laws, measures, dress, language and even writing. The Emperor's Prime Minister Li-Ssu was determined to stamp out these ancient customs so

[1] R. Wilhelm.

that the conquered states should be permanently incorporated in the Empire. One consequence of Li-Ssu's reforms was the well-known "destruction of the books" carried out at his command. His Confucian opponents constantly referred to the sacrosanct authority of the ancient texts and because of this he ordered the destruction of all Confucian historical literature. Every copy in the possession of private owners was ordered to be burnt, but the classical works compiled by Confucius were preserved in the Imperial Library, where they could be consulted under the supervision of officials. This reform also aimed at putting an end to the practice, inaugurated by Confucius, of entrusting education to private teachers such as itinerant philosophers. Education was henceforth to be the concern of the state. Confucius had, however, stressed the need for a unification of all educational institutions, as this was the only way to secure a solid moral basis to society.

This unification was applied, in effect, to every sphere of public life. Throughout the Empire weights, measures and tools were standardised and even vehicles had to have the same length of axle. It is not easy to imagine the difficulties which arose in the imposition of these reforms on the everyday life of the peasant at a time when there was virtually only oral communication and when the only means of getting about was by ox-cart in an Empire stretching from north to south, a distance equal to that between Berlin and Messina. Li-Ssu introduced another system of writing which, developed in the ensuing Han period, became the basis of the present Chinese script.

Later, after the end of the short-lived Ch'in dynasty, when the prohibited books were beginning to appear again from their hiding-places, it was found that they had to be translated into the new script, the old by now having fallen out of use. This brought an alteration of many passages, as the modification of a single character can change the meaning of a whole sentence. This is why Confucianism in the Han period is very different from the original.

Two of the acts attributed to Shih Huang-ti have made his name famous in world history: the destruction of the books, mentioned above, and the building of the Great Wall. As is often the case when historical facts are simplified, the attribution of the Great Wall to the first Ch'in Emperor represents only a part of the truth. Already in the course of the preceding centuries, during the time of the Warring Kingdoms, because of incessant strife between the states and repeated invasions by the barbarians, the northern and western marches had fortified their frontiers facing the steppes with lines of earthworks not unlike the *limes* of the Roman Empire. The Ch'in, a western march, had also strengthened its frontier facing the state of Tai. These fortified lines, therefore, put the origins of the Great Wall back to the fourth century B.C.

During the Ch'in dynasty China was threatened by a new enemy, the Hiung-nu or Huns, who penetrated as far as the steppes of Mongolia. The Emperor had all the defensive earthworks connected up into a single fortified line to protect the northern frontier. He is said to have employed in this gigantic undertaking no fewer than three thousand soldiers and as many prisoners, criminals, tradesmen and unemployed. Any workman who left a crack in the stonework large enough to admit the point of a needle could be condemned to death. As the difficulties seemed to become insurmountable the Emperor consulted a soothsayer who told him that the Wall would not be completed until ten thousand men lay buried underneath it. This was too much even for the tyrant who compromised with the celestial powers by having a man buried alive bearing round his neck a tablet on which was engraved a character signifying ten thousand. From that moment the work progressed more rapidly. This is but one of the many legends surrounding the building of the Great Wall.

Succeeding Emperors consolidated the immense defensive work whose most important sectors in their present state date back to the Ming period of the fourteenth and fifteenth centuries. The Wall never fails to make an unforgettable impression on the tourist who visits it today. Built of granite blocks, stone and brick, and rising to a height of twenty-three feet, it carries on the top a paved military road wide enough to allow two cars to pass and is defended on both sides by crenellated parapets. It runs from Shan-hai-kwan on the Straits of Pe-chih-li to the western frontier of Kansu, a distance of one thousand four hundred and six miles. There is a further extension of the wall from Kansu out into the salt desert. In certain exposed areas, on either side of the great trade routes, there are defensive towers every hundred yards and these are garrisoned. Elsewhere these towers occur only every mile. The Wall does not follow the easiest route, but goes up and down mountain-sides so that in certain places the transit of heavily armoured troops, especially cavalry, is difficult. On the other hand, where it runs through open country it is very vulnerable and requires a large number of troops to guard it.

This fortified line, the oldest in history, which was originally intended to protect the Northern Chinese provinces against the barbarians, was also a solid defence in later years against the great Tartar armies. It was a powerful defensive wall between two peoples and two opposing forms of civilisation, the one sedentary and agricultural, the other nomad and pastoral: the civilisation of Eastern Asia and the barbarism of Central Asia. If the Tartars occasionally succeeded in breaching the rampart it was when China was weak and generally it was done by deceit and trickery. When Jenghis Khan failed at Kalgan he quickly sought out a less well defended point and his invading hordes broke through into China whilst the Kalgan garrison was expecting a second attack. The Manchu troops flung themselves in vain against the Great Wall for many years until at last they succeeded in breaching it by treachery before Shan-hai-kwan.

Spurred on by a superhuman will which would brook no resistance, the Emperor showed himself also to be a great builder of cities and palaces. These have disappeared completely, but the patient skill of the archaeologist will one day reveal some of their foundations. Chinese history mentions a great many palaces and there are pictures of them on the painted rolls of succeeding centuries. The paintings of the T'ang and Sung periods represented not real palaces, but imaginary ones, the abodes of emperors and immortals in grandiose high mountain settings. The Boston Museum has a roll by the famous Sung painter Chao Po-chu (first half of the twelfth century) showing the entry of the first Han Emperor Liu Pang into the Ch'in fortress Kuan-tung in the mountains.

The first act of Liu Pang, shortly after his entry into this fortress, was to abolish the harsh laws of Ch'in Shih Huang-ti. The painting does not show the original Ch'in fortress, long since destroyed, but substitutes instead a contemporary Sung building which does, however, manage to convey the idea of what these castles looked like high up in the Shensi mountains. Reliefs and models of buildings found in Han tombs and dating from the last two centuries B.C. reveal that Chinese architecture changed as little between the Han and the Sung periods as it has done between the Sung period and the present day. The differences between the architecture of the Manchu Summer Palace near Peking and that of the palace of Shih Huang-ti are differences of degree only. The grandiose audience-chamber on Chao Po-chu's roll in Boston must show just what these chambers looked like in the Ch'in palaces.

One architectural creation never surpassed nor even equalled by any other succeeding Empire was Hsien-yang, the capital and residence of the Ch'in Emperors on the banks of the river Wei, west of Hao, the ancient Chou capital and the site of the present town of Hsian-fu (Ch'angan). The city was eight days' walk from east to west, a vast area of private houses and imperial palaces with their parks, zoological gardens and artificial lakes. The Emperor ordered one hundred and twenty thousand noble or distinguished families to settle in the new capital and to have private mansions built. The city was divided by the river Wei into a north part and a south part. These were joined by a covered bridge nearly sixty-five feet wide and two hundred and eight feet long, with sixty-eight arches and eight hundred and fifteen pillars. Water was brought to the town by canals on either side of the river. The plan of the city was supposed to imitate the milky way and each house represented a star.
. The Emperor built two hundred and seventy palaces for his own use. These were joined by covered passage-ways, as

was customary in Chinese palace architecture and as can still be seen in the Peking Summer Palace. These passage-ways were bordered with evergreen trees and they were formed of regularly beaten earth.

"Every time that he (the Emperor) had conquered some prince," says Che-pe, "he built a palace at Hsien-yang similar to the one he had destroyed. He transferred there all the precious objects and art treasures he had taken; he peopled them with the loveliest women in the Empire of whom there were fully ten thousand! Each one of these imperial residences had its provisions, its staff, its courtiers, its musical instruments, and was always fully equipped so that Shih Huang-ti could go there whenever he wished and find everything ready for him. The twelve months of the year were not enough to visit them all. The avenues were decorated with silks and embroideries; everywhere there were hanging gardens, covered alley-ways and everything to rejoice the sight or to satisfy one's curiosity".[1]

The residential palace, surpassing all others in grandeur and magnificence, was called the "City of the Palace". It had taken seven hundred thousand men to build it. The two peaks of the Southern mountain formed the pillars of the main doorway and the avenues which crossed the palace enclosure in all directions were each eighty *lis* long. The great courtyard could hold a hundred thousand men and the great hall ten thousand. The latter was so high that fifty-foot banners did not reach the ceiling. The stone was quarried from the foothills of the Kun-lun mountains, the wood came from the present provinces of Hu-pe and Sze-chuan and was of many kinds: cypress, fir, pine, cinnamon and all species of sweet-smelling woods. From the south had been brought coral trees and others with shiny leaves that grow in Yunnan. The sumptuous decoration and the richness of the interior can only be guessed at, as nothing has survived which might

[1] H. d'Ardenne de Tizac: *La Chine féodale et l'art chinois : Les Ts'in* (Artibus Asiae, IV, 1926).

give us a clear idea of the Ch'in style. The Ch'in period was so short, however, lasting only thirty or forty years, that it can scarcely be held to have produced a style of its own. Shih Huang-ti succeeded to the throne in 246 as Prince Cheng, took the title of Emperor in 221 and died in 210. The predominating style of the period is that of the Warring Kingdoms or Huai style for jades and bronzes. It was elegant, graceful and technically very refined. It bears a certain resemblance to certain modern decorative styles.

Even when faced with death, Shih Huang-ti made his power felt in the building of his tomb. He built a gigantic mound at the foot of the Li-shan mountain. This contained three chambers: an entrance-hall, an ante-room and a burial-chamber in which the coffin was laid. The base of the sarcophagus represented the earth with its mountains and rivers and the vaulted ceiling, the sky and the stars. The miniature oceans were of mercury which was made to flow from a piece of machinery hidden underground. The walls were dressed with metal and round the sarcophagus were arranged models of palaces, summer-houses and court-officials' dwelling-houses, all studded with pearls and precious stones. The whole was lit by huge torches of seal-fat. To prevent any treachery by the workmen they were all assembled in the entrance-hall and shut in by a heavy door which was then sealed off. They were left buried alive and the whole site was covered with a huge mound of earth on which were planted the same kind of trees as grew on the mountain.

The Segalen-Lartigue-Voisins expedition visited the site in 1914. Their account says:

"It is situated two and a quarter miles from Lin-tung in the district of Sian, and is approached by a long climb from the Wei valley, the road running parallel to the Li mountain as far as its base. . . . Between the road and the mountain the ground is undulating and this, together with the arid nature of the soil, causes the site to stand out both from the plain and against the mountain landscape. . . . It was a bold conception to construct an earthwork amidst this proud mountain scenery, but the Emperor demanded it of his architects. The result is that the site has gained in historical grandeur and the mountain has lost some of its splendour, to become merely a framework, a back-cloth, a setting. . . ."

The expedition did not obtain permission to excavate on the tumulus. This had, however, been opened for the first time three years after the king's death and again on several occasions in the nineteenth century, when it was pillaged. It is very unlikely that the French archaeologists would have made any startling discoveries. Even a few modest remains, though, would have given an idea of the style of the period.

Shih Huang-ti died in 210 during a journey to the shores of the Eastern Sea in search of an elixir of immortality said to be found on an island there. Death overtook him one thousand six hundred and fifty *lis* (about five hundred and thirty miles) from his capital. To avoid any disturbances or uprisings which his death might cause, the eunuchs decided to keep it secret. The coffin was transported in the Imperial carriage and hidden behind drawn curtains. Meals were served to the dead Emperor and the mandarins continued to make their reports and present their requests, the answers being supplied by the Grand Eunuch concealed inside. The great heat of the summer, however, soon made the stench unbearable and so a great load of salt fish was purchased and loaded on to the other carriages to disguise it. Thus the all-powerful despot, still commanding in death, took the long road home to his last resting-place where, amidst his inestimable treasure of gold, precious stones and jewels, he continued to reign over the earth and heaven whose images surrounded him.

In 207 a palace revolt, led by Hiang-yu, put an end to the dynasty by assassinating Enh Shih Huang-ti. Hiang-yu opened up the tomb and took possession of the Imperial seal which had been artistically engraved on jade by Li-Ssu. Like all Chinese seals this was square and its handle was formed by five intertwined dragons. It bore an inscription: "By the decree of Majestic Heaven the Sovereign Emperor hath long life and prosperity." It was held to have such magical power that it was preserved by succeeding monarchs and was so hotly disputed in successions and changes of dynasty that on one occasion it was actually damaged. The Sung Emperors claimed to possess it still, but with the last of them it disappeared for ever.[1]

Our journey eastwards has now reached its end. The object of your guide has been to make it exciting rather than voluminous, instructive to the layman rather than comprehensive to the scholar.

One further section must be added to the book. It concerns something which happened a considerable time after this book was first written, something which takes us westward again but which serves nonetheless as a fitting postscript to all that has happened down the centuries. This is, of course, to the discovery of the Dead Sea Scrolls.

[1] From H. d'Ardenne de Tizac: op cit.

15

THE MONASTERY ON THE DEAD SEA

The Persian doctrine of the struggle between good and evil, light and darkness, has come into the lively discussions on the history of religion since the finding early in 1947 of the scrolls in the caves of Wadi Qumran on the Dead Sea seven miles south of Jericho. More than a decade ago the Press reported this momentous event as "the greatest archaeological discovery of modern times since the Renaissance". The story is well-known of how a Bedouin goat-herd boy threw a stone into one of the many caves in the fissured rocks of the west shore of the Dead Sea in the Qumran valley, and by so doing roused from its two-thousand-year sleep a library of scrolls from the pre-Christian era. The light this finding and its consequences has shed on the dark centuries of transition from the Old to the New Testaments, from Judaism to Christianity, must interest not only the narrower specialist circle of scholars but also the whole world, for the origin of our religion is involved.

Two leading Orientalists in Jerusalem, Père Roland de Vaux of the Ecole Biblique, and G. Lankaster-Harding, made a systematic search; they clambered into more than two hundred and fifty caves, and came upon evidence of human life dating back four thousand years, with ten thousand fragments of a library once hidden away from aggressors. The scrolls have crumbled to pieces, the putting together of which will take many years of toilsome, scholarly work. They reach back to the third century before Christ and are, then, more than two thousand years old. To set the fundamental value of these texts in the right light, it should be noted that the then oldest known text of the Bible in Hebrew, the Masora Text, dates

227

from the ninth century A.D. and that till then the Jews used the only two texts: the Alexandrine translation of the Septuagint, which was the Greek version of the Old Testament, begun in the third century B.C., and the Latin Vulgate of Saint Jerome, completed in the fourth century A.D. Knowledge of the Hebrew or Aramaic original texts of the Books of the Old Testament was therefore brought a thousand years nearer their origin by the discovery on the Dead Sea. There has been until now only one similar finding of old manuscripts saved for scholarship. That was in Tun-huang, a Buddhist monastery on the eastern border of the Gobi Desert, where in 1035 A.D., likewise in a period of threatened invasion, monks walled up their library in a remote chamber where in 1900 they were found by chance by a Tibetan monk, and soon after came into the hands of the orientalist Sir Aurel Stein and the sinologist Paul Pelliot.

As well as Books of the Prophets Isaiah, Habukkuk and Daniel found in 1947, there was a further, and, till then unknown, text of the second century before Christ, containing the rules of a religious order of that time. This was published in America in 1950 under the title, *Manual of Discipline*. It was this text that opened the way to the actual sphere of new discovery, which was the study of the Essene Sect whose chief seat this deserted area on the west shore of the Dead Sea was soon recognised to have been. A decisive factor in this realisation was the excavation of a ruin known to the Arabs as Khirbet ("ruin")—Qumran. The excavation exposed an old stone building with twenty or thirty chambers and several cisterns, a large number of which have remained intact. Adjoining is a burial ground with more than a thousand graves. These all lie north to south, not east to west as do Muslim graves, and contain no burial objects. It was concluded that a monastery of the Essene Sect had been uncovered. The Elder Pliny, Flavius Josephus and Philo the Alexandrian all wrote about this sect which has been known of since the beginning of the Christian era. But writings from their time were missing.

Josephus was himself a member of the sect for a few years. The Essenes, he wrote, taught that the soul was immortal, whereas the Sadducees believed it died with the body. They allowed of no blood offerings in the Temple, for they used holier, bloodless purification. For that reason they were denied entrance to the Temple, and conducted their services apart from the Jewish sanctuary. "They are moreover men of excellent character, occupied solely in cultivating the soil. But of all who have any claim to the name of virtue, it is they who have the highest honour and praise for a state of equality among themselves, unknown among the Greeks or any other peoples; and this state they have enjoyed not only recently but for long years past. They have brought about complete common ownership in every respect, and allow the rich man no greater enjoyment of his possessions than the needy one. Yet there are more than four thousand living thus. They neither marry nor keep men-servants, for they deem this wrong and the cause of all quarrelsomeness. So they live apart and serve each the other. By casting votes they choose some from among the priests to administer their harvests and to provide grain and food. They all live in one and the same way, resembling most nearly the Dakian tribes called Polists. They renounce marriage, as they see in it the main danger to the maintenance of community life, and because they remain chaste. They were settled in many towns of Judea, but prefer villages where they can live in strict communities in monasteries, so that all possessions are in common ownership." Their rules resemble those of later Christian monasticism.

In contrast to the Jewish congregation, the Synagogue, this new Israel was added to no longer merely by membership of race, but by the personal voluntary decision of the individual. The members formed a holy community, "a sanctuary in Aaron". By "Aaron" is meant the priesthood; by "Israel", the people. The priests and the people were therefore clearly divided as in ancient Judaism. In the Manual the people are called "'am" ("the multitude") or "harabbim" ("the many"). All questions of law and government were reserved for the priests. The law against offences occupies an important place both in Josephus and in the Manual. The death sentence was imposed for blasphemy, excommunication for serious offences. For an outcast further life was virtually impossible. Baptism and meals were communal. "After they have worked for a period of five hours, they gather at the same place, and girdled with a white linen cloth they bathe in cold water. When they are again seated, the baker gives out loaves and the cook serves food on each man's plate. The priest blesses the food, and no man may partake of it before the prayer is said. The priest gives thanks after the meal. Before and after it they praise God as the giver of life. When they have put off their sacramental wraps, they return to work till evening, when they again take food in the same manner. If guests are present, they sit at the same table. These rites have no purifying effect unless they are performed with devout humility" (Flavius Josephus). The Manual states that only through humility of soul before the precepts of God is the body purified by sprinkling with holy water and by consecration in flowing waters. There exist two scrolls: one, previously known, discovered in an old synagogue in Cairo and preserved in Damascus, the other a scroll found in one of the Qumran caves, the Manual now in the possession of the American investigators. They closely agree textually, and Professor Dupont-Sommer of the Sorbonne, the translator of the Qumran scroll, puts the question as to what sect both scripts may have referred. Could it be the known Essene Sect? Professor Sukenik, the leading archaeologist at the University of Jerusalem, made the same query, and clearly had in mind this sect which, however, is nowhere mentioned by name in the scripts. The very agreement between the information given in the scroll and that given by Philo and Josephus leaves open no other conclusion.[1]

The great importance given to the Essene religious community in the history of religion lies in its function as a transition from Judaism to Christianity within the period from the third century before Christ to the Roman subjugation of Palestine in 68 A.D. This transition from the ancient Jewish Talmud Sect to a metaphysical religion of marked spirituality

[1] A. Dupont-Sommer, *Observations sur Le Manuel de Discipline découvert près de la Mer Morte*, Paris, 1951; *Nouveaux Aperçus sur les Manuscrits de la Mer Morte*, Paris, 1953—Collection L'Orient Ancien Illustré.

was so radical that a new world era was begun with the birth of the Messiah.

A commentary to the Prophet Habukkuk has come to light in Qumran. It is of great importance for our knowledge of the spiritual foundations of the Dead Sea Sect, the Essenes. In this a "teacher of righteousness", a priest endowed with divine revelation, leads a group whose members are poor and call themselves "the new community". The teacher is named "the chosen of God".[1] This leader demands strict observance of the law, is at variance with the priests in Jerusalem, and consequently is persecuted by an evil priest who is denoted as the prophet of falsehood, or man of lies.

Now who is this teacher of righteousness, and who is the evil priest? The first, as Wilson thinks, could refer to a title conferred on a number of men who had appeared as the Messiah, "the anointed one". The belief in the Messiah has been irrevocably centred on and fulfilled in the person of the Christian Saviour, but the belief continued in the Islamic faith where it led to the founding of divine dynasties like that of the Fatimids. Even before the discovery of the Dead Sea Scrolls this designation was known in the Book of Enoch. Later it appears in the Gospels where it refers to Jesus, "the son of man". Further, by the evil priest is meant a high priest who persecuted the Messiah and had him put to death. Various names are claimed for this personage, predecessors of Pontius Pilate of the Gospels.

One of the most important teachings of the Dead Sea Sect, as the Essenes are cautiously named by the investigators of the site, is the moral philosophy of "the two ways", which was unknown to the ancient Hebrews, and which found its way to the Essenes from ancient Persian tradition, probably transmitted through Manichaeism. The "men of lies" were already recognised in the rock inscriptions of the Achaemenian King Darius. The scrolls from the Dead Sea quote time and again the way of light and the way of darkness, the spirits of light and of darkness, the children of light and truth as against

[1] E. Wilson, *The Scrolls from the Dead Sea*, New York (Oxford University Press, 1955).

falsehood. The Messiah, the teacher of righteousness, is opposed by a demon most often named Belial or Beliar (Wilson, l.c.S.78). At the end of time there will be the Last Judgment, a concept which was likewise unknown to Judaism, but was a doctrine of the Avesta. At Doomsday the Messiah and Saviour would divide for ever the two worlds of light and darkness; and this is the belief both of Christianity and of Islam today. The purification at the spring of "living water", or baptism, as well as the holy meal, the Eucharist, are not of Jewish origin either. Professor K. G. Kuhn of Gottingen has emphasised in a treatise on the development of the Eucharist, that the Jewish Passover was and still is a family festival in which both men and women take part, whereas the Christian Communion in its original form was held on the model of the Last Supper at which only a limited circle of men with the head of the church congregation were present. Kuhn believes that the Christian Communion derives from this early Christian ritual, and that Jesus himself introduced it. The correctness of Kuhn's theory that the sacrament of the Last Supper originated with the Essenes seems to be confirmed by the later discovered fragments that complete the Manual.

It may well be that further scrolls, similar to these stimulating documents, are still in existence somewhere, waiting to be discovered and to shed light on the great gaps in our knowledge of ancient history which still remain. It is tempting to the scholar to assume that this will be so and that the greater part, even, of his task lies ahead. As any theatre audience knows, there is no moment so filled with expectation as the gradual lightening of a darkened stage to reveal a great and brilliant spectacle, as the figures of the players emerge from the shadows to speak the first lines which will introduce and illuminate the play.

SUGGESTIONS FOR FURTHER READING

I GENERAL

V. Gordon Childe, *What Happened in History*. Penguin, 1942.

H. Frankfort and others, *Before Philosophy*. Penguin, 1949.

H. Frankfort, *The Art and Architecture of the Ancient Orient*. Pelican History of Art, 1954.

R. Grousset, *The Civilisations of the East*. (2 Vols.) Knopf, 1931.

A. C. Bouquet, Comparative Religion. Penguin, 1942.

The Sacred Books of the World. Penguin, 1954.

II PARTICULAR

B. Rowland, *Art and Architecture of Ancient India*. Pelican History of Art, 1953.

V. Gordon Childe, *New Light on the Most Ancient East*. Routledge and Kegan Paul, 1952.

Sir Leonard Woolley, *Ur of the Chaldees*. Penguin, 1938.

The Development of Sumerian Art. London, 1935.

Seton Lloyd, *Mesopotamia. Excavations on Sumerian Sites*. London, 1936.

Foundations in the Dust. Penguin, 1947.

A. H. Layard, *Nineveh and Its Remains*. (2 Vols.) London, 1849.

Nineveh and Babylon. (2 Vols.) London, 1853.

Discoveries in the Ruins of Nineveh and Babylon. (2 Vols.) London, 1853.

The Monuments of Nineveh. London, 1853.

Autobiography and Letters. (2 Vols.) London, 1903.

Suggestions for Further Reading

G. Coutenau, *Everyday Life in Babylon and Assyria*. Arnold, 1954.

Guy le Strange, *Baghdad during the Abbassid Caliphate*. O.U.P., 1924.

R. Coke, *Baghdad City of Peace*. London, 1927.

A. U. Pope (ed.), *A Survey of Persian Art*. (6 Vols.) O.U.P., 1938.

R. Ghirshman, *Iran*. Penguin, 1954.

Stuart Piggott, *Prehistoric India*. Penguin, 1950.

H. C. Candee, *Angkor the Magnificent*. 1925.

G. F. Allen, *Buddha's Words of Wisdom*. Allen and Unwin, 1959.

Walpola Rahula, *What the Buddha Taught*. Gordon Fraser, 1959.

John Blofeld, *The Wheel of Life*. Rider, 1959.

R. Wilhelm, *A Short History of Chinese Civilisation*. Harrap, 1929.

K. S. Latourette, *A Short History of the Far East*. Macmillan N.Y., 1947.

Sickman and Soper, *The Art and Architecture of China*. Pelican History of Art. Penguin, 1956.

H. G. Creel, *Studies in Early Chinese Culture*. London, 1937.
The Birth of China. London, 1936.

A. Waley, *The Book of Songs* (translations from the Shih Ching). London, 1937.

Liu Wu-Chi, *A Short History of Confucian Philosophy*. Penguin, 1955.

W. Willetts, *Chinese Art*. (2 Vols.) Penguin, 1958.

Rice, *Tamora* (on Central Asia).

INDEX

A-anni-pad-da, 27
Abbas Abad, 121
Abbas the Great, 119, 120, 121, 125, 128, 133, 134
Abbas II, 119, 131
Abbasid dynasty, 100–118
Abd-el-Malik, 100
Abd-ur-rahman, Sheik, 52, 53
Abhayamudra, 172, 173
Abraham, 29, 31
Abu Bekr, 138
Achaemenians, 79, 80, 81, 82, 86, 97, 108, 128, 231
Adad, god, 60
Adhi Buddha, 173
Adshanta, 169
Afghanistan, 18, 138
Africa, East, 15
Ahuramazda (Oramazda), god, 81, 83, 84, 85, 86, 94
Ahwaz, 109
Ajanta, 169
Akkad, 28, 32, 38, 41, 60
Akshobya Buddha, 173
Aksu, 146
Al Amin, 114
Al Kaim, 118
Al Nazar, 118
al 'Ubaid, see 'Ubaid, al
al-Hira, 112
Al-Yahudiyah, 120
Aleppo, 36
Alexander the Great, 27, 38, 64, 91, 138
Ali, caliph, 135
Ali Kapu, 123, 126, 127, 128
Alides, 104, 105
Allah-werdi, 133
Amarna, 41
America, Central, 73
Amitabha Buddha, 151, 154, 158, 173
Amoghasiddha, 173
Ananda, 167, 168
Andersson, J. G., 176
Andes, 15
Andrae, Walter, 59
Angkor Thor, 161, 162, 163, 173
Annals, Book of, 201, 211
Anorchivan, 89
Anshan, 78
Anshar, 67
Antioch, 90, 92
Anu, god, 32, 60, 63, 64, 74
An-yang, 178, 180, 192
Apollo, 143
Apsu, god, 67
Arabian Nights, Tales from, 100, 104
Arahtu, 70
Araxes, 91, 134

Archaeologische Mitteilungen an Iran, 86 n
Ardashir, king, 91
Ardebil, 127
Arsames, 84
Artaxerxes, 82
Arupa, 173
Aryan civilisation, 20
Asankhyeya, 156
Ashur, god, 60, 62
Asoka, king, 147
Aspadana, 120
Asshardon, king, 64
Assur, 36, 41, 42, 51, 59, 60, 62, 79
Assurbanipal, king, 40, 41, 42, 52, 64
Assurnasirpal II, king, 40, 43, 51, 52
Assyrians, 26, 29, 36, 38, 39, 40–62, 63, 78, 80, 81, 85
Astyages, king, 78
Auf Hellas Spuren in Ost-Turkestan, 147 n
Avalokiteshvara, 151, 154, 155, 158, 163
Avesta, 86, 98, 232
Azadhmard, 95
Azerbaijan, 89, 91, 127

Babar, 138
Babbar, god, 32
Babel, tower of, 63–71, 160
Babu, 74
Babylonia, 17, 23, 26, 28, 29, 31, 32, 33, 36, 38, 39, 40, 41, 44, 58, 59, 60, 61, 78, 79, 80, 81, 82, 83, 84, 100, 160, 161, 162, 167
   Bab-Ili, 63
   civilisation of, 63–77
   Jews in, 39
Bactria, 79, 143
Baghdad, 42, 90, 100–118
Bagistan (Behistun), 83
Baktiares, 119
Balbec, 46
Bal-el-Talisman, 118
Bali, 166
Balkh, 107, 138
Balkuwara, 109, 112
Bamiyan, 138, 140, 152
Bardiya, 79
Barkemids, 106, 110
Basra, 29, 58, 101, 115
Bayon, 163
Bedsa, 169
Behistun, 82, 83
Bel, god, 63, 68, 69, 74
Belial (Beliar), 232
Benares, 153
Berlin Museum of Ethnology, 142, 154
Berossus, priest, 38
Bezeklik, 154
Bhumisparshamudra, 172, 173
Bir, 45

235

Index

Index

Index

Index

Index